Frances D. Spargo <u>Williams Crowe</u>
Gincocks, 26A Church Lane
EAST PECKHAM, Nr. TONBRIDGE
Kent TN12 5JH
Tel. no. (01622) 872025

NATIVE TONGUES

NATIVE TONGUES

Charles Berlitz

Charles Berlitz, world-famous linguist and author of more than 100 language-teaching books, is the grandson of the founder of the Berlitz Schools. Since 1967 Mr Berlitz has not been connected with the Berlitz Schools in any way.

GRANADA
London Toronto Sydney New York

Granada Publishing Limited
Frogmore, St Albans, Herts AL2 2NF
and
36 Golden Square, London W1R 4AH
515 Madison Avenue, New York, NY 10022, USA
117 York Street, Sydney, NSW 2000, Australia
60 International Blvd, Rexdale, Ontario R9W 6J2, Canada
61 Beach Road, Auckland, New Zealand

Published by Granada Publishing 1983

Copyright © Charles Berlitz 1982

British Library Cataloguing in Publication Data

Berlitz, Charles
 Native tongues.
 1. Language and languages
 I. Title
 400   P201

ISBN 0–246–12042–8

Printed in Great Britain by
Richard Clay (The Chaucer Press) Ltd,
Bungay, Suffolk

Granada ®
Granada Publishing ®

Dedicated to my grandfather, Maximilian Delphinius Berlitz, multilinguist and language-teaching innovator, who inspired and guided my lifelong interest in languages.

Contents

Preface

My grandfather was M. D. Berlitz, a linguist who spoke fifty-eight languages and who invented a unique system of language teaching. When I first started to speak, I learned four different languages at the same time, each exclusively spoken to me by different members of my family. At this very early age I did not know that these were world languages but simply thought that they were different ways that people had of speaking which, when one considers it, is really a good way of defining languages. I have since acquired about two dozen more languages through language study, research, teaching, travel and residence in various countries, and the writing of language teaching books.

It had often occurred to me during my language career that someone should write a book about languages, not exclusively to teach a language, but to present a series of informative facts and incidents to illustrate the influence that language has had in diplomacy and war, the mystery of its origin, and the circumstances of its spreading and receding. Such a book would deal with curious linguistic customs, including words of love, and even insults and epithets, unusual sound coincidences, and language shortcuts as, for example, how a person who speaks English already has a knowledge, though he may not realize it, of thousands of foreign words.

Such a book would offer an overview of how language has affected the peoples of the world all through history—and does so today more than ever. It would deal with the conflict between languages in the present world and the possibility of a world language for the space age.

Since I have written considerably about some of the great mysteries of the sea, such as the Bermuda Triangle and Atlantis, I have been asked how my study of languages fits in with the element of mystery. My answer is that language itself is one of the world's greatest mysteries—how it originated, how it spread all over the world, how languages are so different, and how writing developed from pictures and counting into the alphabet and the four hundred or more other scripts used in the world. For language, reinforced and immortalized through writing, has been the most important development in the progress of the human species, leading it from family group barbarism, not unlike animal packs, to its present dominion of the earth and a force toward the exploration of the cosmos.

Foreign words are not foreign to those who speak them. Each language group has a distinctive outlook on the rest of the world. When we penetrate this different way of thinking, we have added another dimension to our own personalities. On the world island where we all live it is increasingly important for us to understand the cultures and languages of our neighbors and, through this, how they think. We now have a greater opportunity of doing this than ever before, although perhaps not so much time. We owe it to ourselves—to our own survival—to become more familiar with the languages, and therefore with the cultural outlook, of our neighbors on planet earth.

1. There Are 2,796 Languages in the World

At this moment at least 2,796 separate languages are being spoken on our planet—according to a calculation by the *Académie Française*, the French Academy, whose decisions are the last word, at least for linguistic conservatives, on the French language and linguistics. There may well be, in remote forests and jungles, other languages that have not yet been discovered.

The world's languages are divided into 12 important language families and 50 lesser ones. The Indo-European language family, to which English belongs, is one of the 12 most important—and among languages importance is measured by number of speakers around the world.

In addition to the languages spoken today, there exist 7,000 to 8,000 dialects. A dialect is generally considered to be a variant of a language sufficiently different from the parent tongue in pronunciation, vocabulary, or idiom to cause some difficulty in comprehension. Dialects frequently become languages—modern French, Italian, Spanish, Portuguese, and Rumanian all started as regional dialects of Latin within the ancient Roman Empire. English in its earliest form, Anglo-Saxon, was the dialect of powerful Wessex; modern English, which developed after the Normans conquered England in 1066, grew out of the dialect of London, the capital city.

Some languages are basically so similar in general vocabulary and construction that native speakers can understand, if not speak, the related language. Thus Norwegians, Swedes, and Danes can communicate with each other although they cannot understand Icelandic, the older and more stable language. Dutch speakers can understand English speakers much more easily than English speakers can Dutch, although the languages are closely related; and Portuguese speakers can understand Spanish with greater ease than Spanish speakers can follow Portuguese. Yiddish and German are almost always mutually comprehensible, since Yiddish originated as a dialect based on medieval German.

The Bible—Old and New Testament—has been translated into and published in 275 languages. Selections from the Old and New Testament have been printed and distributed in 1,710 languages.

More than 700 languages are spoken in Africa south of the Sahara. Hundreds more, some as yet unclassified, are still spoken among the Indian tribes of North and South America. In the Republic of India, 18 official languages and hundreds of minor ones coexist.

An official language is the language a government conducts its business in, and only when a government decides to make it so is a language "official." The United Nations has had five official languages (Chinese, French, English, Russian, and Spanish) since its beginning in 1945—and at the UN, "official" means that all speeches are simultaneously translated into those languages. The UN also has what it calls "working" languages, English and French, the tongues in which all documents are published. Recently Arabic has been added as an official language, entailing considerable expense in the construction and wiring of Arabic interpreters' booths in the conference rooms.

More official languages have been allowed in the Soviet Union than in any other country on earth. Each one of the 15 component Socialist Republics of the Soviet Union has its own language, and these republics themselves contain Associated Republics which also have their own languages and often their own alphabets. At least 80 separate languages are spoken within the relatively small area of the Caucasus Mountains, often referred to as the "mountain of languages," where deep valleys and high mountains have isolated language groups swept there by invasion or migration over many centuries.

Although there are only about 50,000 pure Aboriginal Australians left in Australia, they speak more than 200 different languages. These languages are dying out as the small tribes disappear.

The number of world languages has been decreasing, notably during the past hundred years. Several centuries ago the number of separate tongues probably numbered more than 10,000, making the earth even more a Tower of Babel than it is today.

A medieval concept of the Tower of Babel.

The word *Babel* may be traced to the Aramaic *Bab-ilu*—
"Gateway of God"—the place which the Greeks called
Babylon, where the original Tower of Babel was thought to
have been built. In Hebrew *bilbel* means "confusion," a
reference to the dispersion, resulting from insuperable
language barriers, of the building crews of the proposed
tower to heaven. *Babel* has come down to modern languages
as the English "babble"; the Italian *babele*; the Spanish
babel and *balbuceo*; and the French *babil*.

The Spanish *conquistadores* who invaded Mexico in 1517
were amazed to find the Tower of Babel legend already
current there, under another name. The great pyramid of
Cholula was built, according to the Cholulans, to provide a
refuge from a future flood, and its builders had been
scattered through a confusion of languages. The Popol Vuh,
a surviving record of the Maya, contains a striking passage:

> Here the language of the tribes changed—their
> speech became different. All they had heard or
> understood when departing from Tulán became

The huge pyramid at Cholula
(a reconstruction).

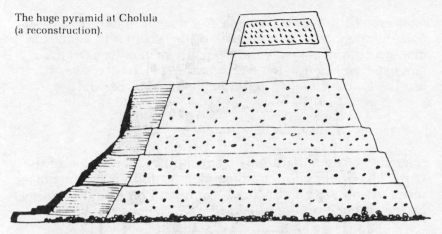

different. . . . Our language was one when we
departed from Tulán. Alas! we have forgotten our
speech. . . .

Over a thousand separate languages were in use in the New
World when the first explorers and colonizers arrived; that
number has now decreased by at least 60 percent. As the
number of spoken languages decreases all over the world,
linguistic scientists are preserving threatened languages
before they vanish altogether, using tape recordings,
vocabulary research, computerization, and memory banks.
This preservation is being carried out among the dwindling
tribes of Siberia, in the Amazon basin, among the Plains
and other Indian tribes of North America, and to a lesser
extent in Central and South America, where the Indian
languages are still strong. The last speaker of the Black
Tartar tribe in Siberia taped examples of his language for
Soviet linguistic scientists, as has the last speaking member
of the Mandan tribe in the United States for American
ethnologists. Ishii, the last surviving speaker of an
unidentified and uncatalogued tribe, died some years ago in
California before scientists could tape his language. It is not
known how many other single survivors of ancient
languages have died with nobody left to understand their
last words.

Although most of the important world languages have
evolved in the last few hundred years, a number of ancient

ones are still in use or have been revived. Speakers of these ancient languages have had to decide whether to adopt the modern technical vocabulary directly or modify it to their language. In Hebrew the decision for "electricity" was to use the Old Testament word *hashmal*, from Ezekiel 1:4,

חשמל

hashmal

referring to the radiating halo surrounding the vision of the Lord. The Navaho for "automobile" is *chidí*, from the noise made by the early Ford cars warming up on a cold morning on the reservation—*chidí-chidí*.

Among the several thousand world languages, only 101 count over 1 million speakers. Of these, the fourteen most important in number of speakers are, in approximate order:

Chinese
English
Hindustani (the spoken form of Hindi and Urdu)
Russian
Spanish
Japanese
German
Indonesian
Portuguese
French
Arabic
Bengali
Malay
Italian

All of these have at least 50 million speakers, including dialects. Chinese is definitely the number-one language, with almost 1 billion speakers. English, second by several lengths—with approximately 300 million native speakers— is nevertheless much more widely spoken over the world's surface than Chinese. Perhaps 200 million additional speakers around the globe use English as a second language.

Since most of the world's population either speaks or is familiar with one of the fourteen languages listed above, or with one of three other widely spoken languages—Dutch, Greek, Swahili—or with a language in either the Scandinavian, the Turkic, or the Slavic group, it is possible for an individual with the time and inclination to be able to communicate with the great majority of the inhabitants of this planet by learning to speak these 20 languages.

Several famous linguists have accomplished or surpassed this feat. Cardinal Giuseppe Mezzofanti, chief Vatican librarian in the last century, reputedly spoke 50 languages fluently, including American Indian and African tongues, and could translate 114 more. Sir John Bowring, once the British governor of Hong Kong, could speak 100 languages and read 100 more, doubtless aided by his collection of dictionaries.

Some of the world's primitive cultures have developed the most complicated languages. At two ends of the temperature scale, the Eskimos and the Zulus possess subtle and complicated languages, until recently unwritten, with inflected vocabularies of 20 to 25 thousand words— thousands of words in excess of the vocabulary used in daily speech by the average American college graduate.

Of all the spoken languages still in use, Basque, a unique tongue spoken in northern Spain and southwestern France, may be the most difficult to learn, being related to nothing on earth except to a small language pocket in the Caucasus Mountains. Basque is probably a remnant of a cave language spoken before the glaciers covered great parts of the Northern Hemisphere. Its extremely difficult structure and vocabulary have elicited the Spanish proverb: "When God wished to punish the Devil he condemned him for seven years to study Basque."

2. *How Languages Started*

No one knows when or where languages started, what the first language was, or which is the oldest language now spoken. It is generally accepted that language evolved from a series of sound signals such as are used by birds, fish, and land and marine animals.

There are a variety of theories concerning the first words uttered by emerging humankind. Perhaps language started with a warning to others, such as "Look out!" "Run!" "Over here!" or "Help!" as a swiftly moving or lumbering beast was approaching. Other "first words" may have been hunting instructions during a group effort or—later—orders from the leader of a war party. On a more personal level, perhaps the first words expressed a warning or a threat to stay away from one's food, or mate, or possession, or warned someone away from a cave or—as animals still do— challenged a rival to combat.

Linguists call another explanation about the beginning of language the "pooh-pooh" theory. It suggests that our first words came as an exclamation of dislike, hunger, pain, or pleasure, eventually leading to the expression of more developed ideas and emotions. In this case the first word would have been an involuntary "Ow!" which, in most languages, still exists as some form of "ow" or "ai."

The "bow-wow" theory postulates that emergent human beings established a beginning vocabulary based on the sounds that certain animals made, as a means of identifying them. This type of naming is still noticeable in childish references to a "moo-cow," a "bow-wow" for a dog, a "quack-quack" for a duck, and the expression "baa-baa black sheep." A cat in Chinese is a *mao*, spoken in a tone exactly parodying the "meow" of any cat.
A striking example for the "bow-wow" theory that has come down through the ages is the word "barbarian," from *barbaros*, originally used by ancient Greek travelers to designate foreigners who did not speak Greek, the language of culture, but who sounded, as they spoke their outlandish tongues, like sheep bleating "baa-baa."

Still another explanation of the beginnings of language is offered by the "ding-dong" theory, which suggests that humans began their ascent to language by naming objects, actions, and phenomena with a recognizable sound, such as "boom" for thunder, "splash" for water, "swish" for a cutting weapon, or "crackle" for a fire. The Japanese *pika-*

pika is a good descriptive word for a flash of lightning, as is
the English "boom!" for any explosion, including the atom
bomb. The word for coining words to echo a sound (or to
give a verbal impression of a sight) is *onomatopoeia,* which
comes from the Greek and means "to make a name."

In the language of the Chinook Indians of Oregon the word
for "heart" is *tun-tun,* an apt description of the noise the
heart makes if you listen to it.

The "yo-he-ho" concept of initial language development is
based on a belief in human cooperation, certainly an
idealistic explanation of the purpose of language. This
theory proposes that the earliest language was chanting to
stimulate collective effort, whether moving great stones to
block off cave entrances from roving carnivores, carrying or
dragging large game back to the tribal compound, or
repeating warlike phrases to inflame the fighting spirit. It is
fairly certain that poetry and song came from this aspect of
beginning speech. Songs of this nature are still with us,
such as the song of the Volga boatman and the sea chanties
of clipper-ship days.

It is probable that humans started their speech patterns in
small family groups and then, as their circles of
communication spread, adopted new words from other
groups. This went on until a common vocabulary or basic
language was formed and proved its worth for cooperative
hunting or raids.

Words which have come down from Neolithic times can
sometimes be recognized in languages spoken today. In
Basque, the word for "knife" is a compound which
translates as "the-stone-that-cuts," and "ceiling" literally
means "roof-of-the-cave."

While theories of basic language origin refer to emergencies,
the hunt, and combat, words for emotions and spiritual
feelings probably derive from applying sounds to emotion—

the "pooh-pooh" theory. "Love" and "hate" are good
examples. In almost all languages the word for "love" is a
pleasant, mellifluous sound, while the word equivalent for
"hate" is harsh and rasping. The same match of sound and
meaning is found in other word pairs ("beautiful" and
"ugly," for example) in many languages.

Language probably derived not from one but from a
combination of the various sources proposed by theorists.
Max Müller, the famous archaeologist and linguist,
suggested that the increasing development and intricacy of
language followed the development of the human brain over
a period of thousands of years.

---

3. *How Languages Spread and Decline*

Languages spread through migrations for food or fertile land, through warfare, conquest, and colonization, through trade or religion, or through a combination of these. The principal languages spread by colonization, for example, are English, French, Spanish, Dutch, Portuguese, and, increasingly, Russian. A language declines when it is literally overcome by a stronger language which, in the long run, proves more useful to the area's population. It is for this reason that numerous emergent states of Africa, former British and French colonies, chose a local African language as their official one and then went back to French or English for communication because of the international advantages and the availability of textbooks and technical works in these languages.

Swahili, a trade language on the African east coast and
interior, has become an important international language
and is official in ten African countries. It has developed an
extensive written literature and is increasingly a must for
anyone working or living in east Africa. If Swahili
eventually takes the place of English completely in the east
African nations, a number of English words already adopted
into Swahili will nonetheless remain—just as English
retained words originating with the Roman legionaries.
English words in Swahili include *eropleni* (airplane), *lori*
(truck), *motokaa* (automobile), *helikopta* (helicopter),
parashuti (parachute), *kapteni* (captain), *jipi* (jeep),
baisikele (bicycle).

———————————

Before India's independence, Urdu and Hindi, now the chief
languages of Pakistan and India respectively, were
considered so similar that they were both referred to as
Hindustani. The principal difference between them is that
Hindi is written in the Sanskritic script Devanagari
("writing of the gods"), and Urdu is written in Arabic
script, the language of the Koran, the holy book of Islam.
Hindi is more influenced by the ancient Sanskrit; Urdu
contains many Turkish, Arabic, Persian, and Pushtu words
dating from the time of Akbar, the great Mogul emperor of
India. Akbar noticed that his army had adopted words used
by different troop contingents to basic Hindustani so that
the warriors could understand commands and each other,
and decided to make this "army" language an official one.
In fact he called the language Urdu, meaning "army." The
word "Urdu" is linguistically related to our English word
"horde," indicating a wild and motley group—not
necessarily an army.

———————————

Hindi speakers in the Republic of India constitute one of
the world's largest language groups. Yet decades after
independence from England, India is still obliged to use
English as a common tongue, since the South Indian
language groups violently oppose the adoption of Hindi as
the official language.

———————————

All European languages, except Hungarian, Estonian, Finnish, and Basque, belong to the Indo-European language family which extends across Europe through the Caucasus to Iran and northern India. The similarity of certain key words in the many languages of this group suggested to early linguists that they were on the trail of an aboriginal world language. It turned out, however, that all these languages belonged to only one group and did not include the Semitic (Middle East) or Sinitic (East Asia) families or the many other language groups of Indian America, Africa, southern Asia, and the Pacific. In other words, we have cataloged only some of the branches and upper limbs of the tree of languages, but have still not identified its lower limbs or its trunk.

Basic Indo-European is thought to have started 25 thousand years ago in central Europe and to have spread all over Europe and through Russia and Iran to the Indian subcontinent. The motivation for this migration was search for food, hunting grounds, and fertile land. In the course of their wandering, these Indo-European speakers developed most of the languages that we, their European, North and South American, and Asian descendants, speak today. However, in the course of the long migrations, the original language changed so much that the speakers of its modified forms could no longer understand each other—a realistic enactment of the story of the Tower of Babel.

Language researchers, in their search for the original homeland of the Indo-European language group, raised the possibility that three words common to all the languages in the group might establish where the basic language began. These three locating words were "beech tree," "turtle," and "salmon." The only geographical location in which all three living forms were found is the area in central Europe between the Elbe, Oder, Vistula, and Rhine rivers. Here there were salmon, turtles, and beech trees, but no turtles north of the Danish border, no beech trees east of the Vistula, and no salmon west of the Rhine. This theory has been supported by the fact that the spoken language closest to the original Indo-European roots is Lithuanian, still spoken in the identified area. Incidentally, the key word for

"salmon," varying but little in all the ancestral languages,
is—you guessed it!—"lox" (or *lachs*).

Another word which has been suggested as a common link
between all primitive Indo-European tribes (also called Aryans,
meaning "noble") is the word for ox-yoke, or *yuk* in old Gothic.
Variants of *yoke* occur in all sections to which the original
Aryans, or proto-Aryans, migrated and worked the patient ox.

Latin is an example of a language spread by conquest.
During the centuries when Roman power covered most of
the known world—or at least the world known to the
Romans—Roman legions, administrative personnel, traders,
and camp followers in colonies throughout most of Europe
developed a slang which mixed with the local Celtic
languages and eventually became French, Spanish,
Portuguese, Italian, Catalán, Romansch (spoken in
southeastern Switzerland), and Rumanian, the last two even
being named for Rome.

Even before the new Latin or Romance languages had fully
supplanted Latin in Europe, Latin itself had been spoken as
a world language for a longer time than any other before or
since.

The new Latin or Romance languages often adopted Roman
camp slang instead of the correct Latin word. *Caput* was
"head" in Latin, but the legionaries used *testa*, a round
cooking pot, jocularly for "head." This ancient slang has
come into French as *tête* and into Italian as *testa*. The
correct Latin word for "head"—*caput*—survives as *capo* in

Italian and American Mafia idiom for "head man" or "chief."

A further change of meaning of the Latin *caput* occurred in German, in which *kaputt* now means "wrecked" or "broken." Germanic burial squads in the Middle Ages counted each corpse as a "head," or *caput*, so the word came to express, in Germany, anything broken, wrecked, or unserviceable.

Roman slang for "horse" was *cavallus*; the correct Latin word was *equus*. The common word became *cheval* in French, *cavallo* in Italian, *caballo* in Spanish, and in the English the plural or collective *cavalry*. The correct Latin word reappears in English only in *equestrian* and *equine*.

The word "mile" comes from the Latin *mille*—"one thousand," referring to a thousand complete paces, left foot and right foot, of the legion's formal parade step, approximately 5.2 feet, the regular Roman way of measuring distance between towns.

Because of the long Roman occupation of England, the Germanic invasions and settlements that followed, and the French Norman conquest in 1066, English is linguistically halfway between the Latin and Germanic languages. (The ancient continental Germans, for their part, managed to oppose the Roman conquest with notable success.) Thousands of Latin-derived words have entered English, as have many words and phrases that are practically unchanged from Latin. Although an ancient Roman might be puzzled by their application, he would easily recognize such words as:

exit	alibi
item	alias
salary	ad hoc
deficit	omnibus
profit	candidate
propaganda	nucleus

sic	calculus
testimony	modus vivendi
habeas corpus	veto
terra firma	subpoena
	persona non grata

Because the use of spoken Latin seems to be receding, there is a tendency to consider it a dead language. Its death may be considered premature, however; it is still used in medical, scientific, legal, and scholarly circles and is studied by thousands throughout the world. It is still the official language of the Roman Catholic church, and publications in Latin are issued regularly by the Vatican.

Like Latin, ancient Greek continues to contribute new words to modern languages. The Greek for "far," *tele,* is used in many combinations:

telephone	far voice (Greek *phone*)
telescope	far watcher (Greek *scopos*)
telegram	far letter (Greek *gramma*)
telepathy	far feeling (Greek *pathos*)
teletype	far impression (Greek *typos*)
television	far view (Latin *visio*, "view," "a seeing")

Greek, a vital language of the eastern Mediterranean, seemed for a while—during the time of Alexander the Great—on its way to becoming the dominant language of the world. Although Greece was later conquered by Rome, Greek was still considered the language of culture and refinement and was taught to young Romans by their Greek slave-tutors. Caesar did not need an interpreter to speak to Cleopatra, nor did Mark Antony—all of them could speak Greek.

Modern Greek is closer to ancient Greek than the Romance languages are to Latin. A literate modern Greek can read and understand the inscriptions cut in stone by his ancestors 25 hundred years ago.

The Semitic language group includes Aramaic, Punic (Phoenician), Hebrew, Amharic, and Arabic. Aramaic was a general language in the ancient Middle East and was the language used daily by Christ.

Aramaic has disappeared as a living tongue except in several small villages in what was ancient Samaria. Phoenician disappeared when the commercial Carthaginian Empire was conquered by Roman armies that destroyed all books and records as well as the cities and their populations.

سلام *salaam*   שלום *shalom*

Arabic and Hebrew are closely related through Aramaic. Among many resemblances, an especially noteworthy one is the usual greeting—*salaam* and *shalom*, both meaning "peace."

The spread of Islam from the seventh century on has been an outstanding example of language conquest through religion. The Arabic language is so tied up with Islam that it has spread over half the world and is still expanding.

The Arabic-speaking Moslems might have conquered all Europe had they not been stopped in central France at the Battle of Poitiers by the Frankish king Charles Martel (Charles the Hammer) in the eighth century. As it was, the Moslems maintained themselves in Spain until 1492, leaving in Spain a legacy of scientific, chemical, medical, and astronomical terms, many of which have come to English through Spanish:

algebra   nadir
alcohol   zenith
chemistry   alkaline
                 cipher

One word adopted from the Moslems of Spain which is used every day by almost everyone in Spanish is ¡*Ojalá!* which means "I hope so!" or "I hope that . . .!" or "May it come to pass!" This expression is an echo of a thousand battlefields, a linguistic memory of the Moslem war cry *Wa Allah!*—"Oh Allah!"

Turkish belongs to the Uighur-Altaic language group, which also includes Finnish, Hungarian, and Estonian. Turkish is similar to a variety of Turkic languages extending through the southern U.S.S.R., central Asia, and western China— essentially the routes of the great invasions from Asia which once swept up to the gates of Vienna. It has long been an axiom that one could travel the caravan routes from Istanbul to Peking speaking only Turkish.

---

4. *1066 and the French Invasion of English*

By some time after the departure of the last Roman legions, England was speaking Anglo-Saxon, a Germanic language. Germanic tribes, coming from the North Sea coast between Holland and Denmark, had invaded and colonized England and established their language as the dominant tongue. The original Celtic language was pushed back to Wales, Scotland, Cornwall, the offshore islands, and Ireland, where the Celtic languages still survive. Then, in 1066 Anglo-Saxon as the preferred language received an almost fatal blow. The Norman French invaded England and William of Normandy vanquished and killed Harold of England—a definite turning point for the English language. More than half of the English vocabulary today is of French-Norman and Latin-via-French origin.

After the Norman conquest the French-speaking conquerors established themselves as the ruling caste. French barons and knights surrounded the new ruler, not Saxon earls and thanes (most of whom had died in their losing battle at Hastings). William doled out the land of these dead Saxons to the warriors who had helped him conquer the country, and favored the new French landholders in his new and heavy tax demands. He treated the native Saxons as socially and economically inferior, a familiar practice in conquered or annexed territory, yet upheld Saxon laws and customs, as he swore to do at his coronation.

The good life, medieval style, of the Norman French overlords is echoed in English speech today, for instance in everyday terms for meat. Meat prepared for the table is still referred to by its modified French name, while the animal from which the meat comes keeps its Saxon name.

THE ANIMAL	MEAT FOR THE TABLE	MODERN FRENCH
steer	beef	*boeuf*
pig	pork	*porc*
calf	veal	*veau*
sheep	mutton	*mouton*
chicken	pullet	*poulet*
deer	venison	*venaison* (from "hunting")

In a word, the Saxons did the raising and slaughtering of the animals, while the Normans enjoyed the eating thereof. Almost all English words that describe food preparation are of French origin, even though they may not look French— for instance boiled, roast, toast, fry, sauce, pastry, soup, jelly, and condiments. Even when English fully surfaced again as the national language of England, tasty dishes were often given French names—a custom evident today on the menus of upper-echelon restaurants in the United States, the British Commonwealth, and indeed most of the world.

Many words which came into English at the time of the Norman Conquest indicate the position of the Saxons after the Battle of Hastings. Their unenviable situation seems to unfold as one considers the following list of French words adopted into English at that time: peasant, trespass, punish, oppress, prohibit, discipline, tax, judge, penalty, prison, torture, supplication, exile, treason, rebel, dungeon, execution. The word *mortgage* (literally "death-pledge"), another Norman contribution to the English vocabulary, is no longer used in conversational French, where it is replaced by *hypothèque*, but it remains a word of considerable importance in English.

———

Other French-derived words of this period reveal the feudal systems and customs introduced by the Norman conquerors: villain, palace, castle, army, armor, lance, tournament, baron, count, duke, noble, tower, domain, mansion, beauty, dance, poetry, rhyme, grace, gentle. English has many other Norman or French derivations having to do with cavalcades, hunting, pleasure, the social graces, the arts, apparel, rooms of mansions, and furniture: parlor, pantry, couch, chair.

———

When the French and Anglo-Saxon tongues blended into a new language, a rare phenomenon occurred that helped give English the world's largest vocabulary: the language offered two words instead of one, a basic Saxon word and a more elegant or formal French word, for many actions and phenomena.

ANGLO-SAXON ORIGIN	FRENCH ORIGIN
smell	odor
sweat	perspiration
eat	dine
dead	deceased
go away	depart
come back	return
want	desire
get	obtain
get	receive
look at	regard

———

Bodily substances that are permissibly expressed by English pronunciation of the adopted French words *urine* and *excrément* are still considered shocking and often unprintable in their original Saxon forms.

———————

In general, almost all the polysyllabic words in English are of French-Latin origin while the one-syllable words come from Anglo-Saxon.

———————

By the fourteenth century, English had again become the written as well as the spoken language of England. Edward I, himself a descendant of the Norman kings, on one occasion formally accused the French king of wanting to wipe out the English language.

———————

Some old French names and expressions have been so anglicized that they have become unrecognizable. The famous riding path in London's Hyde Park, Rotten Row, is a corruption of *la route du roi*—"the king's way." The name of London's Marylebone section and street is a corruption of *Marie-la-bonne*—"Mary the good."

———————

The expression "hoity-toity," for "pretentious," comes from the French *haut toit*—"high roof"—from which the pretentious looked down on the literally "lower" classes.

———————

French began its true ascent as a world language during the golden age of Louis XIV of France, gradually becoming the diplomatic, intellectual, and literary language of Europe. Voltaire, in a letter he wrote from the court of the Prussian king, Frederick the Great, observed that everyone at court spoke French and used German only to soldiers and horses.

———————

Within modern times hundreds of French expressions, of more recent vintage than the early medieval adoptions into English, have become current in English and other world languages: *cliché, rendez-vous, savoir faire, sang-froid, s'il vous plaît, encore, bon voyage, dernier cri, billet-doux, ménage à trois, déshabillé, au contraire, joie de vivre, insouciance, cordon bleu, fin de siècle, dernier mot, nom de* plume, *entente cordiale, coup d'état, détente*. Without these and a multitude of other words it would perhaps be difficult for reporters to write about foreign affairs or theater critics to write their *critiques*.

———————————

5. *How You Can Turn Thousands of English Words into French, Spanish, Italian, German, Portuguese, or Dutch*

André Maurois has recounted an incident between soldiers who met in the trenches during World War I. A Portuguese soldier offered to teach a French soldier a thousand words of Portuguese in less than one minute for 100 francs. The French soldier accepted. "Look," said the Portuguese, "all the words you have in French that end in *-tion* are the same in Portuguese, except that they end in *-ção*, which you should pronounce *-saong*. There are over a thousand of them and they are all feminine gender, just like French. That took less than a minute, didn't it? One hundred francs, please."

Since English is basically a language derived from both
French-Latin and Germanic Anglo-Saxon, it has more
common words in two separate language groups than any
other modern language. Thousands of English words can
easily be converted into French, Spanish, Italian, or
Portuguese. Thousands of others, derived from Anglo-Saxon,
have their cognates in German, Dutch, and the Dutch-related
languages Flemish and Afrikaans, as well as in the
Scandinavian languages, and, with only a little effort, can be
identified like recognizable features in family portraits.

Many English words of Romance origin can be changed
according to their endings into the Romance or Latin
languages. English words ending in -tion, such as "nation,"
"situation," "revolution," and hundreds of others, have
exact equivalents in French and are spelled the same,
except for some written accents: nation, situation,
révolution. (In French as well as the other Latin languages
these are feminine gender.) In Spanish the -tion words end
in -ción: nación, situación, revolución. In Italian the ending
is -zione: nazione, situazione, revoluzione. In Portuguese, as
pointed out by the Portuguese soldier to the gullible poilu,
the ending is -ção: nação, situação, revolução.

Multisyllable English nouns ending in -ty, such as
"fraternity," "liberty," "society," become French by
changing the -ty to -té, to -dad in Spanish, to -tà in Italian,
and to -dade in Portuguese.

ENGLISH	FRENCH	SPANISH	ITALIAN	PORTUGUESE
fraternity	fraternité	fraternidad	fraternità	fraternidade
liberty	liberté	libertad	libertà	liberdade
society	societé	sociedad	società	sociedade

Words that end in -able or -ible in English can be turned
into French or Spanish by using the same endings, into
Italian by changing the endings to -abile or ibile, and into
Portuguese by using -vel.

FRENCH	SPANISH	ITALIAN	PORTUGUESE
possible	posible	possibile	possível
probable	probable	probabile	probável

Many of the multisyllable English adverbs ending in -*ly* are the same in the Latin languages, except that they end in -*ment* in French and -*mente* in the others. "Rapidly," "naturally," and "usually," among others, exist in the Romance languages as follows:

FRENCH	SPANISH	ITALIAN	PORTUGUESE
rapidement	*rápidamente*	*rapidamente*	*rapidamente*
naturellement	*naturalmente*	*naturalmente*	*naturalmente*
usuellement	*usualmente*	*usualmente*	*usualmente*

English nouns and adjectives ending in -*ent*, such as "president" and "evident," have the same spelling in French; in Italian, Spanish, and Portuguese a final e is added. Similar words, like "excellent," vary in spelling but are still recognizable.

FRENCH	SPANISH	ITALIAN	PORTUGUESE
président	*presidente*	*presidente*	*presidente*
évident	*evidente*	*evidente*	*evidente*
excellent	*excellente*	*eccellente*	*exelente*

When the English ending is -*ment*, as in "monument" and "supplement," the French spelling does not change, and the other languages change only slightly.

FRENCH	SPANISH	ITALIAN	PORTUGUESE
monument	*monumento*	*monumento*	*monumento*
supplément	*suplemento*	*supplemento*	*suplemento*

In converting any of these English words of French-Latin derivation into one of the Romance languages, note that in speech, the accent is important and should always be checked with somebody who knows the language. In general, remember the following: the *h* is silent in the Romance languages; the Spanish *j* is pronounced like a strong English *h*; the French *n*, except when it begins a word, has a nasal sound, as do the Portuguese sounds *ã* and *õ*.

As Greek was the ancestor of Latin, and contributed much to the Latin vocabulary, one can turn a number of English medical and psychological words of Greek or Greek-Latin origin into modern Greek simply by prolonging the *ia* ending, pronouncing it *ee-ah* in words like hydrophobia, agoraphobia, kleptomania, nymphomania. In the Greek pronunciation of words like *psyche* ("soul") and *psycheiatros* ("soul doctor"), the p and s are pronounced separately and the *ch* is pronounced hard, like a guttural *k*.

English, German, the Scandinavian languages, and Dutch all descend from a common Teutonic language. It is therefore comparatively easy for German speakers to convert thousands of English words to German, Danish (with the related languages of Norwegian and Swedish), and Dutch (with the Dutch-related languages of Flemish and Afrikaans). Most of the basic words in these languages can be identified with only a little effort, like recognizing familiar features in family portraits. The following comparative listing of some of the thousands of words common to English, German, Dutch, and Danish shows their basic resemblance to each other, despite the linguistic sound shifts of certain letters that occurred many centuries ago as the languages drifted apart from their common ancestor.

ENGLISH	GERMAN	DUTCH	DANISH
bath	*Bad*	bad	bad
best	*best*	best	bedste
blind	*blind*	blind	blind
book	*Buch*	boek	bog
bread	*Brot*	brood	brød
break	*brechen*	breken	braekke
brown	*braun*	bruin	brun
cold	*kalt*	koud	kold
come	*kommen*	komen	komme
dance	*tanzen*	danzen	danse
daughter	*Tochter*	dochter	datter
drink	*trinken*	drink	drikke
false	*falsch*	vals	falsk
father	*Vater*	vader	fader
find	*finden*	vinden	finde
finger	*Finger*	vinger	finger
foot	*Fuss*	voet	fod
give	*geben*	geben	give
good	*gut*	goed	god
green	*grün*	groen	grøn

hair	Haar	haar	hår
hammer	Hammer	hamer	hammer
hand	Hand	hand	hånd
hang	hängen	hangen	haenge
hard	hart	hard	hård
help	helfen	helpen	hjaelpe
here	hier	hier	her
ice	Eis	ijs	is
lamp	lampe	lamp	lampe
land	Land	land	land
man	Mann	man	mand
midday	Mittag	middag	middag
midnight	Mitternacht	middernacht	midnat
mother	Mutter	moeder	moder
mouse	Maus	muis	mus
rat	Ratte	rat	rotte
ring	Ring	ring	ring
sand	Sand	zand	sand
see	sehen	zien	se
send	senden	zend	sende
shoe	Schuh	schoen	sho
shoulder	Schulter	schouder	skulder
silver	Silber	zilver	søl
sing	singen	zingen	synge
sink	sinken	zinken	synke
so	so	zoo	så
storm	Sturm	storm	storm
summer	Sommer	somer	sommer
think	denken	denken	taenke
thirst	Durst	durst	tørst
under	unter	onder	under
wash	waschen	wassen	vashe
water	Wasser	water	vand
west	Western	west	vest
wild	wild	wild	vild
wind	Wind	wid	vind
winter	Winter	winter	vinter
wolf	Wolf	wolf	ulv
word	Wort	woord	ord
young	jung	jong	ung

Of all the languages in the North Germanic subfamily, only Icelandic, isolated as it is in the central Atlantic, has stayed close to the original North Germanic root. For this reason it is practically unintelligible to speakers of the Scandinavian languages, German, Dutch, and English. But if an ancient dragon ship manned by Vikings should sail out of the Atlantic mists to an Icelandic harbor, its crew would have no difficulty communicating with the modern Icelanders.

A Germanic dialect, Frisian—or Fries—spoken in the Dutch province Friesland and on the North Sea coast near Denmark, is so close to English that the following English couplet sounds practically the same in both languages:

> Good butter and good cheese
> Is good English and good Fries.

Comparing English "bath" and German *Bad*, "thanks" and *Danke*, shows that English, alone with Icelandic of the North Germanic languages, has retained the th sound of the Anglo-Saxon letter thorn, þ . In this case English lags behind the other Germanic languages, which have simplified the th sound to d.

---

6. *Language, Gender, and Sex*

Most European languages have a built-in grammatical preoccupation with the gender of nouns which also influences the adjectives used with them. In the Latin languages all nouns are either masculine or feminine; German, Greek, and the Slavic languages go even further—all nouns are either masculine, feminine, or neuter gender.

English is much more gender-free than the Latin languages
in its noun forms. Nouns referring to people and larger
animals are assigned genders, but all other nouns are neuter;
exceptions are (less and less frequently) made for ships,
planes, trains, cars and other large mechanical objects,
which are usually referred to as "she."

Among the Indo-European languages, English puts the least
emphasis on grammatical gender of nouns. Chinese is
probably the most unisex in its pronouns of all languages,
having the same word for "he," "she," and "it."

Latin languages have masculine and feminine forms for
"the" which indicate the gender of the noun. In French
there are two forms, *le* (masculine) and *la* (feminine), for
"the" with a singular noun, and an inclusive neuter form,
les, for plural nouns. Spanish uses *el* and *la* in the singular
and *los* and *las* in the plural. Portuguese also has four forms
for "the"—*o* and *a* in the singular and *os* and *as* in the
plural.

Although Italian has only two genders, it offers eleven
variants for "the," not only to differentiate between
masculine and feminine but to attain the most mellifluous
sound combination with the word that follows.

German nouns are divided into three genders—masculine,
feminine, and neuter. The word for "the" is *der*, *die*, or *das*,
with a common *die* for the plural. In addition, *der*, *die*, and
das change to *des* or *den* or conserve their sounds
depending on the case they are in—that is, how they are
used in the sentence.

Russian has three genders but, in line with its frequent
tendency to briefness, has no word for "the" at all. This is
also true of the other Slavic languages.

Russian nouns are all masculine, feminine, or neuter and all
change their endings according to their place in the
sentence, as do their accompanying adjectives. This is one
of the reasons that Russian is considered so difficult to
learn—except, of course, for a Russian.

Although gender, or the sex of all objects, is so
grammatically important in European languages, no one has
satisfactorily explained how all objects became divided into
categories based on sex. It is thought that this language
concept may have started by classifying living things and
then transferring classification to objects or forces that
seemed male or female.

In most languages "sun" is a masculine word and "moon"
and "earth" are feminine. In German, however, "the sun" is
feminine and "the moon" masculine. "Day" is generally
masculine and "night" feminine. "Light" is feminine except
in German, where it is neuter.

"Child" is understandably neuter in German, but the word
for "girl," *Mädchen*, is paradoxically neuter, and so is
"wife"—*Weib*, a word also used for "female" or "woman."
As Mark Twain said: "In German, a young lady has no sex,
but a turnip has."

The female organ is feminine in all Latin languages but
French, where it is masculine (*le vagin*).

The Latin languages have masculine and feminine forms for
"they"—*ils* and *elles* in French, and *ellos* and *ellas* in
Spanish—usage depending on whether "they" refers to
masculine or feminine objects or persons. If the group
referred to is mixed, "they" takes the masculine form,
whether or not women—or feminine nouns—are in the
majority.

In Spanish, for example, if only one man and twenty women passengers were on a bus, the group would be referred to as *pasajeros* (masculine), not *pasajeras* (feminine), and would become *pasajeras* only after the male passenger had gotten off the bus. Adjectives also follow this male-oriented grammatical rule. In the hypothetical case of a sit-down strike for women's rights in a plaza of a South American city, the word for "seated ones" would have a masculine plural ending if any men at all participated in the demonstration.

Spanish even has masculine and feminine words for "we"— *nosotros* and *nosotras*. Women, however, frequently use the masculine form even when speaking of themselves as a group, so strong is the influence of *machismo* in Spanish.

The word for "man"—*hombre*—is constantly used in Spanish conversation as an exclamation by both men and women. This has been going on for generations, long before "Man!" became a constant interjection in American idiom.

If a Spanish or Italian husband telephones his wife to say that he is with a friend, the ending of the word he uses for "friend"—*amigo* or *amiga* in Spanish, *amico* or *amica* in Italian—would clearly indicate the friend's sex. So would the spoken words in German, *Freund* and *Freundin*. In French the difference between *ami* and *amie* would be harder to detect, and in English, a much more unisex language in its noun endings, the sex of the friend would not be indicated at all.

In French, most names for animals under the size of a rabbit are either masculine or feminine, whereas for larger animals there are two variants. The French word for "mouse" is feminine—*la souris*. Therefore, if one wishes to designate a male mouse, one would have to say *la souris mâle*—"the (feminine) mouse male." "Rat" in French is masculine: *le rat*. To refer to a female rat, one would have to say *le rat femelle*—"the (masculine) rat female."

Some French words have changed gender over the years. When automobiles were first invented the word *automobile* was assigned masculine gender but now the word is classified as feminine.

In virtually all languages, certain innocent-sounding words may bring on a conversational shock. In French one must be careful with the word *fille*, which means "girl" or "daughter." When *fille* is used in context as "daughter" there is no difficulty, but when you use it for "girl" you must qualify it as *jeune fille* ("young girl") or *petite fille* ("little girl"). Without these qualifying words you are suggesting that the *fille* you are talking about is, in the words of the Victorians, a "woman of easy virtue."

In Spanish, to use the sacrosanct word *madre*, "mother," to refer to a person's mother without qualifying it with another word is to live dangerously. *La madre* ("the mother") or *tu madre* ("your mother") suggests a common insult—an involved inference referring to questionable sexual practices by the mother of the person addressed. To avoid anything that sounds like this familiar insult, you should always use the expression *su señora madre*—"your lady mother"—or *su mamá*.

It is curious that in comparatively recent American slang the word "mother" is an insult when applied by one male to another.

By custom, a Spanish woman retains her name after marriage. If, for example, a woman named María Fernández marries a man called Antonio Rodríguez, her name becomes Señora María Fernández de Rodríguez—the *de* implying, linguistically at least, that she is the property of her husband. The last names of their children, however, will be Rodríguez-Fernández until the next generation, when the mother's last name (unless it is a famous one) is usually dropped.

Customary marriage services in different languages contain some surprises. In German the groom is instructed to "love and honor" his bride; in Hebrew, the service enjoins the bride to "love, to cherish, to obey" her husband. The English service was identical until "obey" was changed to "cherish." The Greek marriage service leaves no doubt about the woman's role: "This woman will subject herself to this man." The Spanish version is unexpectedly in tune with ideas on women's liberation—"I give you a wife but not a slave."

The French marriage injunctions stress faithfulness: "The spouses owe faithfulness and assistance, each to the other." This Gallic preoccupation with fidelity reminds one of the curious fact that the French word for "love," *amour*, is masculine in the singular but feminine when used in the plural.

The Prophet Mohammed allowed a maximum of four wives at a time to true believers, and according to Islamic law, any one of them can be divorced by a simple formula spoken by her husband. This formula, which must be repeated three times, is: *Taaleka wallahi wa billahi wa tallahi*—"By Allah the bonds are dissolved." Although this easy divorce formula does not apply vice versa, Islamic law does provide for the financial well-being of the divorced wife.

In recent years considerable pressure has been exercised by proponents of women's rights against the use of English words which contain the word "man," such as "chairman," "spokesman," "anchorman," "layman," "mailman," "workman." One suggestion being followed is that the word "man" in these cases be replaced by "person." This linguistic compromise favors Latin roots (French: *personne*) over the Germanic ones from which Anglo-Saxon got the word *Mann* in the first place.

In German *Mann* is commonly used for "husband." *Mein Mann* means "my husband" and not the somewhat suggestive "my man," and "my wife," in similar fashion, basically means "woman" as well as "wife." German envelopes are frequently addressed to the husband with *Frau* written after the husband's name: *Herrn Heinrich Schmidt, und Frau.* If one is speaking to a man about his wife, one refers to her as "Ihre guädige Frau" (your honored wife).

In the Latin languages the word for "woman" is acceptable and interchangeable for "wife." In French, Spanish, Italian, and Portuguese, respectively, *ma femme, mi mujer, mia moglie, minha mulier* means "my wife," or "my woman."

A woman's choice of words and expressions in any language is understandably different from a man's. Japanese is a good example of this tendency. Japanese women customarily employ a more polite speech and choose the more deferential verb forms. Japanese men are inclined to shorten verbs and to express themselves in short and vigorous conversational bursts, reminiscent of the decisive and forceful manners of the traditional *samurai*.

The Japanese have several words for "I"—*watakushi*, the more feminine *watashi*, and the short, military-sounding *boku*, this last word formerly used only by men. But today, especially among the younger, more liberated generation, some Japanese women now use *boku*, the proud warrior word, to refer to themselves.

The Semitic languages, of which Arabic and Hebrew are the principal survivors, are even more preoccupied with masculine and feminine gender than the European languages. Not only are the nouns, pronouns, and adjectives masculine and feminine, but even the verbs change gender. The simple expression "I love you" has six varieties in Hebrew, depending on whether the speaker is a male or a female, talking to a male or a female, or to several males or females at the same time. If the males or females of such a group are mixed, the masculine gender predominates, as in the Latin languages.

Russian verbs have masculine and feminine forms in the past tense but not in the present or future tenses.

In the Hopi language there are two words for "Thank you," *kwakwha* for use by men, and *askwali* for use by women. Some merriment is caused in Hopi circles when visiting tourists try out these words—they often get them wrong.

In Mexico the Mazateco have developed a private male language of long and short whistles which correspond to the syllables of certain words. Mazateco women are therefore unable to understand what the men are talking about and, so far, no male has apparently betrayed the secret.

Among primitive tribes that are still living far from civilization in such reaches as the jungles of South America, Africa, southeast Asia, and parts of the frozen north, anthropologists have found specialized male and female languages for sex-separate tribal activities and taboos on use of the language by the other sex. Thus women cannot mention weapons or war or hunting or men's activities in general, and the males of the tribe observe the taboo on mentioning cooking, weaving, women's garments, or women's activities. If a woman uses a word belonging to the warrior-hunter vocabulary, she risks bad luck for the tribe and punishment for herself. To get around this taboo, women have sometimes invented a special women's vocabulary for male terms so they can secretly talk to each other about the activities of the males.

---

7. Language Incidents That Changed History

In all of South America, more people speak Portuguese than Spanish. The Portuguese speakers are concentrated in Brazil, the great eastern bulge of South America. They speak Portuguese instead of Spanish because of a pope's decision 500 years ago which was designed to keep the peace between Spain and Portugal. In 1481, when Spanish and Portuguese seafarers were already beginning to explore the Atlantic, the reigning pope—hoping to keep peace between the two powers, issued a Papal Bull awarding to Portugal all undiscovered lands on a horizontal line south of the Canary Islands and all lands north of the line to Spain. In 1493, one year after Columbus discovered the New World under Spain's sponsorship, the pope changed the boundary line. He awarded the "new" lands west of the 38° west longitude (all of South America) to Spain and those east of it to Portugal—prompting Francis I of France to remark: "I should like to see the passage in Adam's will that divides the New World between my brothers, Charles V of Spain and the King of Portugal." A final arrangement in 1494 moved the line west to 46° 37' allowing Portugal to claim the great land mass that became Brazil.

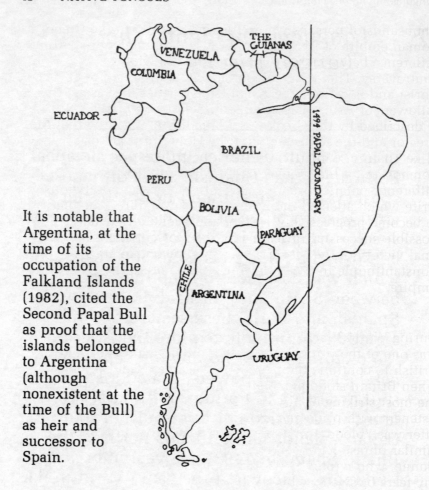

It is notable that Argentina, at the time of its occupation of the Falkland Islands (1982), cited the Second Papal Bull as proof that the islands belonged to Argentina (although nonexistent at the time of the Bull) as heir and successor to Spain.

Hiroshima and Nagasaki might have been spared the atom bomb if a single Japanese word had been translated differently. The word was *mokusatsu*, which can mean either "ignore," "withhold comment," or "have no comment." Before dropping the first atom bomb, the United States warned Japan of a new weapon and gave the Japanese government the chance to surrender in order to avoid overpowering destruction to its cities. The Imperial Government announced internationally that, pending cabinet discussion of the development, it was following a policy of *mokusatsu*. This verb was translated as "ignore"— and the Bomb was dropped.

Thousands of persons were killed or tortured in the Greco-Roman empire of Byzantium because of a one-letter spelling difference between two key words in a religious controversy. The disagreement concerned the nature of Christ and is called "the Arian heresy" after the losers, the followers of Arius. The Arians insisted that Christ's nature is described by the Greek word *homoisian*, meaning that the Creator and the Redeemer and the Holy Spirit are of a "like" nature, while the orthodox belief was that they are *homoösian*, of the "same" nature. The conflict this difference entailed was typical of the internecine religious strife which affected the Eastern Roman Empire, causing it to become progressively weaker and eventually making possible successful invasions by the Moslem Arabs and the final victory of the Moslem Turks, who conquered Constantinople in 1453, putting a final end to the Eastern Empire.

During World War II, Churchill's use of the English tongue was one of the principal morale builders which enabled the British to continue their resistance against Nazi Germany when Britain stood alone after the fall of France. Perhaps the most striking of his phrases, and one that filled his listeners with pride and defiance, was that all he had to offer was "blood, toil, tears, and sweat." By a coincidence a similar phrase had been used 399 years previously by John Donne, who wrote: " 'Tis in vain to do so or mollify it with thy tears or sweat or blood."

German almost became the official language of the United States of America. The Continental Congress, convened in Philadelphia during the Revolution, at one time considered adopting a new language for the future United States, perhaps with the aim of cutting off all ties with England. Among the languages suggested were German, Hebrew, and French. German was the most favored for several reasons: there were many German-speaking Americans in Pennsylvania and other states; Dutch settlers in New York and elsewhere could learn to use German easily; German would be easy for other colonials to learn, since it was basically similar to English; the Hessians, German troop levies "rented" by the British, were deserting to the

Americans and many wished to remain in America.
Nevertheless, when the proposition came to a vote, English
was chosen as the language of the new republic—by the
majority of one vote!

George III, who spoke German fluently, was the first of the
Hanoverian Georges to be fluent in English.

The conquest of the Aztec Empire by Cortés was greatly
facilitated by a language bridge created by two interpreters.
After the Spanish had landed and were engaged in combat
on the Mexican coast, a bronzed Maya warrior about to be
killed suddenly shouted in Spanish, "Don't kill me,
caballero. I am a Castilian like yourself!" He turned out to
be a shipwrecked and very sunburned Spaniard who had
joined the Maya. Later, Cortés acquired an Indian
woman, Malintzín, who spoke both Maya and Aztec,
so that Cortés and his men could communicate with the
Aztecs by using both interpreters and all three languages:
Spanish to Maya and Aztec and the reverse. Malintzín soon
acquired the Spanish language, a new name, Marina, and a
lover—Cortés himself (this relationship ended when Cortés
married her to one of his subordinates). Marina was able to
speak directly to the Aztec rulers and to understand what
they were saying among themselves, while the Aztecs could
not understand the conversation or orders of the Spanish
invaders—so the Aztecs remained ignorant of their
approaching doom.

Malintzín-Marina, in spite of or because of her help to the
Spaniards, is considered by Mexicans to be a traitor to her
people, and even the name Malinche, a local pronunciation
of Malintzín, is a word of contempt. In modern Mexico,
malinchero denotes a Mexican crassly devoted to foreign
interests.

yepolínhq mexiica

Aztec representation of Malintzín translating for Cortés.

The four words which suddenly appeared on the wall during the feast of Belshazzar of Babylon and which were interpreted by the prophet Daniel (Daniel: 5) served as a prophecy and perhaps as a psychological shock to the reveling Babylonians. The four words—*Mene, Mene, Tekel, Upharsin* (in Aramaic: "numbered, numbered, weighed, divided")—were interpreted by the prophet as: "God hath numbered thy kingdom, and finished it. Thou art weighed in the balance and art found wanting. Thy kingdom is divided, and given to the Medes and Persians." This interpretation certainly did not encourage the Babylonians when, during the same night, they found themselves in battle against the Medes and Persians who, even as the banquet progressed, were moving into the city.

Subsequently the Jews fared better under the Persians than they had under the Babylonians and eventually returned to Israel.

The result of an important engagement in the Ardennes during the Battle of the Bulge in World War II was probably influenced by—and certainly sticks in the memory because of—the use of a single word by General Anthony McAuliffe. The word was "Nuts!"—the reply given by the general to a German offer to accept surrender of his command to avoid its annihilation. The panache of this reply raised the morale of his outnumbered troops, who successfully held the line and contributed to the winning of the Battle of the Bulge. The German command post which received the one-word message, not fully comprehending the derisive nature of the word, at first interpreted it in its meaning of "crazy." Only later did they realize its magnificent insolence.

It has often been said, more or less seriously, that World War I was caused by street signs. All the suppressed peoples of pre-war Europe—Serbs, Croats, Slovenes, Czechs, Slovaks, Poles, Rumanians, Letts, Lithuanians, Estonians, the French of Alsace-Lorraine—had a constant reminder of their subject condition in the street signs of their own cities, written in the official language of their overlords, the Austro-Hungarian, German, or Russian empires. Nevertheless, after two world wars and the present freedom to use one's own language in central or Eastern Europe, the national fragmentation has not generally improved the general situation from what it was under the "common market" aspect of the old Austro-Hungarian Empire. In fact, after two world wars the U.S.S.R.–controlled bloc extends, in central Europe, a great distance beyond the old frontiers of the Russian Empire.

The Nazi propaganda minister Joseph Goebbels, in a late effort to exhort Germans to even greater efforts toward final victory in World War II, warned an immense rally that if the Allies won the war the German people would be forced to learn English, an unpleasant sounding and supremely difficult language. This threat probably had no effect on the war effort and, although the Allies did win, German is still flourishing as the most important central European language. After Russian, it has the greatest number of native speakers in Europe.

All French schoolchildren are taught that the commander of
Napoleon's Imperial Guard at Waterloo replied to a British
offer to surrender with the immortal words: "The Guard
dies but never surrenders." This noble statement was
reputedly uttered by General Pierre Cambronne; however,
his actual words are generally considered to have been more
on the order of General McAuliffe's reply to the Germans,
130 years later. Based on reports from participants in the
battle, what General Cambronne really said was:

Merde! La garde ne se rend jamais.

("S---! The Guard never surrenders.")

The sound of the phrase heard through the crashing of
gunfire and the screams of horses and men perhaps lent
itself to the more printable textbook interpretation:

La garde meurt mais ne se rend jamais.

("The Guard dies but never surrenders.")

Cambronne's name is still connected with the second
version. When the offending word is referred to in a polite
conversation in French (the most polite among languages) it
is called *le mot de Cambronne*, "the word of Cambronne,"
or sometimes just *les cinq lettres*, "the five letters." This
word is also used to say "good luck" to an actor when he is
about to go on stage or to someone about to confront a
difficult situation. When the first French astronaut enters
the space capsule for take-off, the last word of farewell and
good luck he will hear will undoubtedly be *le mot de
Cambronne*.

8. Rallying Cries of Conquest, Defiance, or Prayer

At certain moments in history the constant repetition of a few simple words has been effective enough to galvanize a nation to actions which have changed the world. The power of rallying cries or slogans ("slogan" itself comes from the Celtic word for "battle cry") has been obvious to the molders of public opinion from ancient times to the present. The most effective national slogans have pertained to specific aims at certain definite times. They must be short, catchy, easy to remember, and keyed to a real or imagined need—like the catch phrases invented on Madison Avenue. Some of these effective rallying cries of history are still with us; others, having served their initial purpose, have vanished into history.

ORIGINAL MOTTO	TRANSLA-TION	ORIGIN AND EFFECT
Cartago delenda est!	Carthage must be destroyed!	Cato, the great Roman orator, used this as the final phrase in every speech he made in the Senate of Rome. It was successful—Carthage was destroyed, and Rome became the supreme world power.
I tán i epitás! Εἰ τάν εἰ ἐπιτάς!	With it or on it!	A form of farewell reputedly used by ancient Spartan mothers and wives to their sons or husbands going to war, carrying great shields. If killed nobly in battle, warriors would be carried home on their shields. If they lost their shields in battle, however, they would be disgraced. This injunction was an important morale booster to the ancient Spartans and eventually to all Greek warriors from Thermopylae, thousands of years ago, right down to the present.
Le shanah ha ba'ah b'yerushalim! לשנה הבאה בירושלים	Next year in Jerusalem!	A ritual declaration made by Jews at Passover ever since the fall of Jerusalem to the Romans. This repeated wish has been successful—after more than 2,000 years, Jerusalem again belongs to the Jews.
La illaha illa Allah wa Mohammed er rasul Allahi! لا إله إلا الله ومحمد رسول الله	There is no god but God and Mohammed is His messenger!	This Arabic profession of faith fired and inspired the Moslem conquest throughout Asia, Europe, and Africa. It is still repeated five times a day by all Moslems throughout the world in their prayers.
Dieu le veult!	God wills it!	Initially said by Peter the Hermit, these Old French words launched the Crusades, whose aim was to deliver the Holy Land and Jerusalem from the Moslem Saracens. After several Crusades and endless bloodshed, the Holy Land was conquered but, under the pressure of the Moslems, the Crusaders were unable to hold it.

Liberté, Egalité, Fraternité! 	Liberty, Equality, Fraternity!	This was the motto of Revolutionary France, and is today the motto of the French Fourth Republic. It was extremely successful at first, in Napoleon's early campaigns; the troops levied by the monarchies opposing Napoleon readily sympathized with the sentiments apparently motivating the French. This sympathy later cooled when Napoleon's own imperialistic designs became evident.
Proletarier aller Länder vereinigt euch!	Workers of the world, unite!	These words come from the first page of *The Communist Manifesto* of 1848, written by Karl Marx and Friedrich Engels, Germans who wrote and published in German while living in England. This message, which has achieved worldwide distribution in translation, qualifies as successful in half the world's area, although its ultimate success has yet to be determined.
On les aura!	We'll get them!	This slogan, used by French soldiers and civilians in World War I, referred to the Germans. The rallying cry was successful; the French, together with their many allies, did defeat the Germans.
Ein Volk, ein Reich, ein Führer!	One people, one country, one leader!	This rallying cry of the German National Socialists (Nazis) was at first eminently successful in uniting the German people, although it must be counted as finally unsuccessful—as most of the other nations of the world united against the Germans.
¡No pasarán!	They shall not pass!	This Spanish Republican motto used during the Spanish Civil War was an adaptation of a French battle cry used in the Battle of Verdun in World War I, *Ils ne passeront pas!* The Spanish motto did inspire the defenders of

the Republic, but must be judged unsuccessful—the Franco supporters "passed" through and over the lines of the defenders.

Remember the Alamo! Remember the Maine! Remember Pearl Harbor!		Each of these American rallying cries refers to a specific attack on Americans which triggered an official declaration of war (against, respectively, Mexico, Spain, and Japan). The outcome of each war was successful for the United States.
Banzai! 万歳 ！	Ten thousand years!	Although this exclamation was used in Japan long before World War II, in that conflict it became linked to war cries during desperate Japanese attacks. The expression "ten thousand years" came to mean "ten thousand years to the Emperor," or "to Japan," or to both inseparably.

$$E = mc^2$$

Not in itself a rallying cry of conquest, defiance, or prayer, it belongs in this listing as a simple statement that has already affected humanity and the world more than all the others together. It is Einstein's equation, Energy = mass × the speed of light squared, the application of which has brought us into the nuclear age with all its advantages as well as oppressive indications of general doom. An even simpler interpretation of the equation is that "In three letters and one number it explains the working of the stars."

9. *Words of Love and Admiration*

In the languages which divide all nouns
into grammatical masculine and feminine
(or masculine, feminine, and neuter), the
word for "love" changes its gender
according to language. "Love" is masculine
in the Latin languages, and feminine in
German and Russian and its related
languages.

Greek, along with Chinese and related languages, offers a choice of words for "love" depending on whether friendship, family love, love for country, romantic love, or passion is meant.

Although the sound of the word "love" in all languages is usually a gentle and pleasant one, the Chinese *ai* ("love") is an exception to some European ears: in Latin languages, *ai* is the word for "Ow!" or "Ouch!"

The following list of ways to say "I love you" in a variety of languages is offered for linguistic comparison. In the languages that use non-Roman alphabets, the phrase has been spelled out in Roman letters. Most of the expressions can be spoken by man to woman or by woman to man, but where alternate forms exist, the woman-to-man form is given in parentheses. It is recommended that you check the pronunciation with someone who speaks the language before using the phrase.

Amharic: *Afekrishalehou*
Arabic: *Ana b'hibbik (Ana b'hibbak)*
Cambodian: *Bon sro lanh oon*
Chinese: *Wo ai ni*
Danish: *Jeg elsker Dig*
Dutch: *Ik houd van je*
Farsi: *Tora dust midaram*
Finnish: *Minä rakistan sinua*
French: *Je t'aime*
Gaelic: *Tá grá agam ort*
German: *Ich liebe dich*
Greek: *S'agapó*
Hausa: *Ina sonki*
Hebrew: *Ani ohev otakh (Ani ohevet otkhah)*
Hindi: *Maiñ tumheñ piyar karta huñ*
Hopi: *Nu' umi unangwa'ta*
Hungarian: *Szeretlek*
Indonesian: *Saja kasih saudari (Saja kasih saudara)*
Italian: *Ti voglio bene*
Japanese: *Watakushi-wa anata-wo aishimasu*
Korean: *Tangsinŭl sarang hä yo*
Lao: *Khoi huk chau*
Lingala: *Nalingi yo*
Mohawk: *Konoronhkwa*
Navaho: *Ayór ánósh'ní*
Norwegian: *Jeg elsker Dem*
Polish: *Ja cię kocham*
Rumanian: *Te inbesc*
Russian: *Ya tebya liubliu*
Sioux: *Techíhhila*

Spanish: *Te quiero*
Swahili: *Ninikupenda*
Swedish: *Jag älska Dig*
Thai: *Chăn ráte khun*
Turkish: *Ben sevi
    seviyorum*

Urdu: *Mujge tumae
    mahabbat hai*
Vietnamese: *Tôi yêu em*
Welsh: *Yr wyf yn du
    garu*
Zuñi: *Tom ho' ichema*

The expressions in the list for "I love you" in Spanish and
Italian really mean "I want you"—they use the verbs *querer*
(Spanish) and *volere* (Italian)—"to want," "to desire," "to
love"—in preference to *amar* or *amare*, whose only meaning
is "to love."

Words of endearment can generally be applied to male or
female:

FRENCH

mon petit chou ....

mon trésor ....

mon chéri ....

ENGLISH

my little cabbage

my treasure

my dear one

GERMAN

mein Schatz ....

Liebling or *Liebchen* ......

Englein ....

ENGLISH

my treasure

little love

little angel

ITALIAN

tesoro mio ....

amore mio ....

gioia mia ....

ENGLISH

my treasure

my love

my joy

SPANISH

amorcito ....

mi amor ....

mi vida ....

mi corazón ....

mi sangre ....

ENGLISH

little love

my love

my life

my heart

my blood

The word for "dear" or "darling" in the Latin languages
changes gender according to the sex of the person referred
to. In Spanish *querido, querida;* in Italian *carino, carina;* in

French *chéri, chérie* are used for male and female respectively.

A pleasant Russian endearment to a woman is *miloshka,* "very sweet one." *Golubchik*—"pigeon"—can be used for either sex.

The adjective "beautiful" used to describe a woman in Russian is *krasivaya* or *krasnaya,* both of which are derived from *krasniy,* "red." This adjective has nothing to do with politics; red has been a favorite color in Russia for many centuries.

A traditional Japanese compliment to a woman's beauty compares a beautiful face to "an egg with eyes," *tamago kato no kao;* the classically perfect female countenance is oval, flat, with striking black almond-shaped eyes.

When speaking Arabic, a man can get an immediate reaction by referring to a woman's eyes as *yoon al ghrazaali,* "the eyes of the gazelle," bringing to mind the huge, limpid, appealing eyes of the gazelle of the desert. Perhaps this compliment derived from the former custom that allowed Arab males to see only the eyes of any woman not in his own harem. Now that women's features are more exposed in most Arab countries, the prized gazelle image can also be applied, in the more Westernized countries, to a woman's ankles, legs, posture, and demeanor, so that she can be described as completely *ghrazaali*—"gazelle-like" in toto.

In China thousands of years ago, a poet said of the great beauty Hsi Chi that when she went for a walk fish dived deeper, geese swooped off their course, and deer ran into the forest before her beauty. Therefore, instead of saying a woman is as beautiful as Hsi Chi, in Chinese one simply says the four words *ch'en yü, le yen,* "diving fish, swooping geese."

In Latin areas, such as the Spanish peninsula, Latin America, and Italy, a custom that is often misunderstood by women travelers from northern climes is the compliment to female beauty spoken by a male to a female when they pass each other on the street. It generally signifies simple admiration, not an attempted pick-up; it needs no reply. The Spanish even have a name for it—*el piropo.*

A *piropo* may be considerably more inventive than a mere reference to a young woman's beauty, and is often elaborately indirect: "It must be lonely in heaven since one of the more beautiful angels has descended to earth!" Nor are young women the only recipients; an Italian may say, as he passes a more mature woman, *"Vecchia ma ancora buona!"*—"Old but still good!"

10. Insults and Profanity around the World

The names of various familiar animals usually have a derisive and insulting meaning when applied to people. English accomplishes this with rat, louse, pig, skunk, dog, bitch—and in British countries—cow. Other languages use different animals to describe offensive persons. French uses *chameau* ("camel") and *vache* ("cow") for unpleasant individuals; *vache* is also slang for "police." *Cochon* ("pig") is also a strong epithet applied to a low or offensive person. A prostitute is referred to as a *poule* ("hen") and a pimp or procurer in French slang is a *maqueraud* ("mackerel").

A peculiarly French epithet is *fumier*, a reference to the farm manure pile—which "smokes" (*fumer*, "to smoke") in the cold country mornings in the villages of France.

Because in French *les vaches* ("the cows") can mean the police (just as "pigs" does in English), a joke is sometimes played on tourists by recommending a reasonable hotel, the "Hôtel Morovache," with the suggestion that any policeman knows where it is. When the name of this nonexistent hotel is pronounced by the innocent tourist, it sounds like *mort aux vaches!*—"death to the police!"—a familiar cry apt to be unappreciated by the local *agents de police*.

In Arabic the word "dog" has been used as an insult ever since, about 1,350 years ago, a dog barked and alerted the enemies of Mohammed while the founder of Islam was hiding from them in a cave. *Ya, ibn kalb*—"Oh, son of the dog"—are fighting words in Arabic.

Dog-based insults are common in English and the Germanic languages. A German favorite is *verdammter Schweinehund!*—"damned pig-dog!"—and the less explosive *stommehond*, "stupid dog," is a Dutch example. In Vietnam the insult *do cho de* literally means "you dog birth."

Russian speakers use the expression "son of a female dog," *sukin sin*, in much the same way the equivalent English expression is used. But the exuberant Russians can go even further, with the insult *huy sobaki*, "dog's male member," and then can top that one with *huy morshevyi*, "walrus' member."

On a higher cultural level, the Russian term *n'ye kulturniy* ("uncultured") is considered a sufficient put-down. *Durak* can best be interpreted as "village idiot."

"Ass" is used as an insult implying stupidity in all areas where asses are common. In other places a local animal is selected. In Swahili, a stupid person is a *punda*—"zebra"— and instead of using "dog" in insults, another local representative is chosen—*fisti*, "hyena."

Spanish has a special insult-by-animal-name: the word for "he-goat," *cabrón*, which has come to signify an impotent or consenting cuckold or, generally, a fool. To a race preoccupied with *machismo*, "maleness," to be called a *cabrón* is a violent insult indeed; sometimes it is even applied, with supreme illogicality, to a woman—*cabrona*.

The Italian equivalent of "cuckold" is *cornuto*, "horned one," usually delivered with a paralinguistic extra punch— holding the hand upward and folding the middle fingers down, indicating the horns "worn" by the cuckold in question. This same gesture, when pointed out or down in the direction of one's opponent, becomes an invocation of the evil eye against him.

The typically polite Japanese use few insults and those they do use tend to be indirect. *Baka* (fool) is a combination of the Chinese characters for "horse" and "deer" with the implication that anyone who cannot tell a horse from a deer is obviously a fool. Another insult is *kono ya ro*—roughly equivalent to "that field hand" or "that peasant."

One of the gravest insults in Chinese is to call someone a "turtle," *too-tze*, an animal connected with several types of sexual deviation. When streamlined modern cars were first imported into China they encountered customer resistance because they reminded the Chinese of turtles.

Many nationalities express the supreme insult to a person by insulting the memory of the person's mother, from the Chinese *tien ni deh ma*, "----your mother," to the Spanish *¡tu madre!*, "Your mother" (see page 37), and the English "you mother!" In each case the mere mention of the maternal parent implies the rest of the sentence, suggesting immoral and unprintable activities on her part.

The complete form of the Spanish insult ¡tu madre! contains only five syllables, and it is often whistled: one long—two short—one long—one short. It can even be sounded on an auto horn, and this honking insult has frequently resulted in gunplay and sometimes in death.

The word "profanity" is derived from the Latin pro fano, "outside the temple" or "in front of the temple" as an example of ritual swearing or promising. Its present meaning implies disrespect toward or light-handed use of religious words.

Use of the word "bloody" in British countries still causes eyebrows to be raised in an almost inherited linguistic reaction. It is generally considered to be short for the oath "by our Lady" and therefore disrespectful in popular usage.

The Italian word for the Virgin, la Madonna, is also considered out of place as an expletive and in speech is often shortened or slurred into the word marronn!

One can say Mon Dieu!—"my God"—in the most polite French circles, but not Bon Dieu!—"good God!"

Spanish speakers are profuse with references to God, the Trinity, the Virgin, and the saints. ¡Jesús! is used as a polite interjection and is the normal way of saying "God bless you!" when someone sneezes.

When Spanish speakers use the future tense to indicate plans or to arrange an appointment, they often add si Dios quiere, "if God wills"—a reservation exactly comparable to the Arabic Inshallah.

In modern Russia, the word for "devil," *chort*, is still a powerful swear word, even though religious influence in Russia is officially kept to a minimum. But language habits are hard to break: Khrushchev himself often sprinkled his conversation with the expletive *slava Bogu*, "glory to God," a much-used formula in the days of Holy Russia.

"The Devil!"—*Fanden!*—is a common oath in the Scandinavian languages, especially when expanded into a rolling curse, *svarte kockte fanden*, which translates to the inoffensive "black boiled devil."

The first words that come to one's lips in a surprise-pain situation, such as hitting one's thumb with a hammer, are usually scatological or profane. An unusual exception exists in Zulu: *dade wetu*, "by our sister."

A strong Spanish exclamation that is definitely out of place in polite conversation is ¡*carajo!*, the word used for the male member of the bull—in former times often made into a whip used on field slaves, galley slaves, and other prisoners one wished to punish.

Verdammt! ("damned!") and *Donnerwetter* ("thunder weather") are German examples of rather mild swear words which can be intensified to earthshaking proportions when combined with other words. The following example combines "Lord," "God," "the Cross," and intensifiers to create an enormous explosion: *Herrgottkreuzverdampterdonnerwetternochmal!*

---

11. Ethnic Slurs and Their Comparatively Innocent Origins

Many national or ethnic epithets applied to foreign groups, although fairly innocent in origin, have taken on abusive meanings from tone or social context in use. Many of these epithets are based on sounds or mispronunciations of sounds.

Gringo, the Latin American insult for North Americans, has been traced back to a song often sung by the American troops as they invaded Mexico in the U.S.–Mexican War of 1848, "Green Grow the Lilacs." Mexican civilians and troops heard the Americans singing the song as they marched or made camp and ran the two opening words together as *gringo*. The word began to be associated with the constantly advancing Americans and finally became an insult. Eventually the word spread to the rest of the Latin world south of the border, where it is sometimes applied to other foreigners as well as Americans.

The pejorative "spik," applied to Spanish-speaking persons, stems from Spanish speakers saying "No ess-pik English" for "I don't speak English"—which they mangled because the English diphthong *ea* is difficult for Spanish speakers to pronounce. Both "spik" and *gringo* derive from imitations of the sounds made by language foreigners. This tendency to designate strangers by the strange sounds they make is at least as old as the Greek word for "barbarians"—meaning people who seemed to be saying baa-baa like sheep.

The use of "Chink" to designate a Chinese person stems from the mispronunciation of the Chinese word for "China," *chung-kuo* ("Middle Country"). Oddly, the word "Chinaman," now in disrepute as abusive, is the literal translation of the Chinese words for a Chinese person: *chung-kuo-ren*, "Middle Country man or person."

An insulting word frequently used in military parlance for East Asians is "gook," which in Korean simply means "country." The word for "Korea" is *han-gook*, "America" is *mei-gook*. The epithet probably started innocently enough with speakers trying to communicate across language barriers and stressing nationalities.

The word "wop," now considered an insult to Italians, started off as a sort of macho compliment in the early days of Italian immigration. *Guappo* (plural: *guappi*) means "strong," "robust," or "handsome" in the Neapolitan dialect and was applied to some of the groups of young men who came to work in America. "Guinea" is of more misty origin, referring as it does to an old word for the African coast.

"Polak" (for a Pole) or "Hunyak" or "Hunkie" (for a Hungarian) are considered to be ethnic insults, although both are innocently derived from nouns or adjectives denoting nationality in Polish and Hungarian respectively. Curiously, the word "honky," a Black American pejorative for a white American, is probably derived from "Hunyak," originating in a climate of employment rivalry between Blacks and central European immigrants in American industrial centers.

Although the word "Negro" has fallen into positive disfavor in recent years, its meaning is basically the same as that of its successor, "Black." *Negro* means "black" in Spanish and Portuguese, the languages of those who first brought African slaves to the New World. In the native African languages, people are not described as "black" in color but rather as having a—healthy and robust—"people color." White people, from the African point of view, look unhealthy, ill, or dead.

An echo of the epoch of slavery is audible in the word "coon," formerly current in parts of the United States. "Coon" stems from the last syllable of *barracões* (the ō has a nasal n sound), the Portuguese word for buildings constructed for holding slaves pending sale. This word is also related, perhaps appropriately, to the military "barracks."

Three insulting epithets applied to ethnic Jews are "kike," "sheeny," and "yid." All of these have innocent origins but have, through the years, become insults. "Kike" made its appearance during the great nineteenth and early twentieth century immigration of Jews from central Europe and the Russian Empire to America. When they arrived and had to sign papers, those Jews who could not yet write were instructed to sign papers with a cross—a sign they were unwilling to make, for religious reasons. They compromised by signing with a circle, called *kikel* in Yiddish, and a shortened form of this word was applied to Jewish immigrants. "Sheeny" is derived from the Yiddish *shaine* (cf. German *schön*), meaning "beautiful," yet it became an insult through change in tone of voice, accent, and intonation. "Yid," a contraction of "Yiddish," comes from *zhid*, itself a Russian contraction of *Judah*—an example of how a noble and historical allusion can be lost in a contraction.

The Yiddish word for "non-Jew" is *goy*, the Hebrew word for "people," "nation," in the sense of people other than the Jews.

When Europeans and Americans first began to invade the Far East economically and militarily, the Asians were often startled by Western facial characteristics, especially the sharp features and varying hair colors as compared to the flatter and to them more normal-looking Oriental physiognomy. In China Westerners were often referred to as *fan-kuei*, "ocean ghosts" or "devils"; in China white is the color of death and red hair a sure indication of devils. Westerners were also called *ta-bee-tsu* ("the great-nosed ones"), an epithet brought back by U.S. marines on China duty which entered English as "beezer," now somewhat archaic slang for "nose."

In medieval French, from the time of Joan of Arc onward, English people were persistently referred to as *les godons* ("the God damns"), since the English soldiers seemed habitually to say "God damn" in confronting almost any situation.

To this day in Moslem countries, Western Christians are popularly referred to as "Franks." This term goes back to the European invasions of the Holy Lands during the Crusades, an episode of history still very much alive in the collective memory of the world of Islam.

"Yankee" is an interesting example of an ethnic insult converted into a badge of honor, then acquiring new connotations of insult through the vagaries of history. The original word comes from the Dutch and is a diminutive of *Jan* (John). *Janke*, later "Yankee," developed in the former American colonies to describe a sort of country bumpkin of Dutch descent, a resident of the Hudson River valley. During the American revolution sarcastic British military men began to apply this term to the rag-tag American troops who were, in fact, often simple farmers. But, as the Americans began to win the war, "Yankee" became respectable, then increasingly heroic. It is now in familiar use throughout the world. With the Civil War, American Southerners transmuted it into "damn Yankees," applying it to Northerners. And with the growth of American international power since World War II, it has become, in some parts of the globe, part of the admonition "Yankees go home!"

Some national epithets apply solely to eating habits, real or suspected. Germans have long been referred to by Americans as "krauts" because of their affinity for cabbage. For generations the French have been called "frogs" because of one of their favorite dishes, the delicious *cuisses de grenouille* (literally, "frogs' thighs").

"Limey" is a pejorative word for Englishmen, used in the United States and some other places. This goes back to seafaring days and grew out of the health-imposed but initially unusual custom of eating limes or drinking lime juice instituted on His or Her Majesty's ships to prevent scurvy.

The word "eskimo" is an Algonkian word meaning "eater of flesh" (literally "he eats it raw"), an allusion to the prodigious consumption of animal protein by the hunters of the far north. The Eskimos do not use this name but call themselves simply "the people" (*Inuit*).

Parts of the former British Empire had derogatory words for Britons from the home country. The South African Boers called them *rooinek* ("red neck") from their tendency to develop red necks in the African sun. The Australians call them "pommies," from "pomegranates," which sounds like "immigrants." And the Indians covertly called them *vilayeti chuha* ("foreign mice").

The British, for their part, referred to most of the white members of the Empire simply as "colonials," and to almost everyone else as "natives," with some specialized words— such as the one covering Arabs, Indians, and Asians: *wogs* (wily Oriental gentlemen).

Germany, which offers a fine choice of national insults for neighbors and other countries, also offers a popular traditional idiom profoundly appreciative of the life-style of her long-time neighbor and enemy, France. To the question of whether someone is really very happy or contented, the reply is often given, "Yes, indeed, as happy . . . as God in France!" (. . . *wie Gott in Frankreich*).

---

12. Same Sounds—Different Meanings

When you laugh in English you are also saying "mother" (ha-ha) in Japanese. The English "Hi!" or "high" means "yes" (hai) in Japanese; the colloquial "yeah" comes out as "no" (iye). Other English sounds which have different meanings in Japanese include "auto," which sounds like "father" (otoh), and "Ohio" is "Good morning" (ohayo). The fine old Irish family name "O'Hara" spoken in Japanese means "honorable stomach" (o-hara).

The first five numbers in Japanese are easy for an English-speaking person to pronounce—the equivalent English sounds are "itchy," "knee," "san," "she," "go" (*ichi, ni, san, shi, go*).

1   2   3   4   5

一　二　三　四　五

Sometimes an entire English sentence sounds like a basic expression in another language. Americans visiting Japan who would ordinarily experience some difficulty in remembering the Japanese term for "You are welcome" (*dōo itashimashité*) have solved the problem simply—answering the Japanese "Thank you" (*arigato*) with "Don't touch my mustache." Said quickly, this is quite close enough to be an acceptable answer.

To ask "How are you?" in Swedish, an English speaker can simply ask "Who stole the till?" This sounds so much like *Hur står det till?* that any Swede would understand it as an inquiry about his health. By a further linguistic coincidence one may also ask "How goes it with you?" by repeating the following somewhat moralistic English sentence: "Who stole the till may err." (*Hur står det till med Er?*)

If you say "I meant to kill ya" to a Spanish waiter he will not be alarmed but will simply interpret your threatening English statement as a normal request for butter (*¿Hay mantequilla?*). Then you can request, "I, yellow," which is a request for ice (*¿Hay hielo?*).

In Swahili, an important trade language in Africa, the English word "simile" means "Go away!" or "Get lost!"

In Indonesian and Malay the shortened form of "bicycle"—"bike"—signifies "fine" or "all right."

Some Russian words have interesting sound-alikes with somewhat unexpected meanings in English.

SPOKEN ENGLISH	RUSSIAN MEANING
sin	son
brat	brother
look	onion
sock	juice
mere	peace, village council, world
horror show	good

In Czech *Rus* means "Russian" when it is capitalized—but spelled with a small letter it means "cockroach."

Some of the African languages also contain linguistic homophones. For example, if you wish to tell an Amharic-speaking Ethiopian driver to go forward, you could say "What a fit" (*woda fit*), and forward he would go. The hippie-like admonition "be cool" means "direction" in Amharic (*bicool*). The English word for a pig, "sow," means "man"; "lamb" is the word for "cow"; and "kill" means "skull."

The Spanish expression ¡*Eso sí que es!* ("That's exactly it!" or "That's just right!") can be pronounced exactly by anybody who speaks English if he simply spells aloud the word "socks" quickly as an exclamation: *s-o-c-k-s!*

Anyone named Sam Cohen will be interested and perhaps confirmed in his self esteem when he learns that in Lao, the language of Laos, "Sam Cohen" means "three men" (*sam kohn*). The proper name "Kaplan" is Turkish for "tiger."

Because Chinese and English are such different languages, few people would guess that homophones do exist. The childish English expression for "Goodbye," "ta-ta," means either "talk-talk" or "fight-fight" in Chinese, depending on the tone used. The expression "Not so!" or "It isn't true!" comes out as *boo shih!* in Chinese, a curious coincidence

with a colloquial and emphatic American expression
denoting absolute disbelief.

Anyone called Bill has a slight head start in foreign
language vocabulary. If you say that name you are saying:

Russian	"was"	(*bil*)
(or)	"were"	(*bili*)
Norwegian	"motor"	(*bil*)
Zulu..................	"two"	('*mbili*)
Fijian	"to push"	
(or)	"to divide up" ..	
(or)	"out of town" ...	(billy)

Because the human voice can utter only a limited number of
sounds, it is not surprising that the same sound occurs in
various languages but changes its meaning. The sound of
the short English word "so" means a variety of things in
more than a dozen languages:

French	"bucket"............	(*sceau*)
Spanish	"Whoa!"	(¡*So!*)
Hungarian	"word"	(*szó*)
Italian	"I know"	(*so*)
Portuguese	"I am" or	(*sou*)
	"alone"..............	(*so*)
Chinese	"place," "rope,"	(according to
	"demand," or	tone)
	"lock"..............	(*so*)
Vietnamese	"to be afraid" ...	(*so*)
Zulu..................	"face" or "the	
	next morning" ..	(*so*)
Fijian	"to help a	
	person in	
	difficulty" or	
	"to scrape the	
	skin off yams" ..	(*so*)

In Japanese, by a rare linguistic coincidence, "so" has the
same meaning as the English "Is that so?" (*So desuka?*)

The English sound "how" also has a worldwide variety of meanings:

Chinese	"good"	
	"signal"	
	"title"	
	"call"	(*hao*)
Hawaiian	"to smoke"	(*hao*)
Japanese	"an autocrat"	(*hao*)
Algonkian	"greetings"	(*how*)
German	"Hit!"	(*hau*)
Spanish	"bow-wow"	(*¡jau-jau!*)

English written signs sometimes give contradictory impressions to non-English-speakers. French visitors wonder at the sign "Sale" over a display of merchandise in shop windows, because *sale* means "dirty" in French.

Some current and eminently respectable words in the languages of the Far East closely resemble X-rated words in English. American military personnel in China in World War II were surprised and fascinated to learn that there was a city named Fuking in Fukien province. In southern Chinese, Fuking means "Happiness Capital."

Some Japanese words sound equally startling to English speakers. The Japanese word for "restitution" is *fukkyu*. *Fuku* means "good luck," *fukin* means "towel," and *ifuku* means either "clothing" or "subjugation to authority."

Fuku is also the name of a delicious fish, very dangerous to eat if not cleaned by an expert. This poisonous fish has long been a favorite at male banquets where chefs trained in cutting the fish sometimes, through a slip of the knife, miss the strong poison. In spite of this known danger, Japanese men continue to eat the dangerous fish in a spirit of bravura, and every year a number of people die as a result of these banquets, in which the *fuku* might be said to have had the final word.

Shakespeare used the stratagem of foreign-word sound-alikes to provoke laughs from his audience. In *Henry V,* act 3, scene 4, Katharine, the French princess who is to wed Henry V, receives an English lesson from Alice, her lady-in-waiting. As the lesson progresses Alice points to parts of the body and to items of clothing and tells the princess their English names. This provokes a running commentary from Katharine in French, which the audience was expected to follow. After practicing a number of English words, Katharine asks in French how to say *pied* and *robe* in English. Alice tells her "the foot" and "the gown." When Katharine repeats these words with a French accent, they come out as "de fout" and "de coun," sounding exactly like the X-rated French words for sexual union and the female organ, respectively. Katharine is startled and exclaims in French that these English words "sound bad, corruptible, rude, immodest, and not for ladies of honor to use," adding that she would not use them "before the lords of France." But then she hesitates and reflects that they "are nevertheless necessary"—no doubt bringing down the house with this final observation.

Non-Hebrew-speaking Americans visiting Israel have found they can manage an approximation of the Israeli expression for "so long"—*lehit ra-ot*— by saying "let's hit the road."

Two words in Chinese sound exactly like the one-syllable English "my." When it is said like a question, it means "sell," but like a decisive affirmative answer, the same word means "buy." When the two words are said directly together, they appropriately make the word for "business."

The old English "nay" comes out "yes" in Greek. The idiomatic but lazy modern English "yeah" means "no" to a speaker of Japanese.

---

13. *Language Survival and Survival through Language*

India, with hundreds of languages and more than a dozen main ones, has been repeatedly torn by linguistic riots which have caused thousands of deaths since Independence. The government of India has established a variety of dates by which Hindi, the dominant language of north and central India, is to become the official language of India. But the many millions of speakers of other language groups of the south, northwest, and northeast have constantly objected so strenuously, often in serious rioting, that the establishment of Hindi as the official language has been postponed. In the meantime, the common language for the states of India continues to be English, spoken by educated Indians throughout the subcontinent. To the non-Hindi-speakers, English no longer represents domination by the British or any other group and therefore the language of the old imperial power remains the language of India.

In deference to some of the larger language groups, Indian rupee bills contain identification in India's principal languages, including Hindi, English, Urdu, Bengali, Tamil, Gujerati, Marathi, Telegu, Bihari, Punjabi, Rajasthani, Kanarese, and Malayalam.

Constantinople ("city of Constantine") was the capital of the Greco-Roman Byzantine Empire, which lasted over a thousand years before it was conquered by the Turks in 1453—facts ever present in Greek memory. The Turkish name for the city, Istanbul, is a corruption of a Greek contraction of *istin polin* ("within the city"). Greeks, however, still think of Constantinople as their city, often refer to Istanbul simply as *polis* ("the city"), and for years have dreamed of reclaiming it. Even today, when congratulating a brother officer on promotion, Greek military men say: *Ke 'stin polí, stratigós!*—"When [we get] inside the city [you will be] a general!"

References to the conquests of the warlike Turks have even been integrated into the popular speech of several other languages. The alliterative English expression, "the terrible Turk," was common in the World War I era. An Italian exclamation used when a sudden unexpectedly unfavorable situation occurs is *Ai mamma, i turchi!* ("Oh mama, the Turks!").

Belgian currency—one side in French (above), one side in Flemish (below).

Belgium is a country split by language. Half of its inhabitants, the Walloons (*Wallons*) live in the west and speak French. The other half, the Flemings (*Flamands*), live in the east and speak Flemish (*Vlaams*), a dialect of Dutch. All state business has to be conducted in two languages and the king and the government must be especially careful not to favor one language over the other. In principle, everyone is expected to be bilingual, although each group favors its own language and there are frequent riots and threats of secession.

Spain has been repeatedly threatened with partial
dismemberment in recent years as a result of language
differences and related independence movements, one in
the Basque provinces (*Vascongadas*) of the north and
another in Catalonia (*Cataluña*), along the northeast coast of
the Mediterranean, where Catalán is spoken. Under the
Franco regime language restrictions in favor of Spanish were
in force in both these areas. Under the restored monarchy
both Basque and Catalán are officially permitted. Both
languages differ from Spanish. The sources of Basque are
lost in the mists of antiquity. It may perhaps be one of the
most ancient languages still struggling, perhaps successfully,
for survival. Catalán, closer to French than Spanish, is an
important Romance language and is also spoken as
Provençal in southern France. Most of the native residents
of Barcelona, the cosmopolitan capital city of Cataluña,
speak both Spanish and Catalán.

Hebrew is a striking example of an ancient language that
has been successfully revived as a modern language. The
language of ancient Israel, it fell into disuse as a spoken
language as early as the time of the Jews' return from the
Babylonian captivity, when Aramaic, a related language,
was the general language of the Middle East. Hebrew was
conserved as a written language in religious ritual and
scholarship throughout the centuries of the Jewish
dispersion (Diaspora). When Israel was reestablished as a
nation, ancient Hebrew was established as the official
national language. It thus became a unifying force for all
Jews returning to Israel, most of whom had to learn to speak
it either in school or in military service. It was not until the
second generation of Israelis, the "Sabras" (from a kind of
pear, prickly on the outside and sweet within), who were
born in Israel, that Hebrew truly became a national spoken
language. It is still very close to its ancient origins. If the
prophets who compiled the books of the Old Testament
could return to present-day Israel, they would still be able
to read the Israeli daily press—not without considerable
mystification, of course, about its contents.

סברא   Sabra

One of the first modern persons to become a native speaker of ancient Hebrew was Ehud Benyehuda, the second son of Eliezar Benyehuda, the famous reviver of Hebrew as a spoken language. Ehud's parents spoke to him only in Hebrew and, probably because no one his own age spoke the language, he was slow to learn to speak. When he finally spoke his first correct Hebrew sentence, his father remarked to his mother, "Now, for the first time in more than two thousand years, Hebrew has become a natural spoken language." Growing up in what was then Palestine, Ehud at first found it easier to communicate with Arab children, who spoke a related language, than with the Yiddish-speaking Jewish children. One of his childhood playmates later became the Grand Mufti of Jerusalem, a notorious anti-Zionist. When they met after the establishment of Israel, the Mufti observed, "Had I known what you would become, I should have killed you when we were young."

The names "Israel" and "Palestine" serve as banners or battle cries to the contending Israelis and Arabs. The word "Israel" was derived from the Hebrew words for "he who wrestled with God"—a reference to the biblical story of Jacob wrestling with the angel. "Palestine," *Falestin* in Arabic, comes from the names of the ancient Philistines (Phoenicians) whose descendants still live in war-torn Lebanon.

---

an Ṡaeḃiliṡ	Éireannaċ
Irish language	Irishman

Examples of written Irish Gaelic.

The Celtic languages, formerly spoken throughout most of ancient Europe, have survived only along the coasts of France and sections of the British Isles. Breton is spoken in Brittany in France; Scottish Gaelic in the Hebrides, Scotland, and Nova Scotia; Cymric is still spoken in Wales; and Irish Gaelic, or Erse, is an official language of the Republic of Ireland. These Celtic languages are related to each other but are not generally mutually understandable.

Breton, spoken along the coast of northwestern France, has had a revival in recent years; demonstrations for linguistic and political autonomy have often been coupled with destruction of tourists' automobiles and threats of additional violence.

Irish (Erse), normally spoken in the western counties of Ireland and long a rallying point for the anti-British Irish revolutionaries, received an important linguistic boost when it was proclaimed the official language of the Irish Republic. It also became a requirement for civil servants, many of whom did not speak it. Its supremacy has been difficult to maintain because of the constant use of English in Ireland through commerce, movies, books, and periodicals and the fact that practically all overseas Irish speak English.

During a "speak Irish" campaign, signboards throughout the Irish Republic proclaimed "Cut the last tie with England, the language! Use Irish!" (But the signs were written in English.)

Before the Spaniards reached South America, the well-established and populous empire of the Incas extended through most of the four countries of the west coast and parts of Bolivia. The Incas established their language, Quechua, to aid their rule throughout the empire. Although the Spanish conquistadores destroyed the empire and imposed Spanish culture, Quechua still survives in the Andean highlands, spoken by 6 million Indians in Peru, Bolivia, and Ecuador. Radio propaganda broadcasts originating in Moscow and beamed to the Andean areas are spoken in Quechua, the ancient language of the Inca Empire.

Most of the North American Indian languages are vanishing under the pressure of English, although a few are holding their own. Today Navaho is the Indian language with the most speakers in the United States, well over 100,000—a number that is still increasing. News and other radio programs are broadcast in Navaho regularly from Gallup, New Mexico.

At reservation mission schools it was once customary to punish students for using Indian languages during school hours. This trend is now reversed; the study of Amerindian languages is encouraged as these languages approach extinction.

Canada, one of the largest modern nations, faces a possible linguistic breakup. For generations the French-speaking population of Quebec has struggled to protect their island of French language and culture against the encircling English tide, a struggle culminating in agitation for complete separation of Quebec from the rest of Canada. In recent years injuries and deaths have occurred, notably as a result of bombs placed in mailboxes and elsewhere by separatists. One result of the agitation for the French language has been the establishment of French as an official language in the province—and a scramble by public officials to learn to speak French. The French-language movement in Quebec has even taken on a "French only" aspect, peaking in a provincial directive that French be the only language used by air controllers at the Montreal airport. English was restored as the sole language there after both U.S. and English-speaking Canadian pilots declared they would not recognize or accept this directive.

Education for Canada's Eskimo population has generally been offered in English. But recently French-speaking activists in Quebec have strongly urged that the Eskimos be taught French as well, on the grounds that Canada has two official languages—English and French.

Pro-French activists in Canada attack public signs of all sorts at night, repainting them in French. Street and highway signs saying STOP are relettered to read ARRÊT— although "stop" is in the official French dictionary, the sign painters consider the word too English.

Anthropologists have observed that conquered or displaced national groups cling most stubbornly to three principal cultural attributes: language, typical or accustomed foods, and religion.

Somalia is the only African country in which all the inhabitants speak the same language. The Somali-speaking area was formerly split into British, Italian, and French Somaliland (Djibuti) and a Somali-speaking section (Ogaden) in Ethiopia. Somalia has recently pursued a concerted effort to get its people together in one nation, an effort necessary to repair the situation brought about by the former colonial powers' parceling out of Africa without regard for tribal or regional boundaries.

The rulers of Imperial Russia exerted considerable effort to establish a national religion for most of Russia (excluding the Moslem, Buddhist, and animist tribal groups) and imposed the Russian language on the subjugated nations. The rulers of the U.S.S.R. have—like their predecessors— imposed a religious policy, in their case an official antireligion policy, since the Bolshevik revolution (although with some modifications since World War II). But it is in the policy of permitting the use of national languages that the rulers of the U.S.S.R. have displayed foresight and acuity: all regional languages are not only tolerated but encouraged.

To get an idea of the diversity of languages in the Soviet Union, consider these facts. The U.S.S.R. is composed of 15 soviet socialist republics (Russia itself, the Ukraine, Byelo-russia, Moldavia, Armenia, Georgia, Azerbaijan, the Baltic and Central Asian republics). Each of these has its own language as a mark of nationality. Within these large republics are a number of associated republics, also based on linguistic and national groups; and within these, there are smaller national or tribal okrugs which have their own languages as well.

The Soviet separation of constituent areas by nationality in one sense gives a complete freedom of language notably lacking under the Czarist regime. Schoolchildren, therefore, are educated in one or two tribal or subnational languages and also in Russian, the official language, and thus have learned two or three languages before they even start to learn "foreign" ones, such as English, French, Spanish, or German. But the basic message is fairly obvious: to help one's career in the U.S.S.R., where Russian speakers constitute an important and influential percentage of the population of all the republics, one had better become proficient in Russian, however much one prefers one's own national language.

The survival of foreign language groups seems to be decreasing in the United States as second and third generation speakers become proficient in English. Sometimes a foreign language has suffered active discrimination in the United States. During World War I, anti-German feeling caused sauerkraut to be renamed "liberty cabbage," and hamburger to be renamed "Salisbury steak." Operas sung in German were dropped from programs, German courses were dropped from school curricula, and even amiable dachshunds were attacked when their owners took them for walks. During World War II, however, the German language was not *verboten*; there was even an increase in the study of German, especially among the military forces.

The United States, long considered a "melting pot" of ethnic groups, is now experiencing melting-point difficulties over language education for Spanish-speaking children. Older immigrant groups no longer present a problem for the American educational system, since the German and central European groups now mostly speak English, the Irish always did, the French-speaking areas of an earlier era have been absorbed, the third-generation Italians now speak English, and Asian immigrants are usually happy to have their children taught English in school.

Among countries with the greatest number of Spanish speakers, the United States rates as number 5. Only Spain, Mexico, Argentina, and Colombia have more.

Some of the Spanish-speaking sections of the United States cannot be considered the result of immigration since specific areas—California, the Southwest, Texas, and Puerto Rico—represent past conquests by the United States. In all of these areas, Spanish has tenaciously persisted, sometimes defending itself with considerable vigor. The presence of Spanish as a "resident" American language, plus the influx of Latin Americans into the United States, makes Spanish a spreading language in America and one which gives no signs of ebbing.

Recent opposition to the use of Spanish in public signs and announcements has been noted in Florida where a Miami ordinance has been adopted prohibiting the use of public funds for materials to be presented in a language "other than English" or to "promote a culture other than that of the United States." One of the more curious side effects of this ordinance was the decision taken by the Miami zoo to limit posted descriptions of animals to English only, despite the great number of Spanish visitors. An opposed opinion, however, pointed out that, as the scientific names of the animals were given in Latin, signs containing Latin words should also be removed, since Latin is a foreign language too.

Sometimes a Latin American country attempts to curb the use of English, even on signs. In Panama, for example, an ultranationalistic regime in 1945 decreed that even the names of nightclubs and bars, catering principally to Americans, be changed into Spanish. Thus the Happy Land became *Tierra Feliz* and Sloppy Joe's changed its name to *José el abandonado*.

Switzerland has solved the language problem by having three official languages, German, French, and Italian and, as if this were not enough for a fairly small country, the majority of the population uses a dialect—Swiss German, considerably different from standard German. In addition to these four, there is yet another language spoken in the southeast of this mountainous country—Romansch, a linguistic relic of the Roman Empire. The result of all these languages is not confusion but rather a linguistic preparation and national concord that have made Switzerland the banking center of the world and a peaceful united nation of great prosperity. The multilingual Swiss are famous as hotelkeepers, restaurateurs, and, of course, interpreters.

---

14. *Clicks, Whistles, Gestures, and Musical Scales*

According to the International Phonetic
Association, an organization established by
British and international linguists after
World War I, all the sounds used by
different human groups to construct words
can be reduced to about ninety letters and
symbols. These symbols have been assigned
an unchanging sound value, so that if a
linguist learns the International Phonetic
Alphabet he should, in theory, be able to
pronounce words of any language
expressed in this alphabet.

In practice, however, the International Phonetic Alphabet (IPA) lacks public appeal. Some phrase books offered to the public use the IPA to show how the words should be pronounced. A foreigner who does not speak English but wishes to communicate would certainly have difficulty using the IPA as a guide if he had not previously mastered the key. He might be able to figure out how to say "Good-night" in English (gut ′nait) but would have more difficulty in pronouncing "Thank you" [′θæŋk ju]. He would be even more baffled by words needed speedily in emergencies, such as "What's the matter?" [wət iz ðə ′mætə] or "Call the police. I've been robbed." [kə:l ðə pə′li:s, aiv bin ′rəbd]

The International Phonetic Alphabet has been applied to languages lacking an alphabet, such as American Indian and some African languages. Despite its potential for teaching correct accents, the IPA has not been well received by the tribes, which prefer their languages the way they are. In any case, the American Bible Society has already translated the New Testament into 1,100 languages by using the Latin alphabet for tongues that do not have an indigenous system of writing.

The IPA cannot be used for those African and Asian languages, now increasingly important on the world scene, in which a word changes its meaning with the click which accompanies it or with the tone or pitch.

In click languages the click is an integral part of the word. Native speakers seem to pronounce the clicks simultaneously with other sounds—a linguistic feat almost impossible to imitate by anyone who has not started learning the language as a child.

Clicks are a distinctive feature of the Khoisan, Xosa, and Zulu languages of South Africa. Khoisan, the language of the Hottentots or Bushmen, has four clicks and the Zulu languages have three. In Zulu one click is made by pulling the tongue back from the front teeth (like saying "tsk-tsk" in English), another is formed by the click one uses to get a horse to speed up, and a third is made by drawing the tongue down quickly from the roof of the mouth.

In South Africa the clicking sounds are referred to as the "Kaffir click." This is a misnomer because Kaffir is an Arabic and not an African word—*Qafir*, "unbeliever"—and the peoples should be referred to by their tribal names or by the collective Bantu (which means simply "men").

The name Hottentot was applied to the Bushmen of South Africa—whose name for themselves is Khoi, "the people"— by the Dutch, who thought that the tribesmen sounded as if they were stammering and stuttering, *hateren en tateren*, which was shortened to Hottentot.

Kuo-yü, the northern variant of Chinese (also known as Mandarin) which is now the official language of the People's Republic of China, employs only four tones, often designated by the numbers 1, 2, 3, and 4 in books designed to teach Chinese to foreigners. The Chinese themselves usually learn the tone when they learn the ideograph (Chinese symbol for a word). The first Chinese tone is high and short; the second is said as if asking a question, rising at the end; the third tone is like an incredulous query ("Wh-a-a-t?"); the fourth is delivered as if giving an order ("Go! Stop!").

A single word in Chinese may have several dozen different meanings, so the tone used to say the word emphasizes which denotation is intended. Meaning is also communicated by the context in which a word is used.

Besides the use of tones to indicate the meaning of a word when spoken, the Chinese system of writing also establishes the meaning of each word-syllable. The word *chiang*, for example, can mean, according to how it is written and the tone it is spoken in, either "shall," "to command," "a general," "a river," "soy sauce," "mechanic," "to drop," "to descend," "to surrender," or the family name Chiang, as in

Chiang Kai-shek. The word *mao* has even more meanings: "hair," "feather," "rough," "to risk," "to pretend," "counterfeit," "hat," "cup," "anchor," "cat," or "kitten." (Mao Tse-tung's family name is written with the character for hair 毛.)

In Chinese the repetition of *ma* four times with different tones signifies "Mother scolds the horse" (ma^1-ma^1-ma^4-ma^3). If you add the interrogative participle *ma* at the end, you then have five *ma* in a row: ma^1-ma^1-ma^4-ma^3-ma^1, meaning "Is mother scolding the horse?"

Accounts of the unexpected results of mispronunciation of Chinese abound. One famous incident is said to have taken place in southern China during World War II. A local missionary, giving orders in Chinese for the preparation of an assembly hall for a party for American Air Force personnel and other guests, requested the local Chinese *compradores* to furnish national and international flags. Through mispronunciation and tonal mistakes, the party got no flags. What it did have was dancehall girls from port cities—Chinese, Russian, French, central European, Korean, and so on. International enough, to be sure, but definitely not "decorative flags."

A number of languages have a strong *h* sound, comparable to clearing one's throat while saying *h* or *kh*. Anglo-Saxon included this sound, for instance, in the words *night*, *right*, *sight* (pronounced roughly *nicht*, *richt*, *sicht*), and the English words are still spelled with the *gh* even though the sound has been lost. Hebrew words with this guttural *h* sound, when used in English, are sometimes spelled with a *ch*, and sometimes with an *h*—as in the name for a Hebrew festival: *Chanukah* or *Hanukah* ("dedication").

Russian and Greek use the letter x to express the guttural *h* sound. In Greek and Russian, x is the first letter of the name of Christ—*Xristós*, pronounced "hreestos." So writing "Merry Xmas" on a Christmas card is not in fact informal or a time saver but a respectful repetition of the first letter of the Greek word for Christ.

Another unusual articulation is the sound made by contraction of the throat muscles in Arabic and Hebrew. This is the *'ain*, which is typical of the Semitic languages and gives them an expressive character different from most other languages.

In northern and central Spain a distinct lisp is noticeable in the pronunciation of the letter *c* (when followed by an *e* or an *i*) and the letter *z*. In southern Spain both the *c* and the *z* are generally pronounced like an *s*. This rule applies also in Latin America, since many of the first colonizers came to the Americas from Andalucía and Extremadura, in southern Spain. An imaginative explanation is frequently given for this Castilian lisp: a certain Castilian king spoke with a lisp, and his courtiers imitated the royal speech defect and made it fashionable. More likely, the lisp developed from the speech of ancient Greek colonists in Spain, or from classical Arabic speech during the Arabs' 700-year stay in the Iberian peninsula. Modern Greek pronunciation retains the customary lisp for certain letters.

Cuskoy, a town in eastern Turkey, is called the "bird village" with good reason. Its inhabitants have perfected a language system of chirps, tweets, and twitters almost indistinguishable from authentic bird sounds. The people of Cuskoy developed this unique system because of a ravine and a river which bisect their village and an almost daily fog that prevents the use of hand signals. They have perfected their whistling to cut through the fog, like a natural foghorn.

The Gaunches, the mysterious tall white original inhabitants of the Canary Islands discovered on the islands in the fourteenth century by Spanish and Portuguese seafarers, used a whistling language. They could communicate from hill to hill in their mountainous islands with a series of whistles and they used this communication system in their fierce but hopeless struggle against the Spaniards. Both the whistling and the spoken language (thought by some experts to be proto-Greek or a prehistoric language and by others to be a linguistic vestige of lost Atlantis) disappeared along with the Guanches themselves shortly after the islands were conquered. Certain ethnic remnants in the mountains, however, are said still to be proficient in this secret whistled language.

———————

The system of "talking drums" of sub-Saharan Africa is not based on a code but on imitation of spoken words and expressions, marking word emphasis and syllables by drumbeat. With practice the listening drummers, if they speak the same language, can understand what far-away drummers are saying.

———————

Gestures, as an aid to language and as a substitute for spoken words, are in wide use throughout the world, perhaps more so in southern or warm countries than in the colder north. Insults through gestures (see Chapter 10), usually having some specific meaning, are generally understood to be unfriendly in most countries. Wiggling the fingers from the nose in the direction of the insultee; striking the left arm with the right hand, while clenching the left hand into a fist; snapping the teeth with the thumbnail while extending the little finger towards the opponent are all certainly unfriendly gestures and, in the interest of peace and safety, should be avoided in any country.

A number of interesting gestures in certain language areas convey messages or emotions. In Spanish-speaking countries, holding the thumb and first finger together and snapping the wrist repeatedly denotes excitement or appreciation. In Brazil and some Spanish-speaking countries, increasing the size of the right eye by pulling down the lower lid denotes either that someone is listening or watching who should not be, or that the listener doubts what you are saying. Tapping the left elbow with the right hand is a sign that the person being discussed is stingy. To indicate that you have heard the story before, put your right arm behind your head and pull your left ear with your right hand.

The gesture of the pointing-down thumb to indicate the finishing off of a vanquished gladiator has been corroborated by mention in ancient texts. This gesture was often accompanied by shouts of *habet!* ("he has it!"), an expression strangely comparable in similar circumstances to the modern expression "he's had it." It is not certain, however, that "thumbs up" signified pardon. The signal for sparing the life of a fighter who had fought skillfully and lost was possibly given by the waving of scarves. This is sometimes done today to spare a valiant bull in the course of modern bullfights, which themselves are a living vestige of the old Roman games (*ludi romani*).

Many gestures of appreciation and affirmation, such as
thumbs up, are understood throughout the world, but some
seemingly innocent gestures should be avoided. In the
Orient, for example, it is extremely impolite to point at the
person to whom you are speaking and unforgivable to place
the soles of the feet toward him or her.

A physical gesture highly insulting to Greeks, the *mounza*,
consists of holding the hand, palm outward, toward a
person, like a traffic policeman signaling "Stop." This
gesture may provoke violence from the insultees, or perhaps
a double *mounza*—using both palms, or striking the right
palm with the left, as if to push the *mounza* even closer to
one's opponent.

Almost unbelievable coincidence, or lack of information
about Greek reactions, led the advertisers of an American
automobile named the Monza to use a sultry model wearing
a long gown striped in blue and white—the Greek colors—
and holding up her palm to the viewer. Whatever its
success elsewhere, the Monza was not an outstanding
success on the Greek market.

An extensive sign language developed among the Plains
Indians of North America, perhaps because of their
extensive use of the horse, an unexpected and unintended
gift of the early Spanish explorers. In other sections of
North America, either neighboring Indian tribes spoke
related languages, or—where neighboring tribes spoke
unrelated tongues—several members of a tribe might have
learned the language of their neighbors. But with the
mobility acquired by the Plains tribes through the use of
captured or escaped Spanish horses, tribal parties ranged in
their hunts or raids over ever greater distances,
encountering a variety of different tribes who spoke
unintelligible languages. Through this situation a system of
sign language developed from simple gestures to more
complex ideas and Indians from tribes normally separated
by great distances on the western plains could, when they
met, communicate on a basic and even intermediate level.
Union against the invading whites, however, was difficult

because most tribes considered other tribes as natural enemies. There were occasional exceptions to this rule—as General Custer was later to find out.

———————————————

15. Counting—Fingers, Toes, and Computers

When our remote ancestors first invented systems of counting, they unwittingly took a tremendous step toward the development of communication, writing, and the storing of information—eventually leading to our technically developed world civilization. But even today there exist tribal groups who can count only so high, designating all numbers above their counting limit simply as "many."

One Australian tribe calculates numbers by counting the legs of a dingo (wild dog). Eight is "two dogs"; sixteen, the ultimate count before "many," is "four dogs."

Another Australian aborigine tribe counts by pointing to parts of the face—eyes (one and two), nose (three), mouth (four), chin (five), ears (six and seven), going on to the limbs and various parts of the body.

Most counting systems have been suggested by the fact that people have ten fingers. In English we still honor this fact when we refer to the digital system, remembering that "digit" means "finger," just as the Latin *digitus* does. The Amerindian Zuñi word for "ten" means "all fingers."

In some languages on the east coast of Africa, "pointing finger" is the word used for "seven"—aptly named if you start counting your fingers from the left of your left hand.

In the language of the Loyalty Islands of Melanesia the word for "human being" or "person" is also the word for "twenty." This signifies a full count of ten fingers and ten toes—in other words, a complete person.

Prehistoric inscriptions found on pebbles at Mas d'Azil, France.

Early peoples probably kept counting records by using pebbles or by making marks or notches on bones. Some prehistoric pebbles found in caves in the Mas d'Azil in France show a form of markings, or perhaps elementary writing, inscribed on these counting pebbles thousands of years before any form of writing was supposed to exist.

Some languages base their number system on the concept that we have twenty fingers. In French, Spanish, and some other languages, the same word is used for both fingers and toes. The French words for "eighty," *quatre-vingts* ("four twenties"), and for "ninety"—*quatre-vingt-dix* ("four twenties ten")—are both modern descendants of the ancient Gaulish concept, counting by twenties.

The ancient Sumerians of the Middle East and, through them, the Babylonians and Assyrians counted not by tens but by twelves. This system of counting was actually much more advanced than the decimal, or "ten-finger," system—it was based on the twelve constellations of the zodiac, implying that the peoples of ancient Mesopotamia may have changed a former method of finger-counting to one based on astronomical calculations.

The Babylonian use of twelve as a mathematical unit is actually superior to the use of ten, inasmuch as twelve can be subdivided into more units than ten, and multiples of twelve are more mathematically adaptable than multiples of ten.

The Babylonian system of counting still influences the modern world; we have twelve months in our year, twelve to a dozen, twice twelve hours to a day, sixty seconds (five times twelve) to a minute, sixty minutes to an hour, twelve inches to a foot. Until fairly recently, when they instituted decimal coinage, the English counted twelve pence to a shilling (but twenty shillings to a pound), and in India they counted twelve annas to a rupee.

Zero, the non-number which is perhaps the most important number of all for higher mathematics and cosmic calculations, was known among ancient races only to the Hindus of India and the Maya of the Americas, on opposite sides of the earth. There are indications that the Babylonians and the Chinese also once knew about zero, but forgot it.

The ancient Hindu use of special figures for numbers, including zero, arrived in Europe, via the Arab world, in the Middle Ages, an important milepost in the future development of technological and scientific civilization.

Unlike the Hindu and Arabic numbers, the Maya number system—and use of zero—had no influence on the surrounding Amerindian or later cultures and represents a historical enigma. Did the Mayas, as well as the Hindus, inherit it from a common vanished culture, or did they develop it independently? Whatever the case, the Maya were able to carry out incredibly sophisticated cosmic calculations and, of all ancient people, came closest to reckoning the exact length of the solar year. They calculated it at 365.2420 days; the modern count is 365.2422 days.

Before Arabic numbers were adopted in Europe, Europeans were able to count and figure, but not with the ease and flexibility attained through the use of single figures for numbers and—especially—the concept of zero. The word "zero" itself comes from the Arabic *cifr*, from which we also get the English word "cipher."

The Roman numerical system uses letters to stand for numbers: M (1,000), D (500), C (100), L (50), X (10), V (5), I (1). A smaller number before a larger is subtracted—CM is 900—and a smaller number following a larger one is added. The combinations were so topheavy that they may have slowed up Roman scientific development and, in any case, certainly made bookkeeping for the Empire more difficult. Roman numerals, still in formal use on public buildings and clocks, however impressive they may look, do not lend themselves to rapid arithmetical calculations.

MCMLXXXII – 1982

Both ancient Greek and Hebrew employed letters to stand
for numbers, starting from the first letter of the alphabet:
aleph or *alpha* for "one," *bet* or *beta* for "two," and so on.
These numerals are still frequently used on Hebrew and
Greek clocks and watches.

Chinese, Japanese, and other Asian languages originally
used special signs for numbers. Most writing systems now
include the Arabic system of numerals for modern
calculations. In Arabic itself, however, the original Arabic
digital system is still used. This system uses numbers that
do not look like what are generally called Arabic numbers.
The international "1" looks like the Arabic "1"; the other
numbers are different: a circle stands for "5"; a zero is a
dot; a "6" looks like a "7"; and the other numbers are
completely different.

١	٢	٣	٤	٥	٦	٧	٨	٩	١٠
1	2	3	4	5	6	7	8	9	10

Some words for very large numbers have different values
according to the language you are speaking. Everywhere in
the world, "million" means 1,000,000. But the term for
1,000,000,000 in American English, French, Spanish, and
Italian is "billion," whereas the same number is called "one
thousand million" or "one milliard" in the British
Commonwealth, Germany, and the Soviet Union. The
British English word "billion" stands for the number
Americans call "trillion." It is therefore important to
express these large numbers in figures rather than words for
mutual understanding. The convention in English-speaking
countries is to separate each three digits with a comma
(1,999). Elsewhere the convention is to use a period or a
space; sums of money are recorded with a comma to set off
fractions (DM 1.534,22).

For extreme distances in space, the common measure is
light years—based on the distance covered by speeding light
in one second (186,000 miles, or 300,000 kilometers).

In a number of languages, the names of the days of the week are designated by numbers, except for Saturday and Sunday. But there is no agreement about which day the week starts on. Speakers of Russian, Chinese, and some other languages consider Monday the start of the week; speakers of Greek, Portuguese, Malay, Indonesian, and Arabic consider Sunday to be the first day. This linguistic divergence poses a theological problem: on which day of the week was the earth created?

No numbers are used for the days of the week in the Latin languages other than Portuguese or in the Germanic languages (including English). These languages use the names of former gods for days—Greek or Roman in the Latin languages, and mostly Norse or Teutonic deities in the Germanic language group.

In English the names for the days of the week are a direct throwback to the old pagan gods:

> Sunday, the sun
> Monday, the moon
> Tuesday, Tiu, god of war and the sky
> Wednesday, Wotan, king of the gods
> Thursday, Thor, god of thunder
> Friday, Freya, goddess of peace and crops
> Saturday, Saturn, the Roman god of time and
> revelry

English and the other North Germanic languages honor the sun in the name Sunday. The Latin languages, however, call the same day after the Lord (*domingo, domenica, dimanche*).

The word for Saturday in the Latin languages, Greek, and Russian is derived from the Hebrew word for the weekly holy day, *Shabbath*.

The Japanese name the days of the week after the sun, the moon, fire, water, wood, silver, and copper.

In most European languages, four months of the year have names derived from Latin numbers which do not correspond with the position of the month in our calendar: September from "seven," October from "eight," November from "nine," and December from "ten." The discrepancy arose because the Romans who named our months considered March the first month of the year.

Five months are named for gods: January for Janus, the god of doorways who had two faces; March for Mars, the god of war; April for Aphrodite or Venus, goddess of beauty; May for Jupiter Mayo, the god of growth; June for Juno, Jupiter's wife. Two months were named after publicity-conscious Roman public figures—July for Julius Caesar, and August for Augustus, the first emperor.

The German words for 1, 2, 3 (*eins, zwei, drei*) are widely known, but travelers in Germany are sometimes surprised to find that Germans often pronounce *zwei* as "zwo" when giving telephone numbers or addresses. The practice avoids confusing *zwei* and *drei*, which were numbers long before anyone thought of telephones or modern communication.

Chinese and related Sinitic languages have the advantage of being grammatically simpler than Western languages, with no case endings, verb conjugations, or pluralization. The Sinitic tongues, however, are rich in specialized expressions for numbering different kinds of objects, comparable to the English use of "head of cattle" and "sheets of paper." Among the special "numerative" words in Chinese and Japanese are the following:

NUMERATIVE USED	FOR COUNTING
piece	persons or things
origin	books and documents
item	affairs and clothes
extend	tables and papers

clod	money and land
head	oxen and asses
one of a pair	sheep, limbs, horses
reed	anything tubular
fan	doors, windows, screens
mouth..............................	swords, bells, persons
feather	birds

Chinese pidgin English was built up largely from English words adapted to Chinese syntax, creating such constructions as "two piece man" for "two men." (The word "pidgin" is a local Chinese corruption of the word "business.")

Malays count animals by tails rather than heads.

In both Chinese and Japanese, the word "four," *shi*, sounds like the word "death." The Japanese often substitute another word for "four"—*yotsu*, taken from an alternative system of counting. License numbers using 4 in certain combinations are shunned by Chinese car owners in Hong Kong, Taiwan, and Singapore. They especially avoid the number 1414, which in speech resembles the words "definite death, definite death."

In the Western world, 13 is generally considered an unlucky number. Its unfavorable associations may come from the number of guests at the Last Supper. Such is the force of popular credence in good or bad luck associated with numbers that the great majority of hotels, office buildings, and apartment houses in the United States have no floor numbered 13. The elevator goes directly from 12 to 14—not necessarily because builders and owners are superstitious but because they are certain that guests or tenants would not choose to occupy floor 13.

Through the ages, 7 and 11 have been lucky numbers, and
they are as important to players of dice games now as they
were to the dice-throwing Roman legionaries two thousand
years ago.

———————————

Some numbers have strong religious connotations: 3 has
sacred overtones in Christian countries because of the
Trinity; in Islamic lands, 5 conjures up the five fingers of
the hand of Fatima, the daughter of the Prophet
Mohammed, which, according to legend, she once placed
over the sleeping eyes of her father to shield him from the
sun.

———————————

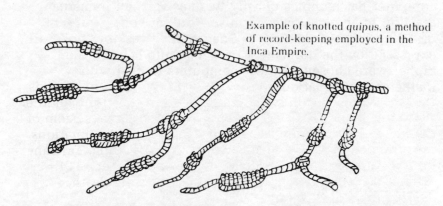

Example of knotted *quipus*, a method
of record-keeping employed in the
Inca Empire.

When the Spaniards discovered the empire of the Incas
there was no form of writing in use. Records and reports of
this highly developed empire came in the form of *quipus*,
large tassels of colored threads whose combination of knots
and weaves indicated information on crops, storage,
population counts, levies of workers and soldiers, progress
reports on public works, and tribute payments. These
quipus were delivered from place to place by special relay
runners called *chasquis*, who covered their routes so
efficiently that they could carry fresh fish from the coast to
the Inca in the mountains, delivering it unspoiled along
with the *quipus*. The count of all property in the empire
was so exact that it was said that if a single sandal were
stolen, the Inca would soon know about it. No one knows
exactly how *quipus* were "read" as the *quipu* readers
disappeared with the death of the Inca Empire.

———————————

The involved color combinations and knots in the *quipus* may have been a way of indicating words or word combinations other than those of formal reports. This theory comes from the fact that poetry, historical records, and entire plays have surfaced from the past, "remembered" from Inca times by Indians living in the Andes. Perhaps some individuals can still be found in mountain villages who have inherited the art of "reading" the *quipus*.

Although computers are increasingly a prime tool in developing technology and probing the secrets of earth and the universe, these machines use only two numbers—1 and 0—a binary (two-part) system. In every question asked, a computer has a choice of only two answers, an immediate reaction to an electronic impulse: "on" or "off," "present" or "absent," "affirmative" or "negative," "yes" or "no"—all expressed by the numbers 1 or 0. The number and the cipher were chosen to allow computers to deal with mathematical equations.

16. *Our Mysterious Alphabet*

Every time we say "alphabet" we are
repeating the first two letters of the ancient
Greek alphabet, which in turn came from
an alphabet first used by the Phoenicians.
In Greek the first two letters were *alpha*
and *beta;* in the older Semitic or Aramaic
they were *aleph* and *bet.*

The first true, not syllabic, alphabet is generally accepted as one found in Byblos in Phoenicia, dating from 1000 BC or earlier. Byblos was a port from which papyrus, for use in writing, was exported to Egypt, where pictorial hieroglyphic (not alphabetic) writing had already been in use for thousands of years. Byblos has been immortalized in the original Greek word for "rolled book," *biblion,* from which Western languages get the words "bible," "bibliophile," "bibliography."

A true alphabet would consist only of letters for individual basic sounds—consonants and vowels—rather than syllables. This alphabet is usually referred to as the Phoenician or Northern Semitic alphabet and is composed of 22 to 30 sounds of letters that combine to make other sounds or words. Other systems of writing have letters that stand for syllables and are therefore not true alphabets but are rather syllabic alphabets, having many more signs than a pure alphabet.

Over 400 systems of writing are known throughout the world today. This does not include scripts referred to in ancient writings whose written records have not yet been found.

In spite of the honor accorded to Byblos as the first known place where a close-to-pure alphabet was used, evidence that alphabetic symbols or letters were used in many other parts of the ancient Mediterranean world has surfaced in discoveries in Italy, central France, western Spain and Portugal, western North Africa, and the islands of the Mediterranean. This evidence suggests that some form of alphabetical writing was used more generally and earlier than previously estimated. Its use was doubtless spread by early Cretan or Phoenician seafarers, who either got it from an earlier culture or who evolved a nonrepetitive sign alphabet for marking days in keeping track of the duration of long sea voyages.

The alphabets, including the variation of certain letters, average about 28 signs. Following the theory of some linguists that the Phoenicians based their letters on the number of days in the lunar cycle, the full alphabet represents a lunar month of 28 days. This lunar explanation of the origin of the alphabet serves to emphasize the moon's influence on earth and its inhabitants, the moon's pull on the outer and inner tides of the earth and on the minds, bodies, and emotions of human beings by periodic mental and physical lunar cycles of 28 days.

If you turn a capital A upside down, you will be looking at a simplified ox head with horns coming from the top of the head and a narrowing chin. *Aleph* means "ox" in Aramaic. *Bet*, the second letter, means "house" and resembles one. *Gimel* (gamma in Greek) means "square" or "camel," according to the linguistic source one accepts; *dalet*, the fourth letter, means "door" in Aramaic. Still other Hebrew letters have forms that can be associated with their meaning: the name of the letter representing the *sh* sound is pronounced *sheen*, which means "tooth," and the letter is shaped like one or more teeth. The Hebrew or Aramaic *kaph* means "palm," and its final form resembles a slender tree. The sound of the letter *mem* resembles the Hebrew sound of the word for "water," *mayeem*, and its written form may represent the enclosed top of a well. Other letters probably derived from picture-symbols whose origins are not as obvious as these. The Greek alphabet uses two letters reportedly representing the male and female primary sexual characteristics—*delta* and *phi*.

Hebrew alphabet.

ת ש ש ר ק צ פ פ ע ס נ מ ל כ כ י ט ח ז ו ה ד ג ב ב א

Greek alphabet.

Α Β Γ Δ Ε Ζ Η Θ Ι Κ Λ Μ Ν Ξ Ο Π Ρ Σ Τ Υ Φ Χ Ψ Ω

It is logical to assume that the Phoenician alphabet came from simplified picture writing which eventually ceased to be pictures and became the tools through which sounds could be reproduced. Whether the Phoenicians were the first to invent the alphabet by simplifying hieroglyphics (pictures and sound syllables) or the cuneiform writing used in Mesopotamia (wedge-shaped marks in wet clay, a combination of pictures and syllables), the result was the same; the Phoenician traders spread the alphabet throughout the Mediterranean world, an early benefit of a free-trade economy.

An ancient Hebrew legend illustrates the importance accorded to the alphabet in antiquity. According to this legend the letters of the alphabet were established by God before He created the world. Islamic tradition has a similar legend, teaching that Allah created the letters of the alphabet Himself, then gave them to Adam—but not to the angels.

Example of Devanagari script.   पाल्याहि जियमझ्ने वसाहि

The original Sanskrit script of India is also attributed to a gift from the gods. The name of the graceful Devanagari script means "the writing of the Gods." Because its vowels, when combined with consonants, form new letters, it does not fulfill the attributes of a true alphabet; but it is widely and effectively used to express the most modern ideas as well as ancient philosophies.

ᚡᚒᚦᚠᚱᚲᚷᛈᚺᛏᛁᚻᛃᚲᚴᛃᛊᛏᛒᛗᚼᚱ
◇ᛦᛗ   Runic alphabet.

Another alphabetic method of writing was runic, developed by the northern Germanic peoples in the third century. Its original 24 letters (2 were later added) were formed by straight lines, probably so written for easier cutting or incising on wood. As Christianity progressed northward, the runic alphabet was superseded by the Latin one.

Ꝩe Old Tea Shoppe

A mispronunciation of an Anglo-Saxon letter, *edh*, probably pronounced *th* as in "thine" or "the," gave rise to a new word. English-speaking tourists seeing signs saying YE OLD TEA SHOPPE misread the word *YE*, which is "the," not "ye." The mistake is understandable, since Ꝩ resembles the modern English *y* with curlicues.

А Б В Г Д Е Ж З И К Л М Н О П Р С Т У Ф Х Ц Ч Ш Щ Ъ
Ы Ь Э Ю Я   Russian alphabet.

To express the variety of sounds in Russian, the Russian alphabet uses 32 letters. After the Revolution of 1917, the Bolshevik regime instituted a reform of the Russian alphabet. One letter that was changed looked something like a church topped by a cross (ҍ). This shape was altered to ë but kept the same pronunciation.

Example of Amharic writing.

አገዜአበሐር ፡ እንደሁ ፡ ዓለሙን ፡ ወደፃልና ፡
እንድ ፡ ልጁን ፡ እስኪሰወጥ ፡ ይረስ ።። በርሱ ፡

The ancient Amharic script of Ethiopia has 33 consonants, all of which can combine with any of the 7 vowels, making a total of 231 letters or signs which typesetters have to consult for setting each page of type.

ى و ه ن م ل ك ق ف غ ع ظ ط ض ص ش س ز ر ذ د خ ح ج ث ت ب ا 1
ى و ه ن م ل ك ق ف غ ع ظ ط ض ص ش س ز ر ذ د خ ح ج ث ت ب ا 2

Arabic, although possessing a true alphabet, is considerably more difficult to write than languages which use the Roman alphabet because most Arabic letters have four different forms, depending on whether the letter stands alone, comes at the beginning of a word, is written between other letters, or is used to end a word. Printed Arabic, essentially the same as the handwritten script, occupies more space on a printed page than Roman type, principally because of the graceful sweeps and loops of the Arabic letters.

A couplet by Sultan Suleiman the Magnificent written in Turkish in ornamental Arabic script (above), and the same couplet written in Turkish in Roman letters (below).

Halk içinde muteber bir nesne yok devlet gibi

Olmaya devlet cihanda bir nefes sıhhat gibi

Although Turkish was written in Arabic letters for more than a thousand years, Mustapha Kemal, the dictator who modernized and strengthened Turkey after World War I, decreed as part of his modernization program that Turks would henceforth use the Roman alphabet. Although the change was at first resisted on religious and aesthetic grounds, it was soon accepted because illiterates were learning to read much more quickly when taught the Roman alphabet.

The Arab countries and Iran and Pakistan are unlikely to give up the Arabic script, especially since it is the written language of the Koran. But a few other Moslem non-Arab countries, such as Indonesia and Malaysia, have taken to using the Roman alphabet, and the Turkic republics of the U.S.S.R., still largely Islamic, now use the Russian Cyrillic alphabet.

Aztec picture writing

A sample of the Cherokee alphabet invented by Sequoyah.

ᏃᎠᏴᏍᏃ ᏂᎣᎨᎩ ᎤᏣᎳᏬᎠᏗ ᏠᏍᎦᎡᎡᏴ
ᏃᏴᎢ ᏉᎦᎡᎦᏨ ᎤᏂᏗᏛᏗᏗ, ᎩᏳ ᏃᏴᎢ

So far as we know, none of the Amerindian tribes north of Mexico had a system of writing other than pictures, before the arrival of the whites. Sequoyah, chief of the Cherokees in the early nineteenth century, reasoning that the power of whites came from their use of "symbols" (letters), invented a Cherokee system of written signs to express all the sounds of the Cherokee language. This written language was used to write the Cherokee constitution and laws and to publish a newspaper in Phoenix, Georgia. Perhaps the magic power of the symbols came too late; the Cherokee tribe was forcibly transported westward by President Jackson along the "Trail of Tears." The Cherokee syllabic writing, however, is still taught in Tahlequah, Oklahoma, where the tribe's oil lands have provided a harvest that President Jackson never dreamed of.

Japanese is written partially with Chinese characters, called *kanji* in Japanese, and usually written, like Chinese, in columns from top to bottom. The Chinese characters are mixed in with two systems of syllabic alphabets with a special sign for each syllable. These supplementary alphabets are really two ways of writing the same series of sounds with which one can represent any purely Japanese syllable. One of these alphabets is the flowery *hiragana* script used for verb endings and in general where the Chinese characters are not used. The other variant, the angular *katakana* syllable alphabet, is used for spelling foreign words and names and often employed on simple signs and advertising. In reading Japanese one frequently finds all three ways of writing on the same page. It would be possible to write all Japanese words either in the wavy *hiragana* or the straight-line *katakana* style, but the Japanese continue to use about 2,000 Chinese characters, dignified by long tradition and ancient culture.

Examples from the two Japanese syllabic alphabets.

	katakana	*hiragana*		*katakana*	*hiragana*
i	イ	い	ni	⇒	に
ro	ロ	ろ	ho	ホ	は
ha	ハ	は	he	〜	へ

The use of *katakana* for foreign words gives considerable elasticity and enables the Japanese to adopt words from English and other languages without translating them but simply adapting the original sound to the Japanese ear. There are hundreds, perhaps thousands of words of foreign origin in Japanese, many of which are easily recognizable to English speakers, such as "rush hour" (ra-sha-wa), "ice cream" (ai-su-ku-ri-mu), "restaurant" (res-to-ran), "floor show" (fu-re-wa-sho), "cigaret" (shi-ga-ret-to), "taxi" (ta-ku-shi), and "motorcycle" (mo-to-sai-ku).

Just as occidental children learn the ABC by rote, Japanese children used to learn the *katakana* and *hiragana* alphabets by reciting a poem in which each separate syllable of the scripts occurs only once. This poem, generally called the *I-ro-ha*, translated below, presented to many generations of Japanese children a fatalistic view of life at an early age.

> Though their hues are gay
> The blossoms flutter down.
> And so in this world of ours,
> Who may continue forever?
> Having today crossed
> The mountain fastness of existence,
> I have seen but a fleeting dream
> With which I am not intoxicated.

Chinese is not as flexible as Japanese in approximating the pronunciation of foreign words and names, since the separate Chinese characters, standing as they do for individual words, do not have the elasticity of the Japanese *katakana* syllable alphabet. Sometimes Chinese equivalents of western names are surprising in literal translation from the original language.

Nixon	尼克森	mud overcoming forest
Reagan	雷　根	thunder root
Carter	卡　特	toll booth special
Kissinger	季辛吉	lucky work house
Ford	福　特	felicity special

Korea, like other ancient nations in east Asia, long used Chinese ideograms, but without a simplifying syllable alphabet like Japanese with its two auxiliary scripts. A Korean king of the sixteenth century is credited with the introduction of a syllabic alphabet to improve the literacy rate among his people. But this ruler, King Sejong, realized that the priestly establishment would probably oppose such an innovation as being contrary to the ancient books, all written in Chinese characters. According to legend, therefore, he invented a syllabic system of 14 consonants and 10 vowels and, instead of writing them on paper to show the priests, he secretly painted them in honey on flat pandamus leaves. During the night ants ate through the honey, leaving exact shapes of the painted letters. King Sejong then called his priests and asked them whether they had an explanation. After deliberating, the priests informed the king that the signs were an alphabet given by the gods to the people of Korea, an interpretation duly accepted and promulgated by King Sejong.

Korean, employing Chinese ideograms (left), and Korean written solely in King Sejong's simplified syllabic alphabet system (right).

17. *An Asian Script of Subtlety and Humor*

Chinese, originally—and still mainly—a system of pictorial ideograms called "characters," is second only to the Indo-European scripts as the most prevalent writing system on earth. In mainland China alone there are over one billion Chinese; among them literacy, aided by a simplification of many of the ancient and graceful characters, has increased considerably in recent years. In addition, Chinese characters are used in Japan, Taiwan, Southeast Asia, and South Korea, and in Chinese overseas settlements throughout the world.

Chinese writing, like the ancient Egyptian and Mesopotamian systems, evolved thousands of years ago from pictures. The ideogram for "sun," originally a circle, is a square with a line through it; the "moon" ideogram looks like a curved half moon. When you write them together as a single character, you get "bright."

日 = sun   月 = moon   明 = bright (sun + moon)

The "tree" ideogram resembles a tree and, when merged with "sun," means "east," depicting the rising sun seen through the trees. Two trees mean "a forest," and three trees written together gives "dense woods" or "luxuriant."

木 = tree   東 = east (sun through tree)   林 = woods (two trees)

森 = dense woods (three trees)

The "horse" ideogram, although simplified through the millenia, is still written with a sign that shows four legs and a tail. The character for "wagon" or "cart" shows a cart seen from the top with two wheels and an axle. When "fire" is written with "cart" the combination means "locomotive." Three carts together means "rumbling traffic." "Cart" with an enveloping or sweeping action line above it gives the word for "army," an interesting reminder of the importance of logistics in tactics developed throughout the thousands of years of warfare in Chinese history.

馬 = horse   車 = wagon   火車 = locomotive (fire + wagon)

轟 = rumbling noise of traffic (three wagons)   軍 = army (wagon + enveloping movement)

The ideogram for "door" looks like the divided gates in traditional Chinese houses. "Mouth" in "doorway" means "ask" or "question." "Ear" in "doorway" means "listen." "Open" and "shut" are suggested by the extended or contracted form of smaller characters within the doorway. "Moon" seen through "doorway" means "leisure" or "repose," and "horse" coming through "doorway" means, understandably, "sudden interruption."   門 = door

問 = ask question (mouth in doorway) 聞 = listen (ear in doorway)

開 = open (door widening) 閉 = close (door contracting) 閒 = leisure (moon in doorway)

闖 = sudden interruption (horse appearing in doorway)

The Chinese ideogram for "woman" and its combinations reflect an often philosophical although male-oriented view of relations between the sexes. The character for "man" or "person" has been simplified to a picture of two legs, the character for "woman" shows a person carrying something. "Woman" and "child" written together is the word for "good." One "woman" under "roof" means "peace"; two "women" means "a quarrel"; and three "women" signifies "debauchery," "fornication," or "adultery." One "woman" with "pig" under "roof" means "giving in marriage," the pig representing not the husband but "household goods." "Woman" combined with "sun" and "big eye" is "envy" and "woman" standing by or listening at a "door" is "jealousy." "Woman" combined with "a thousand" means "faithless," and "woman" and "mouth" is the character for "if."

人 = man, person   女 = person carrying something (woman)

好 = good (woman + child)   安 = peace (one woman under roof)

姦 = adultery (three women)   嫁 = giving in marriage (woman + pig under roof)

娼 = envy (woman + sun + big eye)   妒 = jealousy (woman standing at door)

奸 = faithless (woman + 1,000)   如 = if (woman + mouth)

"Mouth" is a square and, when "vapor" comes out of it, means "word" or "speak." "Solid object" coming out of "mouth" means "tongue," which, written together with "speak," means "language." Three "mouths" together mean "criticism" or "criticize," and "mouth" combined with "beg" gives the character for "eat." 口 = mouth

言 = word (vapor rising from mouth)   舌 = tongue (solid article protruding from mouth)

話 = language (words + tongue)   品 = criticize (three mouths)   吃 = eat (mouth + beg)

The Chinese view of China is aptly expressed in the ideogram for the name, a square with a line going down the middle. This word "middle" has traditionally been the word for "China"—the "middle" country (*chung-kuo*), the middle of the world, the center of civilization. This word is still used for China by Communists, Nationalists, and overseas Chinese. 中 = center, middle, China

A great advantage of the widespread use of Chinese writing throughout Southeast Asia has been that a variety of nations could use the ideograms in their own languages and be understood by a number of other nations within the Chinese sphere of influence. The use of Chinese script is decreasing in Korea and the countries of Southeast Asia. It is still employed in Japan, although the number of characters a student is required to learn in school does not exceed 2,000.

In dynastic times in China, the characters in the language numbered between 40 and 50 thousand; many other words were composed, as they are now, of several separate characters. In modern times 6,000 characters is considered enough to read newspapers or books and, under the present regime, these characters have been simplified in the interest of furthering literacy, despite the resultant loss to art, tradition, and historical continuity.

China may eventually adopt the Roman alphabet, although this is unlikely at the present time, since several important Chinese languages are mutually understandable only through the written language. In addition, Chinese written in the Roman alphabet would be hard to understand because of the four tones, which change the meaning of every syllable. Some syllables have 50 different meanings.

Hân hạnh được gặp ông.   Sample of Vietnamese, written in Roman letters, modified by special signs for accent and tone.

Vietnamese, also a tonal language, has several more tones than the official Mandarin or Kuo-yü. Vietnamese is now written in Roman letters but is complicated by accents, bars, dots, circumflexes, crescents, and commas applied to the Roman letters as a pronunciation and tonal guide.

Chinese writing lends another dimension to painting and poetry; the reader glimpses the suggested shape of many objects while reading a poem or an inscription on a painting. The character for "mountain" suggests a mountain, the word for "rain" shows the sky and raindrops, "flower"

resembles a real one, "dragon" shows its coils and claws,
the word "bird" suggests a real bird about to fly, "fish"
shows the shape of a fish as if seen swimming underwater
from above, as if from a bridge over a garden pool.

One of the most gracefully expressed tributes to the
suggestive effects of the ancient Chinese characters was
made by a poet of the T'ang dynasty thirteen centuries ago.
If Chinese characters are ever replaced by Roman letters (as
is being considered) this excerpt could serve as a reminder
of the subtle beauty that would be lost.

> . . . the beauty of these letters
> Looking like sharp daggers piercing live
> crocodiles,
> Like pairs of phoenixes dancing,
> Like mountain spirits descending,
> Like jade and coral trees with interlocking
> branches. . .

18. Languages Lost—and Found Again

Stone Age pebbles with markings and annotations painted on them have been found in the Mas d'Azil caves in France. What seem to be letters are incised on round and flat stones which have been dated as 12,000 to 16,000 years old. This would put written records back into the Stone Age. Apparent annotations on deer horns and other bones, discovered after these prehistoric bones had long been on exhibition in European museums, indicate that elementary records and astronomical observations date back thousands of years before the writing systems of early Egypt and Sumeria.

The earliest writing probably started from counts or tallies and evolved to complicated picture-writing, and then became a combination of pictures, complete syllables, and some letters. Such a system was used in ancient Egypt, where the hieroglyphic system developed by the Egyptians had a life span longer than any other system on earth.

The use of ancient Egyptian and its hieroglyphic system of writing vanished after the Moslem conquest of Egypt and stayed "lost" for more than a thousand years. The hieroglyphics were forgotten and the language itself went underground, used only in rituals of the Coptic church, a Christian religion still practiced by its native Egyptian believers, whose ancestors survived the Moslem conquest.

Sample of Egyptian hieroglyphic writing.

European travelers to Egypt up to about 1800 often wondered whether the hieroglyphics which they saw on obelisks, the walls of temples and tombs, mummy cases, and sheets of papyrus were writing, pictures, or just decoration. One student of ancient history, the French Abbé Tandeau de Saint-Nicholas, proclaimed, even while Egyptologists were attempting to decipher the hieroglyphics: "It is as clear as day that the hieroglyphics are purely ornamental."

When Napoleon's army invaded and conquered Egypt, Napoleon brought with him a number of scientists and archaeologists; their activity caused some unusual discoveries by the troops—for instance that the Great Pyramid was at exactly the best spot to divide and bisect the delta, that it was exactly aligned to the four directions, and other indications of advanced knowledge of astronomy in ancient Egypt. Napoleon's archaeologists were even more interested in the hieroglyphics but were unable to connect them to any other language. A great breakthrough to the culture of ancient Egypt did come: the troops discovered the Rosetta stone, an ancient royal proclamation incised on a

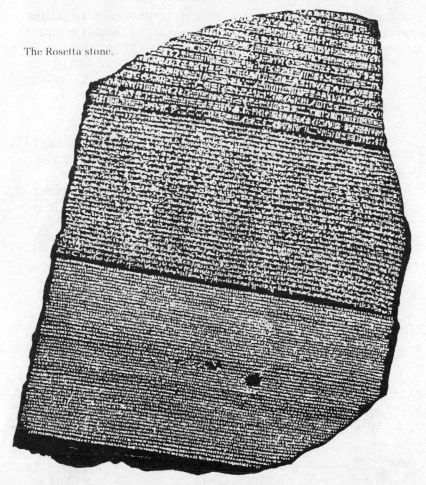

The Rosetta stone.

stone tablet. The proclamation dated from the Ptolemaic
dynasty, established by the Greek conquest of Egypt by
Alexander the Great and therefore employing Greek as well
as Egyptian in its proclamations. The Rosetta stone was
written in three scripts: two versions of ancient Egyptian,
the hieroglyphic and the simplified demotic script, plus the
same message in Greek, which the French scientists could
read. Since the Rosetta stone was broken at both ends, no
one knew where each text started or how the three texts
coordinated. Champollion, a young French linguist and
archaeologist who had dedicated his life to the deciphering
of hieroglyphics, obtained a rubbing of the stone and began
by attempting to solve the meaning of certain hieroglyphics
separated from the others in a flat circle. He assumed they

were well-known names, a supposition that he subsequently proved. The first name he deciphered was Cleopatra and the second was Ptolemy.

Cartouche of Cleopatra's name from the Rosetta stone.

From the moment that the first key to the unknown languages, the name of Cleopatra, was discovered, the decipherment of hieroglyphics became possible, although certainly not easy. Following the theory that church Coptic contained elements of ancient Egyptian, linguists deciphered both the simplified and hieroglyphic scripts. Egyptologists in different parts of Europe made their own translations separately and then compared them, in person or by mail, and found that their translations concurred.

The strain on the human mind of this intensive work was evident in the life of Champollion himself. When he made his first successful translation he shouted "I have it!" then collapsed in a dead faint. Although he drove himself literally to death within the next ten years and died in 1832 at the age of 42, his legacy can be said to be the recovery of a lost language and thousands of years of history.

   Eye of Horus, still used in doctors' prescriptions.

Just one of the ancient Egyptian hieroglyphs is still in day-to-day use throughout the world. It is the ℞ on a doctor's prescription, originally the hieroglyph of an eye—the eye of Horus, Egyptian god of medicine, whose hieroglyph doctors have used through all the intervening ages since the ancient days in Egypt.

Translation of the ancient languages and writing systems of Mesopotamia (present-day Iraq) was accomplished by a number of English and German linguists who approached their translation with an intensity that bordered on obsession. The available language records written in the lost

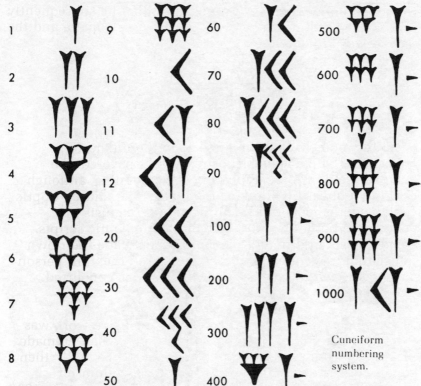

Cuneiform numbering system.

languages of ancient Sumeria, Assyria, Babylonia, and
Persia were written in wedge-shaped (cuneiform) marks
pressed into soft clay tablets and then baked. (For business
transactions the ancient Babylonians used addressed clay
envelopes, also baked, which had to be broken open by the
addressee.) For generations quantities of this cuneiform
writing had been found on bricks and tablets taken from
ancient ruins. Because no one knew how to read it, many
investigators, ignoring the world opened up by the Egyptian
hieroglyphics, maintained that cuneiform was merely a form
of ornamentation.

————————

Since Mesopotamia had been occupied and reoccupied by
so many powers for 5,000 years, potential translators did
not know what language the records that had been found
were written in and therefore were not able to compare it
with any surviving language the way ancient Egyptian could
be compared with Coptic.

————————

Description of triumph of Darius of Persia as carved on the rock of Behistun.

Overhanging rock on Babylonian section of the Behistun inscription.

Translation of these ancient scripts was aided by the desire for self-glorification of the Persian emperors (a tendency among Persian heads of state that has not diminished through the centuries). Certain emperors had erected to themselves practically indestructible monuments inscribed in the many languages of their empire: old Persian, Babylonian-Assyrian, Elamite. One of these multilingual inscriptions was carved on the side of a 300-foot cliff at Behistun in Iran, too high up for anyone to destroy it. But it was not too high for Sir Henry Rawlinson, who let himself down in a bos'n's chair from the top of the cliff and copied thousands of inscriptions. (Copying the Babylonian version almost cost him his life because he could get to the carving only by holding onto the cliffside with his left hand, dangling over a sheer drop of 200 feet and copying the intricate cuneiform letters with his right hand.)

During the wave of interest in deciphering the writings of Assyria and Babylonia that swept European scientific circles in the early nineteenth century, a young German linguist named Georg Friedrich Grotefend was destined to play an important role. Grotefend, discussing Assyrian writing with some friends while drinking in a Frankfurt *Bierstube,* made a bet with them that he would solve the translation enigma. Basing his research on rubbings from stone monuments in Persia written, as he later ascertained, in three languages, he isolated certain combinations at the beginning of each inscription that he surmised were the names of the ruling king, that king's father, and his grandfather. Grotefend knew the Greek names of the Persian kings and from this supposition and his knowledge of spoken Persian he was able, after years of work, to begin to translate Babylonian, Assyrian, old Persian, and Elamite. We do not know whether Grotefend ever collected his bet, but his remarkable research and persistence assuredly belongs in a book of records.

Since a variety of languages were written in cuneiform, researchers originally did not know what language they were going to translate. This problem was largely solved by the incredibly lucky discovery of a deposit of clay books in the ruins of Nineveh in what was once the palace library of the Assyrian king Assurbanipal. By an amazing stroke of fortune, bi- and tri-lingual dictionaries were found, as if the literary king had left them there to help future researchers assess the glories of his empire.

George Smith, an expert in ancient languages employed at the British Museum, made a discovery which shook the Victorian world. In translating a broken-off section of one of the clay books from Nineveh, he suddenly realized that he was reading a partial story of the Flood, written *before* the Hebrew version and interrupted by the break in the tablet.

His discovery caused such a furor that the *London Daily Telegraph* backed him in an expedition to Mesopotamia where, at Nineveh, he actually located the missing segments. The complete story of the Flood almost exactly paralleled the biblical version except for the names of the deity and of Noah, which was Ut-naphishtim. But Smith's strenuous activities destroyed his mind and health. After making one especially difficult original translation at the British Museum he exclaimed, "I am the first man to read this text after two thousand years of oblivion!" He then lapsed into a series of disjointed sounds and began to remove his clothes in the presence of his startled colleagues. He died not long afterward at the age of 36.

Several of the ancient tongues have never been lost. Although Greek has undergone several modifications, Greeks today can still read the ancient inscriptions with much more facility than Italian or other speakers of the Romance languages can read Latin. Ancient Greek texts are hard to read, since there was no punctuation and the ancient writing sometimes moved from left to right and then turned around for the next line, moving from right to left, continuing the back-and-forth movement for succeeding lines. This system is called *boustrophedon*—"as the ox plows"—across the field and then back again.

Latin has been kept alive as a living language through its use in the Roman Catholic church and in scientific and literary circles. Its popular use ceased in the Byzantine Empire as Greek took over. Greeks, however, still refer to themselves in Greek as *Romiós*, "Roman," doubtless remembering the Eastern Roman Empire at Constantinople, which lasted a thousand years longer than Rome.

Latin is pronounced somewhat differently in the languages of northern and southern Europe. No one knows how the Romans pronounced *c*—soft as in the English "Caesar," hard as in the German *Kaiser* (which means "Caesar"), or with a "ch" sound as in "church" and the Italian *Cesare*. This pronunciation difficulty and others—such as whether *v* was pronounced *v* or *w*—could be cleared up if we could go back in time and hear how the Romans spoke Latin, a dream dear to the heart of all teachers of Latin.

The revival of spoken Hebrew as a unifying force in Israel is an outstanding example of the power of language. Like Latin, Hebrew was kept alive for many generations as a religious language and, when it was revived, the matter of a standard pronunciation had to be considered. The main divergence was between the north and central European, or Ashkenazic, pronunciation and the Sephardic pronunciation, developed by Spanish, Portuguese, Italian, and Mediterranean speakers of Hebrew. No one really knew how it was pronounced in ancient times. The Sephardic pronunciation was adopted, perhaps a logical choice since it developed in an area close to the original climate, far from the harsh weather of the cold north.

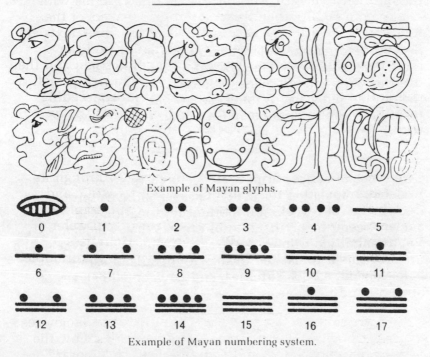

Example of Mayan glyphs.

Example of Mayan numbering system.

Some ancient languages have left records that seem doomed to remain unread. The jungles of southern Mexico and Central America abound with Maya inscriptions. About 2,500 separate signs have been noted, but it is not known whether they are pure hieroglyphics, syllables, or a combination of the two. The Maya even had folded books, which the Spanish conquerors burned under the urging of Bishop Landa of Yucatán—except for four or five copies now in the Vatican and other museums. (Too late, Bishop Landa became interested in written Maya and reconstructed a Maya "alphabet" with the help of Maya survivors. But the alphabet proved to be based on deception by his informants.)

The mystery of the Maya writing system remains largely unsolved, except for the identification of numbers and signs for days and months and, recently, some of the rulers' names. Russian linguists have used computers and published voluminous works on the techniques used, although the meaning of most of the words remains a mystery.

Several Mediterranean languages remain "lost." Etruscan, the language of the Italic civilization that preceded and was overthrown by the Romans, is known through examples of the written language in tombs and other inscriptions, but there has been to date no spoken language to compare it with.

Two types of scripts from Crete, called Cretan A and Cretan B, defied translation for many decades and gave promise, if deciphered, of revealing important information about the ancient seafaring civilization of Crete. When Michael Ventris finally did interpret Cretan B after World War II, the first document translated dealt with details of estate management, assets, supplies, and payments to slaves of olive oil and perfume.

Comparison of inscriptions from the forgotten cities of the Indus Valley (above) and from Easter Island (below), areas separated by half the distance around the world.

An enigma—a startling resemblance between two unreadable writing systems—has been found at opposed parts of the earth's surface, Easter Island in the South Pacific and the excavated cities of Harappa and Mohenjo-daro in the Indus Valley of Pakistan. The Indus Valley cities have been abandoned for thousands of years; their population is estimated to have been hundreds of thousands, even millions. The writings of the Indus Valley cities have been found on seals, the writings of Easter Island on wooden slabs kept in caves. Since there are no survivors of the Harappa culture and no Easter Islander now speaks or reads the old tongue, there is no key to this unusual script, nor is there apt to be. Some of the "letters," however, are so much alike that it seems impossible, as some linguists have maintained, that their resemblance is coincidental.

19. Word Frequency and Some Surprises

There are over a million words in the English language, although the average English speaker uses no more than 2,800 in daily conversation. The vocabulary of the King James version of the Bible is only 6,000 words, and Shakespeare produced all his works with 19,000 words in different combinations. The voluminous Sunday edition of *The New York Times* uses more than either, averaging out at 25,000.

Intelligent and well-read speakers of English can use and recognize between 25 and 50 thousand words; there are even more highly verbal people with usable vocabularies of up to 100 thousand words—four times the vocabulary needed to read the Sunday *New York Times*.

In a study published in 1953—*A General Service List of English Words*—Michael West examined the frequency of certain words in print and conversation by selecting a total of 5 million running words, then counting the number of times each word was used—with some unexpected and interesting results. "And" won first place (106,064), followed by prepositions and adverbs such as "of" (100,511), "in" (48,337), "still" (26,862), "for" (25,951), "as" (23,646), "with" (23,232), and "at" (20,264). The indefinite article "a" rated an 8,972 count. The most frequently occurring verbs were "have" (43,432), "shall/will" (23,466), "do" (12,840), "can" (10,552). "Be" was not counted because of its different forms. The negative "not" and its contraction "n't" had a frequency of 21,587.

Comparing the frequency of each word in pairs of opposites as counted in West's study provokes thought (although some other collection of 5 million running words might yield a somewhat different count). "Peace" (1,544) was used less frequently than "war" (2,468), and "battle" by itself attained a considerable count (1,068). "Man" received 10,388, far outdistancing "woman" at only 1,562 (but this count was made before the women's rights movement started). "Wife" was 866, "husband" was 478. "Widow" had a count of 128, and "widower" did not occur often enough to receive a mention. "Mother" (1,619) scored much higher than "father" (224).

On a more personal note "I" and "me" turned out to be more important than "you" and the other pronouns:

I	21,032
me	5,248
you	12,408
my, mine	7,253

your, yours	3,324
he	31,765
she	4,092
it	35,512

Is it better to give than to receive? West's verb frequency count includes:

give	2,184
take	7,008
receive	1,600

According to the frequency count, religious and philosophical words such as "God" (8,112), "heaven" (690), "soul" (740) did not compare with the high ratings attained by the frequency count of more mundane matters such as "government" (3,165), "money" (2,257), "business" (1,892), "politics" (1,096), and "dollar" (1,074).

Geography, habits, and point of view lead each language group to favor certain words and expressions. For instance, the word for "lion" has a much greater frequency in Swahili (*simba* in that tongue) and other languages of east Africa than in the European languages.

In France "wine" and the names of various wines, and words for the preparation of the delicious French cuisine, enjoy an especially high frequency in conversation. These words are often used in their original French form in other languages.

In American English the expression "OK" is used to mean "yes," or "agreed," or "well, then . . ." or "good." Being impossible to translate, it has entered other languages in its original form.

Spanish, with its tradition of *machismo*, has ¡Hombre! ("man!") as a conversational exclamation—and had it

generations before English-speaking hippies adopted "man!"
as a conversational filler. Spanish terms for phases of the
bullfight defy translation. Just one example is the German
translation of *matador*—*Stierstecher,* "bullsticker"—which
fails to convey the spirit of the *corrida.* Nor is the English
word "bullfight" even literally correct, the Spanish being
corrida de toros, "running of the bulls."

Italian speakers favor terms connected with music and
opera, and Italian has furnished the international
vocabulary of music.

A special Italian word for "hello" or "goodbye"—*Ciao!,* a
favorite expression of the international jet set—comes from
a form of the word "slave": *schiavo,* "I am your slave."

High on the frequency scale in Russian is the word *nichevo,*
whose basic meaning is "nothing" but which also implies "I
don't care," "Don't worry," "It doesn't matter," "What's the
use?"—a sort of reflection of the insouciant fatalism
personified by the "Russian soul."

In horse and cattle cultures, herders or local cowboys are
likely to refer to the important animal by breed or color
rather than an undifferentiated word for "horse" or
"steer"—a natural development fostered by constant
association and the necessity for differentiation. Desert
Arabs, for example, use a variety of descriptive words for
horses, not just a general word "horse."

In the Eskimo language there is no word for "metal" although
there are words for tin, copper, steel and gold. There are words
for separate colors but no generic word for "color."

---

20. *Some Evocative Names for Animals*

The custom of referring to an animal central to the culture in terms that distinguish special features perhaps reaches its apogee among Eskimo groups, who have no special word for "walrus" but must specify the kind of walrus they have just sighted, hunted, or caught, and plan to eat, as follows:

nutara .... "baby walrus"
ipiksaulik .... "two-year-old walrus"
tugar .... "walrus with tusks, male or female"
timartik .... "big male walrus"
aiverk .... "unaccompanied walrus"
naktivilik .... "mature walrus"

Names for animals in a number of languages are descriptive words or phrases indicating what the animal looks like, sounds like, or does. The word for "bear" in Russian and ancient Celtic means simply "the honey eater"; the Finnish word means "honey paw." The Navaho word for "squirrel" is the phrase "it-has-a-bushy-tail," and the Arapaho for "elephant" is "it-has-a-bent-nose."

When Chinese voyagers first saw the kangaroo they did not adopt the Australian name but named it in Chinese the way it looked to them—"pocket rat" or "great rat with a pocket." The Yoruba of West Africa, unused to zebras, called them, with some logic, "striped horses."

The Indian nations of the Americas were astounded at the sight of the horse when it appeared, brought by the early Spanish conquerors. The Aztecs thought it was a hornless deer. The Sioux named it *shuñka wakān*, "supernatural dog," and the Cheyenne (who, like the Sioux, later used horses with considerable success against the U.S. cavalry) referred to it as *mo-eheno'ha*—"domesticated elk." Another animal new to the Cheyenne, the pig, joined their language as *eshkoseesehotame*—"dog with sharp nose."

White people generally consider the zebra to be a white animal with black stripes while the African natives take it to be a black animal with white stripes.

The Narragansett Indians had an appropriate word for a moose. They called it "he trims it smooth."

Because of its human appearance, the orangutan of the South Asian jungles was often mistaken for a wild man living in the trees. In Malay, *orang* is "man" and *utan* is "jungle"; hence "man of the jungle."

Descriptive names do not always seem to fit the animal in question. In Hawaiian, a certain tiny reef fish is called *humohumokunokuapuaa*, and a giant fish of the deep ocean goes by the name of *o*.

The South American llama got its name by mistake. When the Spanish invaders saw the strange animal they asked the Indians ¿*Cómo se llama?*—"What is it called?" The Indians, trying to understand what the Spanish were saying, kept repeating the word *llama*. The Spanish took their own question as an answer, and dubbed the animal they had been calling "Indian sheep" a llama.

Lest speakers of English begin to feel superior to the quaint custom of naming animals for what they resemble, we should remember that many English appellations for animals came about in the same way, although the names seem more scientific because they come from Greek. "Hippopotamus" means "horse" (*hippo*) "of the river" (*potamus*). "Rhinoceros" is a combination of "nose" (*rhino*) and "horn" (*karas*). "Elephant" comes from the Greek for "ivory" (*elephas*), not the other way around, since the Greeks had ivory before they encountered elephants. And "dinosaur" is a combination of the Greek *deinos* and the Latin *saurus*, meaning "frightful lizard"—which, of course, the dinosaur was.

21. *Do Animals Have a Language?*

For countless generations humans have
listened to the chirping of birds, the
chattering of monkeys, the roaring and
howling of the larger carnivores, the
various noises made by domestic animals,
and wondered whether these sounds were a
form of animal speech. Zoologists generally
accept that the sounds made by animals are
a means of communication, but not yet a
form of articulate speech, at least speech as
we know it.

Peoples in different parts of the world have created written sounds to mimic the noises they hear animals making. These human interpretations of animal noises differ from language to language although all over the world the animals themselves are making identical sounds. A listing of words for dog, cat, and bird noises in eight languages shows that cat noises sound the same in the various languages, whereas bird and dog sounds differ (at least linguistically):

	DOG	CAT	BIRD
English	bow-wow	meow	chirp-chirp
French	ouah-ouah	miaou	cui-cui
Italian	bau-bau	miao	chip-chip
Spanish	jau-jau	miau	chíu-chíu
German	haff-haff	miau	piip-piip
Russian	gaf-gaf	myaou	tyu-tyu
Chinese	wu-wu	mao	tü-tü
Japanese	wau-wau	n'yao	pi-pi

A watchdog from antiquity, this Roman mosaic is the oldest representation found to date warning passersby to "beware of dog."

When animal sounds are expressed in print, the early rising cock has *panache*, the cow is resigned, the pig is individualistic.

	COCK	COW	PIG
English	cock-a-doodle-do	moo	oink-oink
French	cocorico	meuh	groin-groin
Italian	chichirichì	muù	gru-gru
Spanish	quiquiriquí	múu	tru-tru
German	kikerike	muh	quiek-quiek
Russian	kukuriku	mu	kroo-kroo
Chinese	kong-shi	miu	oh-ee oh-ee
Japanese	kokekoko	moh	bu-bu

Direct human communication with work animals
throughout the ages has usually taken the form of a series of
verbal orders emphasized with whips, spurs, and a variety
of goads. Horses, for example, have been trained to respond
to these commands:

	GO!	STOP!
English	Gee-up!	Whoa!
French	Hue!	Oh!Oh!
Italian	Arri!	Fermo!
Spanish	¡Arre!	¡So!
German	Hüt!	Brr!
Russian	T-t-t-t!	Tproo!
Hungarian	Elöre!	Hoh!
Arabic	Skee!	Khef!
Urdu	Chull beta!	Bus!

Elephants have long been considered to possess the most
retentive memory among the larger animals. They seem to
justify this claim; in India, for example, they have been
trained to obey more than a hundred words and phrases in
a unique "elephant language" used by their mahouts. These
Indian elephants function as living carriages (the mahout
rides between the animal's ears, astride the head), hunting
platforms, derricks, hoists, trucks, and even troop carriers.
(In an earlier day they fulfilled the function of armored
tanks.) The specialized vocabulary of the mahouts is used
only with elephants and has been handed down through
generations of mahouts. It is reputed to derive from an
ancient language of India, now lost, but in use when
elephants were first trained.

Too many instances of cooperation and common effort
between animals have been observed—the construction of
beaver dams, rabbit warrens, and the enormous communal
nests of the weaver finches in Africa, insect "buildings"
such as anthills and beehives, and the activities of herd
leaders and food scouts—to allow us to deny that animals
and insects use some form of communication. What these
non-humans employ may be a combination of signals,
instinct, and telepathy. If the communicating is based on a
series of signals understood by members of the same
species, it would seem to confirm one of the theories of how

human beings first learned to speak. It would also suggest that certain animal species may, if they survive the depredations of man, eventually learn to express more complicated ideas going beyond their current repertory— alarm, distress, fear, hunger, pain, attack, defense of territory, and mating calls.

In the complex social organization of bees, with its divided work assignments for the maintenance of the queen and the hive, one system of communication is based on motion, or informative ballet. A worker bee can report the location of a new source of food by "dancing" on the inner wall of the hive, its dance patterns centering on the direction of the sun and indicating not only the direction of the new food supply but even the distance from the hive.

Neither the herding and milking of groups of aphids by specialized ant teams to provide nourishment for the colony (an almost exact parallel with human dairy farming) nor the construction of ant skyscrapers in Africa and Australia could be accomplished without some form of communication, telepathic or through signals.

Wolves hunt in packs and also send out scouts to locate prey. One wolf cannot bring down a moose but a wolf pack can. When a moose, elk, or deer is located by a wolf scout, his ululating signal, a wolf "Tally ho!", brings reinforcements.

Some birds of the same species apparently understand "foreign" bird cries from other migratory groups. Some American crows, those from Pennsylvania, for example, can understand cries of alarm from French crows; but Maine crows, who generally do not migrate from their natural habitat, either do not understand "international" crow signals or are indifferent to them.

Some students of "animal" languages believe they have isolated actual vocabulary patterns of animal speech. A German researcher, Erich Bäumer, claims to have identified at least 30 phrases in chicken language. Japanese researchers in spoken or chattered monkey communication have also suggested a figure of 30 spoken signals or phrases. These include: "There is food over here (over there)," which is said something like *howiaak*, and "We'd better go!" or "Let's leave!" which sounds like *kawa'ah*.

When the manlike gorilla, only a legend until fairly modern times, was first seen, described and exhibited (by the French-born American explorer-zoologist Paul du Chaillu) in the 1850's and '60's, and when its existence was confirmed by other African explorers, many people expected that such a manlike creature would possess a simple language roughly comparable to a human one. A later French explorer-zoologist, a student of the great African apes for many years, claimed to be able to talk to gorillas in the Paris zoo, asking them about the circumstances of their capture and the conditions of their captivity. Although he seemed to be conversing with gorillas and uttering gorilla-like sounds, conclusive proof of his knowledge of the gorilla language, if it existed, never culminated in a French-Gorilla phrasebook.

Herodotus, the Greek historian called the Father of History, writing about 450 BC, noted that baboons were trained by Egyptian priests to use brooms to sweep out the huge temples of ancient Egypt. Troops of modern baboons have attacked African villages, throwing stones and using sticks as weapons. In these attacks certain larger baboons have been observed to direct the efforts of the others in the manner of commissioned officers and noncoms in combat situations.

Monkeys have been trained to differentiate between foods and other objects pictured on punch keys to obtain favorite foods, a basis for language or picture communication with human beings. Initial successes with gorillas and chimpanzees, however, including advanced concepts such

as "good" and "bad," "I like," and "I don't like," and
certain other simple verbs and adjectives, have been
followed by a period in which the animals seemed to stop
learning or even to regress. This stopping point may be due
to the relative size of the brain as compared to humans.

_____

The human brain is considerably bigger by weight (average
1,600cc) than the brain of the three most intelligent apes,
the orangutan (500cc), gorilla (600cc), and chimpanzee
(600cc). Among the small animals, rats and pigs rate higher
in intelligence than dogs and cats (approximately equal) and
horses (relatively low). Surprisingly, humans are not quite
at the top of the list. The brain of the porpoise is effectively
larger than the human brain; both organs have an average
weight of 1600cc, but the porpoise brain has twice the
number of convolutions (which means a greater potential
brain power) and has three-and-a-half times as many brain
cells.

_____

Some animals cooperate with each other to help or protect
members of their group, a reasoning activity that implies
communication. Elephants in danger will form a ring
around the young of the herd, like the circle of a pioneer
wagon train formed against Indian attacks. Elephants will
bracket a wounded comrade between them to convey him to
safety and porpoises will support an injured one with their
bodies, holding it at the surface so it can breathe. Porpoises
act together in dispersing menacing sharks. Human beings
have often been saved by porpoises or dolphins from
drowning and from attacks by sharks, a rather unusual
preoccupation with the safety of humans considering the
constant nettings and killings to which dolphins have long
been subjected by mankind.

_____

Dolphins seem happy to play games with humans. The way
they learn some performing tricks has tended to prove not
only that they have retentive memories and intelligence but
also that they communicate with each other either by sound
or by telepathy. In the Miami Seaquarium, dolphins in one
tank learned to identify and balance floating cubes, balls,
and triangles in a sequence chosen by their trainers and

communicated through signs held up over their tank. On the following day, dolphins in a separate tank some distance away showed, when their turn came to learn the trick, that they already knew it. Somehow the trained dolphins in the first tank had managed to describe the trick to the untrained dolphins—as well as to communicate that a reward of fish was forthcoming for correct performance.

Dolphins have been trained to deliver material and equipment under water, a training that enables them to perform in submarine warfare, perhaps to deliver underwater explosive charges to enemy vessels. Prominent underwater explorers including Jacques Cousteau, Hans Haas, and Jacques Mayol have tried to arouse world opinion against using dolphins as unwitting allies in sea warfare.

Dolphins seem to have a sense of humor and often, without being urged, try to copy the speech of their trainers. In Miami in the '60s, Dr. John Lilly directed an attempt to establish two-way communication with dolphins, under the assumption that the size of the dolphin's brain and range of sound indicates a speech potentiality. Dolphins can imitate human sounds and, in addition, can make a variety of noises beyond the range of the human voice, such as barking, metallic beeping, creaking noises, and a number of bubbling sounds at different pitches underwater. Many experiments have been made with electrodes on a captive dolphin's brain; understandably, some of these experiments elicit hoarse and rasping sounds.

In late 1979, a small vessel designed to train captured dolphins for naval service disappeared without trace in the Bermuda Triangle. It contained six dolphins in tanks, and had a crew of four. Beyond the various dangers of ocean travel in a small ship, there still exists the intriguing possibility of a dolphin mutiny—despite the usually friendly nature of these amiable marine animals.

---

22. *Undiplomatic Translations*

As the African nations continue their progress toward modernization, statements by African delegates to the United Nations tend to underline the abandonment of old tribal ways. One French-speaking African delegate, for example, made this declaration: "Africa no longer erects altars to the gods" (*L'Afrique n'érige plus des autels aux dieux*). But the interpreter, thinking that the word *autels* was *hôtels* and that *aux dieux* was *odieux*, translated the delegate's phrase as "Africa no longer builds horrible hotels" (*L'Afrique n'érige plus des hôtels odieux*).

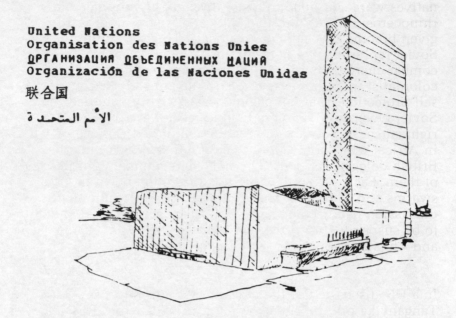

```
United Nations
Organisation des Nations Unies
ОРГАНИЗАЦИЯ ОБЬЕДИНЕННЫХ НАЦИЯ
Organización de las Naciones Unidas
```
联合国

الأمم المتحدة

At the UN, a Russian jibe that "in the U.S. over 50 million people live in slums" was rendered in Russian-to-English simultaneous translation as "In the U.S. over 50 million people live in caves"—an observation which passed uncontested in an ambiance not unwilling to believe almost anything about America.

UN simultaneous interpreters translate—through an elaborate hook-up—the speeches of delegates at the same rate the delegates normally speak. If a word central to a debate is incorrectly translated, it has to be revised as the debate progresses or the discussion risks becoming a Mad Hatter's tea party. Such an incident occurred during the era of decolonization when a representative of the rapidly contracting British Empire was reading a progress report in the Assembly on activities in a former East African trust area administered by the United Kingdom. When he was dealing with the attempts of indigenous personnel (formerly called "natives") to combat plagues of rhinoceros beetles, the Russian simultaneous translator caught the word "rhinoceros" (in Russian, *nasaróg*) but not "beetle" (*zhook*). The Soviet delegate therefore interrupted to ask how the natives were equipped to resist invasion by innumerable rhinoceros. He was told that indigenous personnel were given brooms and pails of chemicals. This seemed to the Soviet representative not only insufficient weaponry to combat charging hordes of rhinos but also evidence of colonialist unwillingness to distribute guns to Africans for self-protection from rampaging beasts. "Also," queried the Soviet delegate, with more than a trace of ecological righteousness, "there are only a few hundred rhinoceros left in Africa; why should they be exterminated?" To this the British delegate replied, "Oh, no! There are many *millions* of them. Each spring they fly down from the north in great swarms and eat the bark off the trees." By this time the discussion had become so complicated that the session had to be suspended until the word for "beetle" was located and—finally—appended to "rhinoceros."

In a UN discussion of the Organic Act introduced in Tanganyika prior to independence, the English-to-Russian translator, the daughter of Russian émigré parents, fluent in Russian but educated outside of Russia, translated the law as *Organicheskiy Akt*—literally a correct translation but a phrase that in modern Russian also means "sexual intercourse." Perhaps primly unaware of this generally accepted meaning, she captured her audience's undivided attention. She continued to develop, in Russian, the ramifications, modifications, and positions taken on this *Organicheskiy Akt*. The fascinated Russian delegates first chortled, then laughed outright, even exchanging waves with the Ukrainian, Byelorussian, Bulgarian, Polish, Czech, and Yugoslavian delegates of the Slavic fringe who, delegation by delegation, joined in solid Pan-Slavic hilarity. The final clincher was a question to the English delegate from a non-Russian speaking delegate: "What do the natives think of the Organic Act?" The reply, which brought down the Slavic side of the house, was: "In general, they maintain a passive attitude."

An attempt by an interpreter to improvise or adapt a familiar saying or proverb can also lead to disaster. An English-Spanish interpreter, attempting to express "there is more than one way to skin a cat," in Spanish, became suddenly inspired to adapt the basic meaning to bulls, considerably more important to the *macho* Spanish psyche than mere cats. Carried away by his enthusiasm, he invented what he thought would be an apt equivalent in Spanish—"There are more ways to catch a bull than by grabbing him by the horns"—before he realized from the hilarious outburst among the Spanish-speaking delegates (astonished that it would occur to anyone to catch a bull by his alternate outstanding characteristics) that something had gone amiss with his reference to that apogee of Spanish machismo, the patently well-endowed *toro*.

A UN representative from India, fluent in English but steeped in the curious accent of English-speaking Indians, was criticizing the Western powers over a matter of "decolonization." He observed that "The colonial powers remain unchanged, still holding in their hands their long-standing fallacies." He was happily unaware that his regional Indian pronunciation had rendered "fallacies" as "phalluses" and therefore failed to understand the explosion of laughter and comment which broke out in the English-speaking delegations. This masterpiece of mispronunciation soon spread to the other delegations and converted what had been a sleepy afternoon session of the General Assembly into an interlude of shared amusement among the three worlds.

Occasionally not just a mispronounced or mistranslated word, but an inadequately translated proverb can prove a source of misunderstanding and almost provoke a diplomatic incident. At the time Khrushchev visited the United States and the United Nations, he appeared on television with David Susskind. During the interview, Susskind said Khrushchev was "barking up the wrong tree." Khrushchev's translator, searching for a Russian rendering of this idiom, told Khrushchev that Susskind had said he was "baying like a hound," a translation that required considerable elucidation before the Soviet premier regained his calm. There does exist, however, an equivalent saw in Russian, having to do with the *trepak*, a lively Ukrainian dance: "Cousin, you started the trepak on the wrong foot."

Language interpreters have been used for thousands of years and frequently have been known to modify purposely what they are interpreting when they consider it convenient. A leader of an embassy from one of the Swiss cantons to the court of Louis XIV knew enough French to realize that what he was saying to the French monarch in German was coming out as an overly servile and unashamedly flattering accolade. After his speech he reproached the interpreter, saying, "Look here, I understand French and you did not translate what I said." "That is true, Monseigneur," admitted the interpreter calmly. "But I did indeed translate what you *should* have said."

The translator's bête noire—a machine that will automatically translate the spoken word, rendering human translators unnecessary—is still a long way from actuality. Any such machine would have to execute the process of simultaneous memory search, reasoning, selection, and judgment necessary to select the correct and most appropriate of several meanings applicable to almost every word in a "foreign" language, and then make the same judgment in the "native" language. If such a machine were possible, the heavy metallic steps of thinking and reasoning robots would soon be audible down the long corridors of the UN.

---

23. *What's in a Name: Places*

The names of some countries in the New World are derived from the languages of the original Amerindian inhabitants:

COUNTRY	LANGUAGE AND ORIGINAL MEANING
Mexico	Aztec: *Mextli,* war god
Guatemala	Maya: *Quauhtemalán,* "Place of wooden pillars"
Nicaragua	*Nicarao,* name of an Indian chieftain at the time of the Spanish conquest
Haiti	Carib: *Ahti,* "Mountain"
Cuba	Carib: *Cubagua,* "Place where gold is found"
Panama	Cuná: "Abundance of fish"
Jamaica	Carib: *Chymaka,* "Well-watered"
Peru	Quechua: *Peru,* name of a coastal river
Chile	Araucanian: "End of the land"
Uruguay	Guaraní: "River of the painted bird"
Paraguay	Guaraní: "River that makes the sea"
Bahamas:	Carib: *Bahama,* "Shallow reef"

The peninsula of Yucatán in Mexico owes its name to a misunderstanding. When the Spaniards landed in Yucatán they asked the Mayans what the country was called. The natives, not comprehending what the invaders were asking in alternate Spanish and Latin, responded, in Maya, "What did you say?" To the Spaniards, this phrase sounded like "yucatán." (Curiously, practically the same thing happened in Alaska: to questions about what the locality was called the Eskimos replied *ka-no-me*—"I don't know"—a phrase shortened to Nome).

Spanish and Portuguese place names in the New World commemorate religious ideas or people or describe European expectations or observations in the area.

COUNTRY	MEANING
Argentina	From the adjectival form of "silver," La República Argentina is literally "the silver republic." The great river which flows past Buenos Aires ("Good airs") is called by the noun form of "silver," La Plata.
Barbados	From *barbudos* ("bearded") referring to the vines hanging from trees, which looked like beards.
Bermuda	From the family name of Juan Bermúdez, a Spanish colonist aiming for another area, but shipwrecked in the "Bermuda Triangle" and washed up on an island with a cargo of pigs.
Bolivia	From the name of Simón Bolívar, hero of the nineteenth-century revolution against Spain.
Colombia	Named in honor of Columbus
Costa Rica	"Rich coast"
Curaçao	Portuguese for "heart" *curação*— referring to the Sacred Heart.
Ecuador	Named for the equator, which passes through it.

El Salvador	"The Saviour"
Honduras	From *las honduras,* "the depths."
Patagonia	*Patagón,* "Big foot." The first Spanish explorers of this section of what is now Argentina, noting big tracks in the snow, concluded that the as-yet-unseen inhabitants had abnormally large feet. But the tracks were left by primitive snow shoes used by the indigenous Patagonians.
Puerto Rico	"Rich port"
Santo Domingo	Saint Dominic
Trinidad	The Trinity
Venezuela	"Little Venice"; the Spanish discoverers found the Indians living along canals.

Columbia has frequently been used as another name for the United States in songs and declarations. It is obviously unfair that the general term America repeats the given name of Amerigo Vespucci, an Italian geographer at the time of the discovery of the Americas who contributed his name to the continents that, logically, should be North and South Columbia.

––––––––––––

Although the term "American" designates an inhabitant of the United States in many languages (with some variant spellings), it is also applied, especially in Spain, to anyone from the New World. "United States" to designate "America " also poses a certain problem in Spanish, because there are other United States in the Spanish-speaking New World—specifically the United States of Mexico, Brazil, and Venezuela. To avoid confusion in Spanish, therefore, the United States is often referred to as the "United States of the North"—*Los Estados Unidos del Norte*—and a person from the country is an *estadounidense* ("United Stater") or *norteamericano* ("North American").

––––––––––––

Most names of European nations stem from the names of tribes who initially inhabited or subsequently conquered them; many countries in Africa and Asia have names that describe the area or its people. (The name Africa itself comes from Latin *Aprika,* "sunny.")

COUNTRY	MEANING
Aden	"Eden" (the garden of)
Cameroon	Portuguese: *camarão,* "shrimp"
Ethiopia	Greek: *aithiops,* "burning face"
Congo	*kong* ("mountain")
Cyprus	From the Greek word for "copper." (Cyprus was an important source of copper in the ancient world.)
Hong Kong	"Fragrant Streams" or "Smelly Streams," depending on the translation of the character for "smell"
India	From the river Indus. In Hindi, the country is named *Bharat.*
Iran	Old Persian: *ariyan,* "noble." This is the same word as the German word *Arier* (Aryan), familiar to all observers of recent history, related to Old Persian through the Indo-European language group, frequently referred to by linguists as the Indo-Germanic group. Erin (Ireland) is also derived from *ariyan*—"noble."
Israel	"The Wrestler with God"
Japan	Chinese: *ji-pen,* "sun-root," since, to the ancient Chinese, the sun rose over Japan. In Japanese, "sun-root" is *ni-hon,* often rendered as Nippon.
Jordan	"The coming-down" (of rivers)
Kenya	*Kilinya,* "White Mountain"
Malagasy (Republic)	"Island of the Moon"

Malaya	*melayu,* "those who fled" or "the fleers"
Morocco	*maghrib,* "the west"
Singapore	"Lion City" (from the many statues of the British Lion)
Somalia	"Land of Hospitality"
Sudan	"Land of the Blacks"
Taiwan	"Terrace Bay"
Tanganyika (now Tanzania)	"Land of Many Tribes"
Thai (Thailand)	"Free"
Togo	"The other side of the lake"
Vietnam	"The Far South." The older name for the area, Annam, meant "the peaceful south," something of a misnomer.
Volta	Portuguese for "turn," referring to a large turn in the Niger River

---

The name Pakistan was constructed as an acronym. Its letters stand for its component parts: *P* for the Punjab, *A* for the Afghani border tribes, *K* for Kashmir, *S* for Sind, and the final *-tan* for Baluchistan. Coincidentally, the Persian word *pak* means "pure" and also "holy"; *-stan* is Urdu for "land." Hence the name Pakistan has the additional connotation of "Land of the Pure" or "Country of the Holy Ones."

Another striking example of a mistake in the name given to a country by explorers or mariners who misinterpreted what they were seeing or hearing is in Africa. Sierra Leone owes its name to Portuguese seafarers who thought they saw a great chain of mountains along the west African coast and also imagined that they heard the roaring of lions in the hills. But the roaring sound came from the surf, and the towering mountains later proved to be cumulus clouds forming great cliffs in the sky. This erroneous designation for Sierra Leone—"Mountain Range of the Lions"—

nevertheless became the permanent term for this part of the coast and for the now independent country of the same name.

Guinea (French: *Guinée*) and Guinea-Bissau are neighboring countries on the African west coast which was formerly called the Guinea Coast. One explanation of the name (the origin is not clear) is that when white seafarers asked, with wide gestures intended to bridge the language gap, the name of the coast, the local tribesmen thought the foreigners were pointing to a group of nearby women. The tribesmen replied using the word for "woman" several times (*guiné* in the Susu language). The explorers named their landing spot Guiné, and by extension, the whole western African shore became known in Europe by that name.

Whatever the origin of the name Guinea, it was adopted into English, for instance in "guinea hen," "guinea pig," the "guinea gold" of the old African trade days, the monetary guinea of England, and even an opprobrious term for Italians or those of Italian descent. (This last example is appended simply as a linguistic note with the admonition that its use may prove dangerous to the health of the potential user.) It was also used to name several new lands, such as New Guinea.

The name China also stems from a misunderstanding. The Romans, who in antiquity purchased so much silk from China for the use of Roman women that speeches were made against this foreign import in the Roman forum, were not personally familiar with China. From time to time, however, they would meet China traders in Persia and would ask them what country they were from. The Chinese, instead of replying *Chung-kuo* ("Middle Kingdom," or "The Central Country"), would diplomatically give the name of the powerful reigning dynasty of the time—the Ch'in. The Romans Latinized the name of this mysterious country of the Ch'in as Sina for easier pronunciation.

The original Latin word Sina reappears in such English words as sinology, sinologist, Sinitic, sinophile. The word China in its various international versions has immortalized the relatively short-lived (221–207 B.C.) Ch'in dynasty.

In Russian, China is called *Kitai* (English version: Cathay), commemorating another dynasty—the Khitan (AD 900–1100)—with which the Russians had frequent contact, mostly warlike.

The Chinese often prefer to call themselves after the great Han dynasty, which ruled from 202 BC to AD 220. Even in Communist China, listings and differentiations of nationality groups such as Mongols, Tibetans, Uighurs, Lolos, and so on refer to the Chinese as belonging to the Han nationality. The southern Chinese, for instance the Cantonese, remember with even greater pride the T'ang dynasty (AD 618 to 906), during which Chinese art and literature attained its apogee. Most of the Chinatowns in the United States and Canada are peopled by southern Chinese, who refer to "Chinatown" in their own language as *T'ang yen fao*—"[The] T'ang people's town."

A Canadian province, Manitoba, is named for the Great Spirit of the Algonkians, Manitou—in other words, God.

American Indian place names include:

Chicago	"The Place of the Skunk Cabbage"
Manhattan	"The Place of the Great Drunkenness" or "The Place Where We All Got Drunk"
Mississippi	"Very Big River"
Missouri	"Canoe River
Oklahoma	"The Red Man"
Omaha	"Upstream People"
Wyoming	"Upon a Great Plain"

The Grand Teton mountains in Wyoming looked to their French discoverers like great nipples (*grands tetons*).

New Jersey, the island of Jersey, Jersey cattle, and the type of sweater called a jersey all perpetuate the last name of Julius Caesar. The Latin name of several Roman cities, from which Jersey is derived, was Caesarea, named in honor of the first Caesar.

Many southern and western state and city names in the United States are of Spanish origin with meanings which are unknown to some inhabitants.

NAME	MEANING
Amarillo	"Yellow"
Arizona	"Arid Zone"
Boca Raton	"Mouse Mouth"
Colorado	"Red"
El Paso	"The Pass"
Florida	"Flowery"
Montana	"Mountain"
Nevada	"Snow Fall"
Palo Alto	"High Pole
Palomar	"Dove Cote"
Pasadena	"Strolling Place"
Reno	"Reindeer"
California	The name of the queen of the Amazons, since the conquistadores had heard that there were female Indian warriors on the west coast of America near what is now Los Angeles.

Vladivostok, the Russian-Siberian port on the Pacific, means "Lord of the East."

Cairo—al *Khaira* in Arabic—translates as "The Conqueror."

Persons who, to save time, refer to Los Angeles ("The Angels") as LA are properly following their local tradition. Los Angeles has already been considerably shortened from its original name, *El Pueblo de Nuestra Señora la Reina de los Angeles de Porciúncula*—"The Town of Our Lady Queen of the Angels of Porciúncula."

In the Thai language Bangkok means "the village of the wild plums."

The name Jerusalem can be translated in at least two ways: the Aramaic designation *Uru Shalim* "City of Peace"; or the Old Greek *Hierosolyma*, "Holy Fortress." Some other meanings of place names in Israel include:

Negev	"South"
Petach Tikvah	"Open Gate of Hope"
Rehoboth	"Paths" or "Roads"
Tel Aviv	"Hill of Spring"
Beersheba	"Place of the Seven Wells" or "Place of the Oath"

According to legend, Rome was named as a consequence of a fight between the twin brothers who founded the city, Romulus and Remus, in which Remus was killed. Romulus, affected by remorse, decided to call the city after his

La Lupa Romana (the Roman wolf), legendary foster mother of the founders of Rome.

brother, using the two-syllable form Roma and a slight modification of his brother's name. By coincidence the name of Roma also echoes the name Romulus, making us wonder if his remorse was as great as supposed.

The Canary Islands in the Atlantic are not named for canaries but for dogs (in Latin: *canis*). When the first Spaniards and Portuguese arrived at the end of the fourteenth century, they saw a great number of dogs, as well as white-skinned natives of mysterious origin and incomprehensible language—but no canaries.

One of the world's most beautiful cities was originally labeled a swamp. In Roman times Paris was called Lutetia Parisianorum—"mud flats of the Parisi tribe." Fortunately for its subsequent reputation, the reference to "mud flats" was dropped after the Roman occupation, preserving the name of the tribe. In French, however, Lutetia and Lutèce are still used as fanciful or poetic names for Paris. A host of hotels and restaurants, in France and throughout the world, use one or the other of these archaic names.

The names of a variety of different residences or focal points of government pertaining to presidents, kings, or other rulers have, when translated or traced, some interesting meanings:

Argentina	La Casa Rosada ("the pink house")
Italy	Il Quirinale (in Roman times: "house of the god of war")
China	Tien An Men ("gate of heaven's peace")
USSR	Kremlin (from *kreml*—"fortress")
France	L'Élysée (from Greek, "Elysian Fields," abode of the blessed after death)
The Philippines	Malacañan ("the ruler lives here")
Spain	La Zarzuela ("musical comedy"—currently the residence of the king, although not the palace)

---

24. *What's in a Name: People*

In European languages the majority of first names come from the Bible. By far the most popular of first names is the one that comes from the Hebrew *Yohanan,* "God is gracious." Its metamorphoses in various languages include John, Jean, Hans, Juan, Giovanni, Ivan, Johann, João, Yan, Sean, Ioan, Ian, Yannis, Johannus, Yahya, as well as the feminine variants Juana, Jean, Jeanne, Janet, Joan, Joanna. The same name is perhaps the second most common last name, taking such forms as Johannes, Janowski, Johnson, Jones, Jennings, Jenkins, Shane, Valjean, Giannini, Jensen, Jantzen, Ivanov.

The most common family name in the languages of Europe is the one that means "Smith"—either blacksmith or any worker in iron. Like many family names, it derives from an occupation (Baker, Tailor, Farmer, Shepherd, Shoemaker, Barber, are also common). All the following names mean "Smith":

Le Fèvre, La Farge, La Forge, Fernand	French
Ferrari, Fabbri, Fabroni, Ferraio	Italian
Herrera, Herrero, Hernández, Fernández	Spanish
Ferreiro, Ferreira	Portuguese
Schmidt, Schmied	German
Smed	Swedish
Kuznetsov	Russian
Kováć	Czech
Kovács...........................	Hungarian
Kowak, Kowalski	Polish
Kovac	Bulgarian
Haddad	Lebanese and Syrian Arabic
Magoon	Irish

Mary, one of the most popular feminine names, means "rebellion" (*Maryam* in the original Hebrew).

One of the Spanish terms for a noble—*Hidalgo*—is a contraction of the words *hijo de algo*, "son of something," "son of somebody."

For centuries peasants had only first names. Some identified themselves more specifically by occupation or a description of where they lived, such as "of the bridge"—or "of London." (Oaks, a pine tree, the river, the church, the mountain—all are incorporated in family names today.) Another method of identification was to use a second name that told people what your father's first name was: "John, son of Peter"—John Peterson. Such patronymic forms include:

Russian:	Ivanov
Spanish:	Rodríguez
German:	Tirpitz
Polish and Russian:	Kowalski
Greek:	Papadapoulos (*poulos:* literally, "little bird of")
Scottish:	*Mac*Gregor, *Mc*Neill, *M'*Leod
Irish:	O'Shea, O'Reilly, O'Rourke

In Scotland and Ireland the "of" precedes the father's name, as in the examples above. In medieval England the father's name or designation was frequently preceded by *Fitz*, a method of preserving the father's name if the child was born illegitimately. The name Fitzroy of aristocratic aura implies that the person bearing the name was either an illegitimate offspring of a king, or a descendant of one who was. In Anglo-Norman, the word for "son" was *fitz* (from French *fils*), and *roy* is an old spelling for *roi*, king.

All over the world, place names honor founders, discoverers, and rulers. But fame is transient and local opinion changes. Some honorific place names, especially in Africa under the aegis of decolonization, have been relatively short-lived.

FORMER NAME	PRESENT NAME
Léopoldville	Kinshasa
Stanleyville	Kisangani
Elisabethville	Lubumbashi
Rhodesia	Zimbabwe
Salisbury	Harare

In the U.S.S.R., where the cult of personality turns on and off, some place names have changed three times since the revolution. Tzaristsyin (named for the Tsar) became Stalingrad, and is now Volgograd; St. Petersburg was renamed Petrograd, then Leningrad. (Scores of localities were named after Stalin; most of them have reverted to their former names.)

In the Dominican Republic the name of the capital, Santo Domingo ("St. Dominic"), was changed to Ciudad Trujillo ("Trujillo City") while Trujillo was alive but quickly reverted to its original form after his death.

Some family names, especially those of pioneering physicists, have been adopted nationally and internationally as the names of physical units. When we speak of watts, amperes, roentgens, curies, herz, ohms, or volts, we are repeating the exact family names of the physicists who measured them ("volt" is an exception; the originator's name was Volta).

Many medical techniques are named for their principal developers as in pasteurization (Louis Pasteur), Salk vaccine (Jonas Salk). The Caesarian section is named for Julius Caesar, who was delivered at birth in this manner.

Objects, techniques, ideas, and movements have all been named for inventors, founders, or popularizers. Some name survivals are evident: Christianity, Buddhism, Marxism. Other nouns and verbs based on people's names have been used for so many years that the origin has been forgotten. All of the following are derived from the family names of outstandingly good—or bad—individuals.

bloomer	Amelia Jenks Bloomer (1818-1894), a suffragist, wore and lectured in the short skirts and billowing trousers gathered at the ankles invented by Elizabeth Smith Miller. Bloomer also advocated the costume in her magazine, despite widespread condemnation of any woman who wore them in public.
bowdlerize	Thomas Bowdler (1754-1825), in a desire to protect the reading public from pornography, edited Shakespeare by purging the texts

of all sexual jokes or allusions (he published *The Family Shakespeare* in 1818). His name is applied to any editorial "cleanup," whether of classics or other written material.

boycott

Charles Boycott resigned his captaincy in the British Army and obtained employment as an agent for absentee landowners in Ireland during the famine years of the mid-nineteenth century. He imposed army discipline on the impoverished Irish tenant farmers, refused to reduce rents, and, when the rents were not paid, dispossessed the tenants from their homes. The surrounding population reacted against him by refusing him services and food delivery and cutting off all contact with him. He had to call in British troops to protect him before he decamped for England. The word "boycott" was in instant currency in 1880.

cardigan

The seventh earl of Cardigan who led the charge of the Light Brigade at Balaklava, wore a sweater that buttoned down the front during his service in the Crimean War. The cardigan achieved a renewed burst of fame by being frequently worn by President Jimmy Carter at the White House.

raglan

Lord Raglan, who had lost an arm at Waterloo, was field marshal in the Crimean War and in that campaign he wore a coat without the usual shoulder seams—the sleeves continued up to the neck. Any garment made this way is said to have "raglan sleeves." (Considering the disaster suffered in the Crimea by the Light Brigade, both Raglan and Cardigan might well have paid less attention to their sartorial comfort and more to cavalry tactics.)

chauvinist   Nicolas Chauvin, a French veteran of Napoleon's campaigns, famous for his irrepressible patriotism. Originally the term had nothing to do with alleged male superiority.

chesterfield   A nineteenth-century earl of Chesterfield was responsible for the popularity of a long black overcoat with a velvet collar, dubbed a "chesterfield."

guillotine   The French physician Joseph-Ignace Guillotin (1738-1814), invented the guillotine in 1789 as a "painless" method of chopping off human heads.

hooligan   Hooligan was the name of a quarrelsome Irish family portrayed in an English play at the turn of the century. This play was seen by Czar Nicholas II during a visit to London. From his comments on the play on his return to Russia, the word "hooligan" entered the Russian language, where it is still used— as it is in English—to describe a destructive vandal or young ruffian (*huligán*).

lynch	Charles Lynch (1736-1796) was a wealthy Virginia planter and justice of the peace. In this office he achieved a sort of immortality for his outstanding record in condemning malefactors to be hanged.
macadam	The Scottish engineer John L. MacAdam (1756-1836) invented a road paving of nearly pulverized stones. Macadam that is bound with tar is called "tarmac."
martinet	General Jean Martinet, a French general who served Louis XIV in the seventeenth century, and who distinguished himself as an especially severe disciplinarian.
sadist	Donatien Alphonse François de Sade (1740-1814), commonly called the Marquis de Sade, wrote novels describing sexual satisfaction derived from inflicting pain or degradation on others. Some of his books were written during long spells in prison, where he had been incarcerated for trying out his theories.
masochism	Leopold von Sacher-Masoch (1835-1895), an Austrian novelist, specialized in writing about an abnormality wherein one takes pleasure in being abused, hurt, or dominated.
mesmerize	Dr. Franz Mesmer (1734-1815), a Viennese physician who practiced hypnotism on his patients, has given his name to a form of hypnosis.

sandwich   The fourth earl of Sandwich, who lived (and gambled extensively) during the reign of George III, used to have his servant bring him slices of meat between pieces of bread so that he could continue at the gambling table without leaving for lunch or dinner. This earl is doubly immortalized—Captain Cook named some newly discovered islands in the Pacific after him. These islands were first called the Sandwich Islands before they became Hawaii.

silhouette   Étienne de Silhouette, whose extremely short career as French controller-general (only 8 months in 1759) seemed to commentators to pass as a fleeting shadow—like a silhouette.

All the Chinese in the world (now calculated to be more than one billion people) share not many more than 100 family names among them. In Chinese literature the Chinese race is often referred to as the "hundred names," encompassing all Chinese. Even though persons of the same family name are not necessarily related, it used to be considered bad form or bad luck for two people with the same clan name to marry. However, if the written form of the clan name diverged—so that the meaning is different even though the pronunciation is identical—marriage was all right.

The written characters for most Chinese family names
denote an object or quality or action:

Chang	expand
Chen	ancient
Chou	thoughtful
Chu	red
Li	plum (or) profit
Lin	forest
Ma	horse
Mao	hair
Pei	white (or) treasure
Sun	grandson
Teng	climb
Wang	yellow (or) king
Wu	fifth clan; name of one of the "three kingdoms" (AD 220-265)
Yin	because
Yuan	beginning

When Chinese people learn one another's names they often
ask in which character the name is written, phrasing the
question "Is the character of your honorable name the Pei of
'treasure' or of 'white'?" or "Is the Wang written as 'yellow'
or as 'king'?"

A grim pun is recorded as responsible for the building of
the Great Wall of China. A soothsayer informed the
tyrannical emperor Ch'in-Shi-Huang-Ti, who was having the
wall built, that he would not be able to finish the structure
(which had already cost many lives) until ten thousand
more men had been buried in it. To solve the problem the
emperor found a man whose family name was Wan (the
character means "ten thousand"), had him buried in the
wall, and went on with its construction.

After the Spanish kings completed the reconquest of Spain
from the Moors by taking the last Moorish citadel, Granada,
in 1492, Moors and Jews in Spain were ordered to adopt

Spanish names. However, the Moors had occupied Spain for seven centuries, and many of the Spanish names forcibly adopted by the Moors were of Arabic origin anyway.

The Arabs who left Spain before and during the Inquisition went to Africa. The Jews went principally to the eastern Mediterranean, where their descendants still bear Spanish and Portuguese names and speak a form of Spanish (Ladino).

Many of the rulers of the principalities, dukedoms, and kingdoms of medieval Germany devised a system of taxing Jews by requiring that they adopt German names and pay for them—on a sliding scale. The most expensive names in this medieval shakedown were pleasant, beautiful, or poetic:

Rosenberg	"mountain of roses"
Himmelblau	"the blue of heaven"
Morgenstern	"star of the morning"
Blumenthal	"valley of flowers" or "blooming dale"
Silverberg	"mountain of silver"

Occupations were less expensive:

Meier	"farmer"
Schneider	"tailor"
Goldschmidt	"goldsmith"
Wechsler	"exchanger"
Fischer	"fisherman"
Kaufmann	"merchant"

Names of colors were also available:

Grün	"green"
Weiss	"white"
Schwarz	"black"
Braun	"brown"
Roth	"red"
Grünfeld	"green field"

Animal names included:

Löwe	"lion"
Wolf	"wolf"
Fuchs	"fox"
Haase	"hare"
Katze	"cat"
Vogel	"bird"

Still others were assigned names of cities, designating origins:

Berliner
Hamburger
Frankfurter

Many of these names were also shared by German gentiles— but not those names given to people who could pay very little or not at all, which carried an insult. They have since been dropped as family names but are recorded in the chronicles of some of the German cities, where we find names of the Middle Ages like Schwanz ("tail"), Eselkopf ("ass head"), and Schmutz ("dirt").

Many Jews who settle in Israel abandon their European names for Hebrew ones: Dayan, Ben-Gurion, Sapir, Avron.

Some Italian names indicate that the first bearer of the name started life by being left in a basket at the door of a convent or church and was adopted and brought up by the religious. The signal is a name that suggests a gift from the angels or blessing by the church:

NAME	TRANSLATION
Angeli	the angels
della Croce	of the cross
Benedetto	blessed
della Chiesa	of the Church
Diodonato	given by God
Santangeli	holy angels

A curious use was made of the name of the operatic composer Giuseppe Verdi during the civil disturbances in a partially Austrian-controlled Italy before, under the military leadership of Garibaldi and the diplomatic direction of Cavour, Italy became a united nation under Vittorio Emanuele II. Anti-Austrian riots were often started by the repeated shouting of the name Verdi at performances of his operas in Milan and other north Italian cities occupied by Austria. This shouting of Verdi seemed to the Austrians to be connected with Italian revolutionary activity. Their suspicions were justified: the name Verdi is also an acronym for *Vittorio Emanuele, Re d'Italia* ("Victor Emmanuel, King of Italy") as the Italians very well knew. The police interdicted the chant *Viva Verdi* until the Austrians were expelled from most of northern Italy in 1857; Victor Emmanuel was crowned King of Italy in 1861.

25. *The View from the Tribe*

Tribal and national groups naturally and understandably associate themselves with a name that extols their strength, superiority, importance, and uniqueness. *Türk* is the Turkish word for "strong"; the translation of *Zulu* is "heaven" or "sky"; the word "German" is traceable to *Herrmann*, "warrior," a description amply reinforced by history.

From one end of the world to the other, tribes have often labeled themselves simply "the people," as if other tribes did not even belong to the same human category. Even the German word for "German," *deutsch, stems from "people."*

A small hairy bear-worshipping remnant of the white race in northern Japan, the Ainu, call themselves in their own language "the human beings," thus distinguishing themselves, to their own satisfaction at least, from both bears and Japanese.

A number of the names by which Amerindian tribes are popularly known were originally nicknames—usually derogatory—given to them by other tribes. White explorers adopted the first name they were told and not the real one. (The white settlers also often "bought" land occupied by one tribe from a neighboring tribe that neither owned nor occupied the land and was therefore quite happy to sell it.)

Indian tribes tended to refer to other tribes by the general catch-all term "the enemy," differentiating between outsiders as "the enemy to the north," "the enemy from the east," and so on to the other points of the compass or specific locations.

The Eskimos are so called from the word applied to them by the Algonkians (*eskimo,* "he eats raw flesh"), who cooked their meat; but the Eskimos refer to themselves simply as Inuit, "the people." The name Mohawk, applied to the tribe by their neighbors, means "flesh eaters," but the Mohawks called themselves Ankwehonwe—"the real people."

The name of the Seminole tribe of Florida translates as "The People Who Wandered Off"; that of the Cherokee as "Different Language People"; the non-warlike Hopi as "People at Peace"; and the Creeks simply as the Creek word for "People." The Iroquois were so named by the French, who noted that spokesmen for the tribe customarily ended their speeches with the word "hiroqoué"—"I have spoken with emotion (joy or sorrow)," which sounded like Iroquois" to French ears.

Many of the Indian nations referred to themselves by their own word for "people," implying in a sense that other tribes were not on the same level of humanity. The Algonkians called themselves "The People"—Ashinabe—but were called Algonkian ("a place to spear fish") by their neighbors.

The Navaho tribe, the largest in the United States, referred to themselves as *Diné,* "The People," but got the name Navaho from other tribes who viewed the large land holdings of the Navaho with so much envy that their expression *tewa navaho*—"great planted fields"—was adopted by the white settlers to designate the Navahos.

Apache (*apachu*) means simply "The Enemy." Mohegan means "wolf" and Arapaho is derived from *araxpéahu,* "tattooed skin."

The word used by members of the Sioux tribe to describe their nation was *Dakotah,* "the allies." But they were called *Nadowessioux* ("little snake, the enemy") by surrounding tribes. When Europeans arrived in the Dakotah area, they adopted the last part of this name as the name of the Dakotah nation.

Many of the Amerindians' difficulties with the settlers were caused by language problems. For one thing, the Indians thought the white colonists spoke like snakes because of the frequency of the hissing s sound in English. Besides a fairly general term "palefaces" applied to the whites in Indian tongues, terms such as "pale-colored-and-scrawny" or "spirit-white-and-thin" were also used.

In the Republic of South Africa, a notable center of racial unrest, native African Blacks are officially referred to as Bantu. Although the Africans are manifestly at the bottom of the totem pole, the appellation Bantu is not inherently derogatory but has a proud origin, meaning "the men." When the white settlers first came to South Africa, they heard the parties of Blacks they encountered referring to themselves as *bantu*. The word is constructed from *mtu*, "man"; the plural form *ba* precedes the noun, exactly the opposite of the convention in European languages. Variants of the word *mtu* occur in other African languages such as Ki-Swahili (*mtu*), Zulu (*uminto*), Toro (*omuntu*), Umfunda (*omunta*), and Luganda (*muntu*). These and some 90 other African languages are all classified as Bantu tongues, which are spoken by about 70 million Africans.

"Bantu" is not derogatory, but the word "Kaffir" has certainly become so, although its use by whites as applied to Blacks is abating. As late as November 1981, the minister of mines of Zimbabwe (formerly Southern Rhodesia) announced that white residents who persisted in using the word "Kaffir" to describe their Black compatriots should leave the country immediately. The word "kaffir" came originally from the Arabic "qafir," meaning "unbeliever," which was long applied by the Arab traders and slavers along the east coast of Africa to Africans who had not yet accepted Islam. Although the Arabs used the word in a basically religious sense, the white settlers were apt to use it as a pejorative epithet, usually in the tone of voice with which former British colonialists pronounced "the natives."

The words "Slav" and "Slavic" are related to the word "slave"—in Roman and Byzantine times a large percentage of slaves came from southern Russia, or Scythia as it was then called.

The Viking raids are remembered in other parts of the world as well. Spanish-speaking mothers warn their children that if they do not behave, *el noruego*—"the Norwegian"—will carry them off.

The Russian word for Russia—*Rossiya*—is connected with the establishment of a Russian kingdom by Norsemen or Vikings from the north. The founders of this first Russian state were known as Rus, derived from the Viking word *rothsmen*—"rowers."

Spanish-speaking peoples still remember the Moorish pirates and raiders in popular speech. The Spanish warning for a suspected plot, spies, or impending trouble is the centuries-old expression, *Hay moros en la costa*—"There are Moors on the coast."

As the European tribes and their American descendants became nations, a tendency to identify tribes and nations with uncomplimentary real or fancied characteristics persisted. Some national nicknames disparage a group's taste in food. In American English, the French are "Frogs," the Germans are "Krauts," the English are "Limeys." The French for Italians is *"les macaronis,"* and the Germans use the horrifying *"Katzenfresser"*—"eaters of cats"—although anyone who has visited Italian cities would be inclined to modify this to "feeders" instead of "eaters" of felines.

Sometimes uncomplimentary names for other nationalities are based on facial, linguistic, or physical characteristics. American slang for Scandinavians is "squareheads," Latin Americans and Spaniards are referred to as "spiks," the Irish are often called "micks," derived from the name Michael and its common short form among the Irish, Mick.

The taller Chinese often refer to the less tall Japanese as "island dwarfs"; when the Japanese invaded China, they became "dwarf bandits." The Chinese often refer to Americans or Europeans as "big noses." The Chinese have a less than complimentary term for Russians: *lao-mao-tsu*, "old hairy ones."

Among French slang names for the Germans used in both
world wars we find *les schleus* and *les boches*. *Schleu* is
not a real word but a combination of consonants common in
German (*schl* occurs in hundreds of words) but unpleasing
to the French ear. *Boche* is thought to derive from *caboche*,
medieval slang for head and, as an alternate possibility,
from a dialectical pronunciation of *bois* (wood) as *boche*.
Thus *tête de boche* would mean "head of wood," even more
pejorative than the first suggested derivation.

The Turks refer to Russians as *Moskof* (Moscow), the
nucleus of the early Russian state, which for centuries
opposed the Tartar or Turkish hegemony over Russia. Each
of the two groups has a folk saying that keeps the ancient
antagonism alive.

> Russian: "An uninvited guest is worse than the Tartars."
> Tartar-Turkish: "When you deal with a Russian, keep an
>   ax handy."

Bad habits, wickedness, even diseases are often credited to a
nearby nationality. The English term "to take French
leave"—leaving suddenly without attending to one's
obligations—has a French counterpart: *filer à l'anglaise*, "to
rush off in the English manner."

Italians refer to the Greeks disparagingly as *i levantini*, "the
Levantines," implying that they are apt not to pay their bills
and to engage in all sorts of dubious commerce. They call
the French, fellow Latins, *nostri cugini antipatichi*—"our
disagreeable cousins."

The Greeks recall their long association with the Turks in
two popular expressions, both indicating trouble or disaster.
When trouble appears to be imminent, a Greek is likely to
say "The Turks are coming," *Erhunde i Turki!* When things
have attained the proportions of disaster, the same Greek is
apt to say "The Turks have arrived"—*Sthasen i Turki!*

There is no special pejorative word in Greek for "Turk"; the word *Turkós* itself being considered by the Greeks to be insult enough. As for the Turks, they refer to the Greeks simply as "unbelieving dogs."

Much misunderstanding and hatred between tribes, nations, and supernations has originated in the strangeness of one group to another, the foreignness of one culture to another, largely caused by the language barrier. Generally, speakers of a single language tend to regard the use of other languages as alien, confusing, and somehow unnatural. One is reminded of the elderly and rather insular American lady who objected in principle to the use of foreign languages in America (and, by extension, everywhere) who is reported to have said, "If God had not wished us all to speak English, He would not have written the Bible in English."

The disease of syphilis (thought to have been brought to Europe from the New World) was called the "French sickness" or "French pox" in England for generations. The Germans also called it the "French disease." For their part, the French called it the "English sickness," or sometimes the "Neapolitan sickness" or the "Spanish gout." Mainland Greeks called it the "Corinthian sickness."

The word "syphilis" has a curious derivation. It is the name of the leading character in a Latin poem of that name written by Girolamo Fracastoro, a poet and physician of Verona who lived in the sixteenth century and was reputedly the first victim of this veneral disease, probably imported from the New World.

In a number of languages, a speaker confronted with something too difficult to understand can blame another language for the confusion.

English	It's Greek to me.
Spanish	That's Chinese to me.
German	That seems like Spanish to me.
Russian	That's Chinese grammar.
Italian	You're speaking Turkish.
Polish	I'm hearing a Turkish sermon.
French	It's Hebrew to me.
	or
	That's lesser Negro.

26. *There Were Others Before Columbus*

A historian of American origins,
Charles Michael Bowen, once coined a
phrase for any historian's reluctance to
recognize that voyagers from Europe had
made the trip to America before Columbus.
The phrase was "No Europeans before
Columbus," NEBC for short.

The historical tradition that Columbus discovered America is certainly deep-rooted, and we may certainly accept it *if* we consider that "discover" means "unveil." It is undeniable that Columbus' voyage was the important one in that it gave form to the misty continent which many Europeans considered to be on the other side of the western ocean. But research and discovery, especially in the last century, has gradually revealed that Columbus was preceded by a variety of transoceanic travelers in historical times. These earlier discoverers have left their mark, and perhaps their names, in the traditions of the Amerindian tribes. Almost all the tribes and nations preserve traditions of white men who landed, taught the tribe, and then departed. In Mexico the white god Quetzalcoatl ("feathered serpent") came from the Atlantic. Among the Inca peoples of western South America it was Viracocha ("windy sea"), who came from and departed on the western ocean. Among the Maya, the godlike stranger was Kukulkan, and in other Mayan tribes the stranger was Gucumatz—names alternately suggesting possible Irish (the hero Cuchulain?) or Babylonian origins.

The Kensington rune stone.

Records incised on stones discovered in North and South America and written in the languages of Europe, Asia, and Africa seem to contradict, by their very existence, the neat arrangement of the dates and circumstances of Columbus' discovery. The Kensington rune stone, discovered in Minnesota in 1898, was inscribed with details of an attack by *skerlings* (Indians?) on a group of Vikings. This stone has long been derided by exponents of NEBC, since it was found by an American of Scandinavian descent, obviously suspect of being anti-NEBC and disposed to believe in Viking exploration of America.

Even the evident Viking remains at L'Anse-aux-Medeaux,
Labrador, and other stone ruins in Canada and New England
seem insufficient to establish public acceptance of
Scandinavian exploration of America. A cartographic
hoax—the "Vinland" map, purporting to be written proof of
Viking awareness of North America—was "shot down"
several years ago when it was ascertained that the ink used
on the map was of modern composition.

———————

Numerous inscriptions in Phoenician and Carthaginian
found along the banks of the Amazon and in the jungles of
Brazil, describing voyages from Tyre or Carthage, or
messages of thanks to the gods, have been classified as
pranks, although placing them in such remote areas, with
slight expectation that they would ever be found, would
have required a considerable number of expeditions by truly
dedicated pranksters—with, of course, the ability to write
ancient Phoenician.

———————

The Paraíba stone, a tablet inscribed in Phoenician found on
a ranch near Paraíba, Brazil in 1872, described an
expedition of ten ships from Sidon in Phoenicia that had
sailed from Ezion-Gerber (near Elath) around Africa. The
ships were at sea for two years, and of the whole expedition
only seven men and three women survived. One part read
rather plaintively: "We are from Sidon . . . commerce has
cast us on this distant shore, a land of mountains." The
message went on to invoke the help of the gods. The Paraíba
stone, long attacked as a forgery, had to wait for almost 100
years before being grudgingly reconsidered as possibly
genuine. One of the reasons it was previously considered
fraudulent was the spelling of certain Phoenician
constructions which were not verified from other sources
until after the middle of this century.

———————

In Mechanicsburg, Pennsylvania, over a thousand stones
marked with what appear to be Phoenician letters have been
discovered since 1948. The incised lettering would have
been made by either Phoenicians or Carthaginians, since
stone cannot be dated. It has been suggested that the stones
were cut and grooved and identified by numbers (letters

were used for numbers by the Phoenicians) with a view to reassemblage at a new site, much as European castles at a later time were shipped to America for reassembly.

An unusual pictorial indication of a visit to the coast of the United States by ancient Phoenicians, or perhaps by Minoans of the Cretan sea empire, was found in Lake Assawampset, Massachusetts, carved on the side of a boulder normally underwater but exposed during a drop in the water level during a prolonged drought. The rock carving represents a well-delineated ancient galley, possibly carved thousands of years ago, when the water table in the entire area was considerably lower.

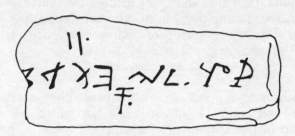

The Bat Creek stone.

One of the more striking examples of inscribed stones found in America was discovered in a burial mound in Bat Creek, Tennessee, in the late nineteenth century. An illustrated report was sent to the Smithsonian tentatively identifying the language as Cherokee, although no one was able to translate it. The inscription remained untranslated for more than half a century, until Joseph Mahen, a linguist and researcher from Columbus, Georgia, discovered that the picture of the inscription was published upside down and, if turned right side up, became Hebrew Canaanite script. When he verified the inscription with Cyrus Gordon, a leading specialist in languages of the ancient East, Gordon suggested that the inscription should be translated: "Year One of the Golden Age of the Jews." A possible explanation of the inscription would be that a number of Jewish survivors of Simon Bar Kochba's revolt against the Romans escaped to what is now the southeastern United States. This

theory has been borne out by the discovery in Tennessee
and Kentucky of caches of Roman coins of the right period
(circa AD 135), along with Hebrew inscriptions on the
coins.

The authenticity of some finds by amateur archaeologists
and treasure hunters in Indian burial mounds has been
challenged because of time anachronisms, differences
between the origin of found objects and the reputed history
of the ancient peoples. In Wisconsin a mound was opened
and a silver bracelet with an obscure inscription on it was
found. When cleaned, however, the inscription turned out
to read "Montreal." Writing resembling Chinese found on a
metal disk in an Illinois mound proved to be, as suspected,
Chinese—but it was an advertisement for a brand of tea.
Evidently modern Indians had continued to use these burial
mounds and followed tribal custom, burying personal
effects of the deceased with the body.

Besides stone inscriptions and traditional Indian legends of
pre-Columbian white visitors, a variety of Amerindian
languages offer rather convincing linguistic evidence that
individuals or groups from across the two oceans came to
America and left, almost as a proof of their visits, words
and expressions in the native languages which were still
being used at the time of Columbus' "official" discovery and
which still survive today.

As the Spaniards extended their conquests in the New
World, their priests examined and learned Indian languages
as an aid in their conversion of the Indians. They were
often surprised to find resemblances of sound and meanings
with Greek, Latin, Hebrew, even Basque words. (Later
researchers were to find even more unusual linguistic
resemblances embracing Babylonian, Sumerian, Phoenician,
Japanese, and Maori.) One explanation that seemed logical
to the Spanish priests was that these words were remnants
of the dispersion of the world's peoples at the time of the
Tower of Babel. Another theory was that the Amerindian
races were descendants of the ten lost tribes of Israel.

Greek words and expressions seem to occur especially in the languages of Central America. The Maya priests used an exorcism for protection against strangers: *konex oman panez.* They said the phrase meant "Stranger go away!" (It did not work on the Spaniards.) By an extraordinary coincidence this expression, in the form *konex om panex,* was used as an invocation in the celebration of the Greek religious mysteries.

The lofty Aztec pyramid temples were called *teocalli,* meaning "houses of the gods," in Náhuatl, the language of the Aztecs. By coincidence (if it were one) this sounded very similar to the Greek *theou kalia*—"[the] god's house," an instance of a phrase not only having the same sound but having the same meaning.

The Maya word for "cloak," *quetón,* sounds like the Greek *chiton* (the *ch* is pronounced gutturally), which means "tunic." The Aztec word for "cloud," *mixtli,* resembles the ancient Greek word *omichli,* "cloud."

Greek and Amerindian sound-alike words have been found far north and south of Mexico. The Delaware Indians called their river the *Potomac;* in Greek the word for "river" is *potamos;* and *poti* means "river" in the Guarani languages of Brazil and Paraguay. In Guaraní the word for "home" is *oko,* comparable to the Greek *oika,* also "home." One wonders how far Greek galleys traveled along the coasts of the Americas in the long centuries before Columbus.

Tepec, which means "hill" in Náhuatl, is almost the same as *tepe,* meaning "hill" in the old Turkic languages of southwest Asia.

The written Egyptian word for "crocodile," *s-b-k* (vowels are not written) essentially resembles the Aztec word *sipak* ("crocodile"), followed by the ending *tli,* a curious trans-

Atlantic name migration for an animal common to both widely separated regions. Even the Latin word for "butterfly," *papilio*, exists in Náhuatl, as *papalo-tl*.

To the surprise of some of the Spanish priests who spoke Basque, several Basque words turned up in Quechua, the language of the Inca Empire. For example, *garua* means "dew" in Basque and "drizzle" in Quechua, and the word for "father" is *aita* in Basque and *taita* in Quechua. *Tata* is also the word for "father" in several of the Indian languages of Mexico; a related form, *atey*, exists in Sioux.

The Quechua word for "high crest," *andi*, which is the origin for the name of the Andes mountains, is similar to the ancient Egyptian word for "high valley," also *andi*.

The ancient Sumerian word for "lie" (an untruth) was *lul*, fairly recognizable in Quechua as *llu-llu*.

The Quechua word for "milk," *ñu-ñu*, and the Japanese word for "cow milk," *n'yu-n'yu*, are the same sound. The word for "heron" in Quechua, *llake-llake*, was *lak-lak* in Babylonia; this similarity may simply represent simultaneous invention of a sound to express the flapping of wings.

Quechua was used in an area extending for thousands of miles along the west coast of South America and inland through the Andean plateau, where it is still spoken. Besides a variety of words from trans-Atlantic languages, it also contains numerous words from islands in the Pacific. The similarity of some Quechua words to words with the same meaning in Maori, the indigenous language of New Zealand, located several thousands of miles away, is notable.

ENGLISH	MAORI	QUECHUA
chieftain	kura	kuraca
sweet potato	kumara	kumara

```
skin ..................... kiri ..................... kara
between ............. pura ................... pura
love ..................... muna ................. munay
mutilated .......... mutu ................. mutu
```

What has not been established, however, is the direction of the migration of these words. Was it from Peru to New Zealand, or vice versa? Or did both languages come from a large island somewhere in between, since covered by the waters of the Pacific? A number of Pacific islands—Easter, the Carolines, the Marquesas, and the Marianas—show vestiges of a former advanced culture whose development is difficult to explain in terms of present size and population potential.

Words from the ancient East and Pharaonic Egypt can be recognized in the languages of widely separated regions of Indian America. The Araucanian Indians of Chile use the same word for "sun" as the ancient Egyptians—*anta*—and the same word for ax, *bal*, as the ancient Sumerians. The Araucanian word for "town," *kar*, resembles the Phoenician word for "city," *cart* (as in *Carthage*, or *Cart-hadash*—the "new city").

Malku, which means "king" in Aimará, a language of the Bolivian Indians, is *melekh* in Hebrew and *melek* in Arabic. The Hebrew word for "magician" is *bileam*; in Maya *balaam* means "priest."

The Maya word *thallac*, meaning "not solid," is curiously similar to *Thalath*, the Babylonian goddess of chaos. There is an additional linguistic and conceptual resemblance to the Greek word for "sea," *thalassa*, and the Aztec god of rain, *Tlaloc*.

The word for "water" in Náhuatl is *atl*, the same word for "water" used by the Berbers of North Africa.

Certain planetary-religious concepts seem to have crossed the oceans. Shapash was the sun god of the Phoenicians and appears among the Klamath Indians of Oregon as the word for "sun." The Hopi sun god is Taiowa, and the Japanese subject form of the word "sun" is *taiyo-wa*.

Sometimes the presence of European words in tribal languages is fairly easy to explain, although perhaps not to the satisfaction of believers of the NEBC theory. One outstanding discovery occurred at the end of the eighteenth century when a British military surveying party was operating in what is now Missouri in the unsettled Louisiana territory (then under Spanish control, under the terms of the 1793 Peace of Paris). The party reported that several of its Welsh-speaking members had found that they could speak with and understand members of the Mandan Indian tribe who appeared to speak a language in which about half the words were Welsh. The Indians were of light complexion and many had gray or blue eyes, and the women were, according to the British commander, "exceeding fair." The commander theorized that the Mandans were descendants of a historical expedition led by Prince Madoc of Wales, who sailed westward in 1170 to found a kingdom in lands across the sea and had not been heard of since. The similarity of words in Welsh and Mandan seems to support this theory.

ENGLISH	MANDAN	WELSH
bread	bara	barra
partridge	chuga	chugjar
boat	jurig	corwyg
paddle	ree	rhwyf (ree)
old	her	hen
great	ma	mawr
blue	glas	glas
head	pan	pen

When the incident became known and the British authorities evinced a lively interest in the reported "Welsh" Mandans, Spanish officials in New Orleans began to fear that Great Britain might claim the area as being already inhabited by people of Welsh racial blood. The Spanish authorities defrayed the cost of a second expedition by the officer who had reported the discovery so that he might reassess his findings, which he did. On his return he reported that his first conclusion about the "Welsh" Indians had been erroneous and then he resigned from the British army and accepted an extremely lucrative post with the Spanish customs and tax administration in New Orleans. The Mandan tribe was subsequently decimated by disease and the remnants merged with the Dakota Sioux to the north, where the survivors continued to use their Welsh words and to preserve certain Welsh traditions until the remnant disappeared.

The origin of the name Brazil is intriguing—and suggestive in itself of pre-Columbian visitors to the Americas. *Brzl*, with the proper vowels added, means "iron" in Hebrew, Phoenician, and Aramaic, and was applied in this sense to a land rich in iron lying in or across the Outer Sea. The name of this land came to be used in other European languages; in England and Ireland the name became *hy* (or "high") *Brazil*, *hy* probably a modification of "isle." Therefore when the coast of what is now Brazil was first discovered by the Portuguese, the name Brazil was already a familiar one and so the coast was named. A provoking question remains to be answered: did ancient Phoenicians or Carthaginians know about the iron deposits in Brazil, the most extensive in the world, and for that reason call the western land, thousands of years ago, by its present name?

---

27. *The Local Coloring of Proverbs*

National groups throughout the world have evolved proverbs in their own languages that embody folk wisdom. Many proverbs have counterpart proverbs in other languages that share the same basic premise but describe it in different terms. The following comparative sampling shows how the peoples of earth tend to think the same but express themselves differently, under the influence of their surroundings, culture, and habits (the English proverb is given first, then translations of the foreign versions):

English: When the cat's away the mice will play.

French: When the cat is absent the mice dance.

Italian: When the cat is out the mice are dancing.

German: When the cat is out of the house, the mice have a feast day.

Chinese: Cat gone, old rat comes out.

Portuguese: When the master goes out there is a holiday in the shop.

Greek: When the boss is not around we know a lot of songs.

English:	Too many cooks spoil the broth.
French:	Too many cooks ruin the sauce.
Spanish:	A ship directed by many pilots soon sinks.
Japanese:	With too many rowers the ship will crash into a mountain.
Russian:	When there are five nurses the child loses an eye. With seven nurses the child finally is found to lack a head.
Chinese:	Seven hands, eight feet.

English:	Don't count your chickens before they're hatched.
German:	You can't hang people before you've caught them.
French and Italian:	Don't sell the bearskin before you kill the bear.
Spanish:	Don't eat the sausages before you kill the pig.
Japanese:	Don't count the badger skins before you kill the badgers.
Russian:	You can't count chickens before autumn comes.
Swahili and other African languages:	Don't curse the crocodile before you have crossed the river.
Jamaican English:	Don't curse the crocodile's mother until you have crossed the river.

The Turks have a somewhat different proverb about a bear and a bridge. It goes, "If you meet a bear while crossing a bridge, address him as 'my uncle' until you have crossed to the other side."

| English: | Look before you leap. |
| French: | Turn the tongue seven times, then speak. |

Japanese:	Have an umbrella before getting wet.
Arabic:	Before you drink the soup, blow on it.
German:	First weigh (the consequences), then dare.
Russian:	If you don't know the ford, don't cross the stream.
Italian:	Be careful bending your head— you may break it.

English:	Everyone to his own taste.
French:	Each to his own taste.
Latin:	Concerning tastes there can be no disputing.
Japanese:	Ten men, ten colors.
Arabic:	Every person is free in his opinions.
Russian:	Every baron has his own special fantasy.

English:	Something is rotten in the state of Denmark.
German:	There is something rotten in the state of Denmark.
French:	There is an eel under the rock.
Spanish:	There is a cat shut up inside.
Japanese:	There is a worm in the lion's body.
Arabic:	There is a snake under the hay.
Portuguese:	There is a cat in there.
Russian:	There is a needle in the bag.
Chinese:	I don't know what kind of medicine is inside this melon.
Malay:	Just because the river is quiet, don't think the crocodiles have left.

English:	Little drops of water make the mighty ocean.
French:	Little by little the bird makes his nest.
Japanese:	Grains of dust pile up to make a hill.
German:	Dripping water hollows a stone.
Italian:	Drop by drop the sea is filled.
Russian:	Single threads from all over the world can make a whole shirt for a man.
Arabic:	A hair from here and a hair from there finally make a beard.
Chinese:	Fu Chien's army stopped the river's course when each soldier threw in his whip.

English:	A bird in the hand is worth two in the bush.
Spanish:	A bird in the hand is worth a hundred flying.
Italian:	Better an egg today than a chicken tomorrow.
French:	One "here-it-is" is worth two "you-will-have-its."
German:	A sparrow in the hand is better than a pigeon on the roof.
Russian:	Don't promise a pigeon in the sky but give a tomtit in the hand.

English:	You cannot make a silk purse out of a sow's ear.
Russian:	If you're born to crawl, you can't fly.
French:	There's no way to turn a buzzard into a hawk.
Spanish:	You can't find pears on an elm tree.
German:	From an ox you can only get beef.

Shakespeare has contributed a number of popular sayings to English, a much-used one being "Much ado about nothing." Portuguese expresses this same thought with "A great vineyard and few grapes." In Italian it is "Much smoke but a small roast"; in Spanish, "Much noise (of cracking), few nuts"; in German, "Much bleating, little wool." A French equivalent has a medieval origin. The Sieur des Barreaux ordered a bacon omelet on a church fast day and, just as he began to eat it, a violent thunderstorm began. The nobleman looked pensively at the sky and observed, "So much noise for an omelet!", an expression which has lasted to this day.

Each language has a store of proverbial expressions for specific situations. When two persons are discussing a third person who immediately appears, English and Portuguese speakers say "Speak of the Devil . . ." In French the phrase is "When you speak of the wolf, you see his tail." An Arabic speaker says, "Thinking of the cat, it came leaping."

Short rhymes in German and Spanish comment on this situation. The German jingle goes:

> *Wenn man den Esel nennt,*
> *Kommt er gerennt.*
> ("When you speak of the donkey, he comes running.")

The Spanish version is:

> *Hablando del rey de Roma*
> *Pronto se asoma.*
> ("Speaking of the King of Rome, suddenly he appears.")

Short sayings, adaptable to everyday occurrences or offering advice, are easy to remember when expressed in verse. One known to almost all English-speaking people is:
Early to bed and early to rise,
Makes a man healthy, wealthy, and wise.

This has an equivalent in German which ignores the need
for an early bedtime:
> Morgenstunde
> ist Gold im Munde
> ("The morning hour is gold in the mouth.")

French has a catchy rhyme for "He who hesitates is lost":
> Celui qui hésite
> Perd son gîte.
> ("He who hesitates loses his place.")

Italian offers rhymed advice about taking one's time while
hurrying:
> Chi va piano
> Va lontano—
> E va sano.
> ("He who travels slowly goes far and goes safely.")

A German couplet that emphasizes the importance of getting
things done now translates exactly into an English rhyme—
> Morgen, morgen nur nicht heute
> Sagen alle faule Leute.
> ("Tomorrow, tomorrow, but not today
> All the lazy people say.")

A rhyming couplet dating from the dark days of medieval
England typifies the sort of male-dominated thinking once
in vogue:

> A woman, a dog, and a walnut tree
> The more you beat them, the better they be.

This theory is echoed in an old German maxim, "When you
approach a horse or a woman, don't forget the whip," and
in the three Ks recommended as the sum of woman's
activities—Kirche, Küche, und Kinder ("church, kitchen,
and children").

The Romance languages emphasize that "woman's place is
in the home." In French the phrase is La femme au foyer; in
Italian, Il posto della donna è in casa.

The Romance languages are less violent than the languages of northern Europe about keeping women in an alleged place, but still speak clearly, as in the Portuguese and Spanish saying: "When the cock crows, the hen keeps silent."

The localized English expression "bringing coals to Newcastle" is meaningless in any literal translation. Both Germans and Greeks can interpret this idea in their own languages, however, by saying "taking owls to Athens" (where there is, or was, a plenitude of owls). Italians use a reference to antiquity—"taking jars to Samos" (an area famous in ancient times for the manufacturing of jars). In Russian the expression is, "He's going to Tula, taking his own samovar"—a pointless action, as all Russians know, since Tula is traditionally the place where the best samovars were made. The Germans have yet another—more debonair—variant, "He is going to Paris with his *own* wife."

---

28. *The Levels of Politeness*

While most languages use the equivalent of the word "please" or some form of the conditional ("would you," "could you") for requests, the Japanese may have established a record as the world's most polite language. *Dozo* is an omnipresent word for "please" but is not really enough for a request. To ask for something, *kudasai* is used: literally the word means to hand something down from a superior height to a lower level. But when you give something to somebody else, you use the word *agemasu*, implying that you, from your inferior level, are handing it up to the recipient, who is on a superior level.

The word *arigato*, Japanese for "thank you" (literally, "it hurts") indicates that you feel deeply the obligation that someone has put you under for the service rendered. And the equivalent for "you are welcome," *dōo itashi mashite, is* literally, "how is it possible? (to be thanked)."

Moshi-moshi ("pardon, pardon") is a way to get someone's attention and also a way to answer the telephone. The custom of saying *moshi-moshi* on the telephone often leads to parties at both ends of the phone saying "excuse me" at the same time.

When the first missionaries came to Japan and tried, as they frequently did, to understand the strange native language in terms of the European concept of grammar, they interpreted the Japanese verb ending -*masho*, used for the probable future, to mean the definite future, causing generations of linguistic misunderstandings. The Japanese concept of a probable future was perhaps more correct than the European idea, since no one can say that a certain action will definitely happen in the future. (Arabic and Spanish speakers also qualify any future action; in Arabic you say *inshallah*, "if Allah wills," and in Spanish you say *si Dios quiere*, "if it is the will of God.")

Japanese offers a choice of honorific words when speaking to others about parents, spouses, children, etc. One refers to one's own wife as *tsuma*, to another person's wife as okk'san, to one's own husband as *shujin*, and to another person's husband as *go-shujin* ("honorable husband"). One's own mother is *ha-ha* and one's father is *chi-chi*; other honorific terms are *oka-san*, for the other person's mother and father, and *oto-san*, for the other person's father. Completely different constructions are used for a son and a daughter, for the children of the other person, and for brothers and sisters, older and younger, of each speaker. The elder always gets more respect; even in calling a waitress one says *ne-san*, "honorable elder sister."

The suffix *san* or *sama*, appended to personal names, does not correspond exactly to "Mr.," "Mrs.," or "Miss," but to the general connotation of "honorable." If you are talking to Mr. Yamaguchi, you address him as *Yamaguchi-san*. To be properly humble, though, you must never use *-san* with your own name.

The Japanese are polite even on their subways, which are so crowded that they employ special packers to push people on and others to untangle them when they get into a station and get them off. The pushers-on are addressed as *oshiya-san* ("honorable pusher") and the pullers-off as *hagitoriya-san* ("honorable puller").

Another word meaning "honorable" is *o* placed before certain nouns, including *o-cha* ("honorable tea"), *o-tera* ("honorable temple"), *o-kane* ("honorable money"), *o-sake* ("honorable sake"), *o-tenki* ("honorable weather"), and *o-kami* ("honorable gods").

The levels of politeness in Japan are reinforced by the custom of bowing, the bow modified in depth by the rank and importance of the person you are greeting—but even the Emperor bows to return a reverence. Westerners tend to wonder whether the extreme conversational politeness of the Japanese and the custom of bowing might not justly be considered something of a waste of time. However, considering the ability of the Japanese to get along so well with each other under crowded conditions, this custom may have considerable advantages for export, along with the cars and computers of Japan.

Just as the Japanese are accustomed to constant bowing, a form of paralinguistics indicating respect, continental Europeans bow less but shake or kiss the hand of ladies more often—a custom shocking to Asians. In Europe and European-influenced countries, a habitual phrase of greeting can substitute for the actual kiss. In southern Germany, Austria, and other parts of central Europe, the expression *küss' die Hand* is a customary spoken greeting to a woman, whether or not her hand is actually kissed.

In France and other European countries, it is proper for a man to kiss the hand (lightly and with a bow) of a married woman to whom he is presented and on other formal occasions.

Spanish speakers incorporate the concept of hand-kissing in their letters, even in business correspondence. Sometimes at the end of a letter one finds the abbreviation S.S.S.Q.B.S.M., standing for *Su seguro servidor que besa su mano*—"Your sure servant who kisses your hand." This is often shortened and modified to Q.E.S.M., the E standing for *estrecha* ("presses"), instead of *besa* ("kisses").

An extremely polite way of acknowledging an introduction to a lady in Spanish is to bow and say *A los pies de Ud., señora*," meaning "I am at your feet, madam."

Chinese has simpler verbal constructions than Japanese, but the honorifics in traditional speech are both imaginative and picturesque—or were until Communist rule on the mainland discouraged honorifics. The traditional indicators of respect are still used by the many millions of Chinese living outside China. The Chinese equivalent for "Mr."—*hsien-sheng*—literally "born before," means "you are older than I am," showing the deference due to age; the real age of the speaker is not relevant. "Mrs." or "Madam" is *tai-tai*, meaning "very very" and implying "very beautiful," "very graceful," "very virtuous." The word for "Miss"—*hsiao-chieh*—means "little sister."

The son of the person you are speaking to can be referred to as *kung-tsu*, "the young prince," and a daughter is called *chien-chin* "one thousand pieces of gold." The speaker's own son is referred to casually as *hsiao-chuen* ("small puppy") and a daughter is *hsiao-nü'rh* ("small girl child").

Exaggerated honorifics are applied in referring to the parents of the person addressed; a father is *ling-tsun*, "the august prince," and a mother is *ling-tang*—"the august hall."

A wife referring to her own husband, however, calls him *chia-chün*, "prince of the house," or—less formally—lao yeh ("old grandfather") or even *lao-pang* ("old stick"), a reference to his power to discipline.

When a man refers to his own wife he uses the expression *nei-ren*, "the inside person," a title which tells much about the former status of Chinese women.

Most of these honorific words have been abolished in "classless" China, where the term "comrade" is applied to all citizens, male or female. The Chinese translation of "comrade," however, conveys a different impression than the Western version, with its connotations of the original Russian revolution. The Chinese word is *tung-chih*, literally "same thought" or "thinking alike"—an apt and understandable term for those who share the same socio-political theories.

Changes in titles and ways of speaking directly to a person have also occurred in the former European colonies of Asia and Africa. Natives in these former colonies are no longer addressed as "boy" or even "young fellow"—*djongos* in Malay Dutch. All readers of Somerset Maugham remember that white men were formerly addressed by Malays as *tuan* ("master"), which also means "you" when addressing a superior male person. With independence, a change was obviously called for, and former colonialists often found themselves obliged to use *tuan* for "you" when addressing their erstwhile charges. Indonesia, the largest Malay nation, adopted the democratic custom of expressing "you" as *saudara* ("brother") or *saudari* ("sister"), as well as conserving the words *tuan* ("Mr." or "master"), and *njonja* ("Mrs.") and *nona* ("Miss").

In India the use of *sahib* ("master"), formerly applied by the local inhabitants to British or Europeans (*memsahib* was used for women) has also lost its exclusivity.

The word *bwana*, familiar to generations of moviegoers from film versions of African life, is now applied as a title to Africans as well as to white people in most languages of sub-Saharan Africa, except in the Republic of South Africa. *Bwana*, a title of respect, implies "boss" or "master," although its real meaning is "father of sons." A white person calling an African "boy" is likely to cause the same sort of reaction in Africa as it would in the United States if used to Americans of African descent.

All European languages have familiar and formal ways of saying "you," ranging from two to seven forms to express the single modern English word "you." The proper use of these variant forms depends on a choice between familiarity and formality, between politeness and what might be considered to be impolite.

English used to have another word for "you"—"thou" and its forms "thy," "thee," and "thine." These forms have disappeared except in prayer or in the Bible and other books written in past centuries. It is used today only by certain religious sects, such as the Quakers. The English word "you" was originally used only to address more than one person; in other words, "you" (or "ye") was the plural form of "thou." Other European languages have not yet simplified the use of "you" to the extent that English has, and students of European languages are faced with a choice of which "you" to use when speaking a European language. The choice of the second person "you" is based on the Greco-Latin plan, shown below and giving the conjugation of the English verb "to be" in the present tense with the singular and plural divisions of the first, second, and third persons:

TO BE	SINGULAR	PLURAL
1st person	I am	we are
2nd person	you are .... (formerly "thou art")	you are
3rd person:	he, she, it is	they are

The English division of persons is the easiest among the European languages, because of the elimination of what was the familiar form, "thou," which was once the second person singular.

French has two forms for "you"—*tu* (singular) and *vous* (singular or plural). *Vous*, however, is not exclusively plural but is the word used for speaking to one person in a formal fashion. *Tu* is used for one person but only to address one person with whom you are on quite familiar terms; a good rule of thumb is to use *vous* when in doubt. Use *tu* when speaking to children, your wife or husband, intimate friends, and animals (should you have occasion to give commands to dogs, cats, or horses, for example). The use of *tu* does not necessarily mean that you like someone—it is simply informal. In some French families, the husband and wife still use *vous* to each other when others are present. *Tu* is generally used among students, younger coworkers, and soldiers to each other, although in other situations where respect is implied *vous* would be used.

The Scandinavian languages and Dutch, like French, have only two words for "you." German has three: the familiar singular *du*, the familiar plural *Ihr*, and the formal singular or plural *Sie*. When German-speaking friends decide that they are good enough friends to address each other as *du* instead of *Sie*, the custom—between males at least—is a toast of mutual esteem over a stein of beer, often drunk with elbows interlocked.

Russian has two forms for "you," the formal *Vih* and the familiar *tih*. In both the Russian and the German military, despite a long history of strict discipline and class differences between officers and enlisted men, officers are no longer allowed to use the familiar form, but must use the formal *Vih* when giving orders to enlisted men.

In Spanish there exist five ways of saying "you"—the familiar singular form *tú*; the familiar plurals *vosotros* (masculine) and *vosotras* (feminine); and the formal singular and plural *Usted* and *Ustedes* (usually written *Ud.* and *Uds.*). *Usted* comes from the archaic construction *vuestra* merced, "your grace," and most probably came into being as a formula for an inferior speaker to a superior, much as an enlisted man speaking to a captain, for example, might ask, "Does the captain wish . . ."—thereby avoiding the direct "you." English has similar forms for addressing people on superior levels—"your honor," "your eminence," "your highness," "your majesty."

Portuguese leads the other Latin languages with seven different words for the pronoun "you." There is the familiar form *tu*, a somewhat less familiar *vôce*, resembling the French *vous*, but unlike the French, having a plural form, *vôces*. Then, as in Spanish, there is the still more polite and formal "you"—*o senhor* ("the lord" or "the gentleman"), *a senhora* ("the lady"), both singular, with plural forms *os senhores* and *as senhoras*. (For a man and several women addressed as a group, the plural "you" is a masculine one.) Speakers of English may be thankful that they have only one form of "you" for daily use.

Italian has a choice of four words for "you." The familiar *tu* form for one person and the *voi* which, as with the French *vous*, can be used for one or more persons. The polite form is the singular *Lei* ("you" or "she"—"you" when capitalized) and the plural *Loro* (which also means "they" when written with a small letter). When Mussolini was in power in Italy, he attempted to simplify these choices by taking a linguistic step backward in time. He decreed that the polite forms should be dropped and that Italians should restrict themselves to the *tu* and *voi* forms. This language reform lasted, under protest, until the disappearance of Mussolini and his regime.

Some of the Latin languages have special terms of respect for age or special achievement, used before a person's first name. In Spanish these terms are *don* and *doña*, (*don Antonio, doña María*); in Italian, *don* and *donna*; and in Portuguese, *dom* and *donha*. These words come from the Latin *dominus* ("lord") and *domina* ("lady"). The modern equivalents can be used with the first name without repeating the person's last name, once you know the person, without implying overfamiliarity, even when used by younger to older persons. They are also used frequently in making introductions or in referring to another person in a conversation, but never, of course, applied to oneself.

Russian also offers a comfortable way of addressing people you have been introduced to. The person's first name (*imya*) is combined with a modified form of his or her father's first name (*ochestvo*). If a man's first name is Ivan and his father's first name is also Ivan, you would call him *Ivan Ivanovich*—"Ivan, son of Ivan." If he has a sister called Natasha, you would call her *Natasha Ivanovna*—"Natasha, daughter of Ivan." The *-ovich* and *-ovna* suffixes are always appended to the father's first name, not the mother's. Sometimes this custom produces a mouthful. Stalin's first name was Iosip; his father's first name was Vissarion. Stalin's close associates therefore called him Iosip Vissarionovich—for short.

Of all the modern languages, English is the only one to capitalize the first-person pronoun "I." Other languages capitalize the first letter of the word for "you": German (*Sie*), Italian (*Lei*), Spanish (*Ud.*), Dutch (*U*), Russian (*Vih*).

---

29. *Hello and Goodbye*

If an extraterrestrial were to monitor earth
sounds from space in order to establish the
frequency of communications sounds in
earth languages, the word that would show
up at the top of the list is "hello." What
boosts the count of this greeting is
telephone and radio communication
throughout the world; most telephone
conversations are held in English, and
English phone conversations begin with
"hello."

"Hello" has been variously traced to the French *hola* ("stop")
and to the Old High German word *holla*, a call for
summoning a dog or a horse. In the United States and
British Commonwealth countries where most phones are
located, "hello" is the accepted way of answering the
phone. French-speaking countries use *allô*; Germany,
Holland, and the Scandinavian countries use *hallo*; in many
Arabic-speaking countries the word is *aló*; and one of the
accepted Spanish words for phone answering is *hola*. Even
in the U.S.S.R. and the Eastern Bloc countries, the first word
on the phone is often *hallo*.

The first telephone operators, who worked in Connecticut in
1878, answered the telephone ring not with "hello" but
with a nautical "Ahoy."

Language groups other than English have a variety of ways
of answering the telephone. In addition to *hola*, Spanish
speakers have considerable choice: *A ver* ("Let's see"),
¿Quién habla? ("Who is speaking?"), *Oigo* ("I am
listening"), *¿Con quién?* ("with whom?"). *Dígame* ("Tell
me") is usually preferred in Spain. In Mexico, the
preference is for *¿Bueno?* used here in the sense of "Well?"

The German response to the ring of the phone—*hallo*—is
usually followed by *Wer spricht?* ("Who is speaking?").
Instead of saying *hallo*, the person answering may state his
or her last name. In Scandinavia, the person being called
will repeat his own telephone number before saying *hallo*.

In Italy one answers the phone with *Pronto* (meaning
"Ready," not "soon," as often mistakenly interpreted by
Spanish speakers and Americans), followed often by *Con chi
parlo?* ("With whom am I speaking?").

One answers the phone in Russia sometimes with *hallo* and
sometimes with *Slooshayu* ("I am listening").

Some nations preserve their own way of answering the phone because they wish to establish the national language firmly or reinforce the national way of thinking. During the Hitler epoch in Germany, it was advisable to answer the phone with a resounding *Heil Hitler!*

In several of the Swahili-speaking nations of Africa, one answers the phone with *Jambo,* a Swahili greeting which means "nothing the matter."

The central government in India is constantly trying to promote Hindi as the national language for all India, and encourages use of the Hindi word *Hanji* ("greetings") to begin a phone conversation, although "hello" is still in general use.

In the more conservative Arab countries, *na'am* ("yes") is preferred over the international "hello." In Iran and Afghanistan, the local word *baleh* ("yes") is preferred over the international "hello." Where "hello" or *allo* does not sound natural, other words are used. In Greece *embros* ("come in"), in Japan *moshi moshi* ("excuse, excuse") and China *wei* (also used to call animals to their feed) are used.

Most words for leave-taking fall into three categories— commendations to the care of God, an implied wish that the people talking will see each other again, or an exchange of wishes for peace, health, or happiness.

The English "goodbye" is a contraction of "God be with you." The French *adieu,* which has a connotation of finality, literally means "to God," as does the Italian *addio,* the Portuguese *adeus,* and the Spanish *adiós.* The Swedish *adjö* is an adaptation of the French *adieu.* The Greeks have adopted the Italian *addio,* converting it to *addio-sis.*

In Spanish, *adiós* is sometimes used as a greeting or in recognition, especially in a passing greeting without other speech—in effect saying "hello" by saying "goodbye" to people as they pass.

The English expression "so long" implies that it will be too long a time until the speakers see each other again. The idiomatic American greeting "long time no see" is a Chinese "pidgin" phrase that exactly translates the Chinese expression *ch'ang chih mei kan-chien.*

A common French way of saying "goodbye" is *au revoir,* which is also the exact translation of the German *auf Wiedersehen,* the Russian *doh svidania,* the Chinese *ts'ai chien,* the Spanish *hasta la vista,* the Afrikaans *tot siens.* Italian has two words for "see you again"—*arrivederLa,* "until I see you again," and *arrivederci,* "until we see each other again." The Italian word *ciao* can be used to say an informal "hello" or "goodbye."

The English "farewell" offers a wish for good fortune to the one who is leaving, and the word has almost the same sound as the equivalent in some north European languages: Dutch *vaarwell,* Norwegian and Danish *farvel.* A Swahili word also expresses a desire for good fortune: *kwaheri.*

The beautiful Japanese word for "goodbye," *sayonara,* implies a poignant realization of separation; it really means "if it must be so."

A Greek word for "goodbye"—*khaire!*—has come down from ancient times and expresses the agreeable order "be happy!"

The Hawaiian word for greeting and farewell is *aloha,* meaning simply "love."

In Turkish the word for "goodbye" depends on whether one is going or staying. *Allaha ismarladik* is said to the one leaving, putting him under the protection of God; the departing one answers *güle güle* ("laughingly, laughingly"), no doubt referring to the pleasure he has enjoyed during his visit.

———————

The Hebrew *shalom* ("peace") is used as a greeting and to say goodbye. *Shalom* has a linguistic cousin in the Arabic word for "peace," *salaam*, used in greetings: *es-salaam aleikum* ("may peace be with you"), to which the answer is *wa aleikum es salaam* ("and on you be peace"). Leaving a host, you say, *Allah ysalmak!* ("God keep you in peace") and the host responds, *Mae es-salaam!* ("Go in peace!")

———————

This ancient word for "peace" occurs in place names around the world, from the Salem in Massachusetts to Dar es-Salaam ("harbor of peace") in Tanzania.

———————

"Peace"—*selamat*—figures in almost all Malay and Indonesian greetings, day and night:

Good morning!	*Selamat pagi*	("peace in the morning")
Be welcome!	*Selamat datang*	("peace in arriving")
To your health!	*Selamat minum*	("peace in drinking")
Enjoy your food!	*Selamat makan*	("peace in eating")
Goodbye (to one going)	*Selamat djalan*	("peace in going")
Goodbye (to one staying)	*Selamat tingal*	("peace in staying")
Good night	*Selamat tidur*	("peace in sleeping")

———————

30. The World's Shortest Phrasebook in the Most Languages

Mark Twain once observed that he had been able to enjoy a walking tour through Germany using only four German words, *bitte, Bier, Kuss,* and *danke* ("please," "beer," "kiss," "thanks"), not always in that order. These four key words could be modified into a basic language guide for today's international travelers by dropping "beer" which is internationally understood in any case and by eliminating "kiss" which is likely to be misunderstood.

This leaves us with "please" and "thank you." Some sort of polite introductory word indicating peaceful intentions and a desire to be helped should be added. "Excuse me" does the job, and can also be used if you bump into someone, nick somebody's fender in a rented car or, in a tropical nation, step on someone's bare toes. "Where is . . ." is an important basic addition, remembering that many of the places, objects, and trademarked products that a traveler might wish to ask about have foreign names similar to the English one (for instance: "restaurant," "pharmacy," "airport," "taxi," "hotel," "hospital," "police"). When you use English words, say them slowly, separating the syllables clearly. (It is not necessary to shout, despite the proverbial advice of an English lady tourist: "The natives will understand English if you speak it loudly enough!")

Because of the worldwide interest in money which is, perhaps, more general than in the time of Mark Twain, the expression "how much?" as well as words of assent and negation—"yes" and "no"—should be added to the basic list. "Good," an alternate for "yes," is an important addition because with it you can express not only assent but also admiration, liking, or satisfaction. Pronounced in a questioning tone, it can also elicit a response of "yes" or "no."

"Hello" and "goodbye" are surveyed in Chapter 29. The more formal or elaborate ways of saying "hello"—"How do you do?" "good morning," and so on—are really forms of politeness which can be dispensed with in this functional eight-word list; a gesture of salutation, such as a slight bow, can take their place.

These eight words constitute an introduction to getting along in a foreign language. Even if the person you speak to knows some English, or produces someone who does, the fact that you have tried to communicate in the local language makes people more friendly.

Although thousands of languages and dialects are spoken today, most of the world's peoples speak or recognize basic words in 25 principal languages. The rock-bottom basic eight-word vocabulary in 25 languages is enough, especially if supplemented with gestures, to establish an initial communications breakthrough any place in the world. Words in languages customarily written in non-Roman Alphabets are given in the Roman alphabet in simple phonetic form. Some guides to pronunciation are included. In languages other than English, the vowels *a, e, i, o,* u are generally pronounced *ah, eh, ee, oh, oo.*

	EXCUSE ME	PLEASE	THANKS	WHERE IS...?	HOW MUCH IS...?	YES	NO	GOOD
FRENCH	Pardon*	S'il vous plaît	Merci	Où est...?	Combien...?	Oui	Non*	Bon*
	*final n pronounced nasally							
SPANISH	Perdón	Por favor	Gracias	¿Dónde está...?	¿Cuánto...?	Si	No	Bueno
GERMAN	Verzeihung*	Bitte	Danke	Wo ist...?*	Wieviel...?*	Ja	Nein	Gut
	*v pronounced f; w pronounced v							
PORTU-GUESE	Perdão*	Faça favor*	Obrigado (mas) Obrigada (fem)	Onde...?	Cuanto...?	Sim	Não*	Bom
	*ão pronounced like nasal on; ç pronounced ss							
ITALIAN	Scusi	Per piacere*	Grazie*	Dov'e...?	Quanto...?	Si	No	Buono
	*ce pronounced cheh; z pronounced ts							
SWEDISH	Forlat*	Var vanlig	Tack	Var...?	Hur mycket...?	Ja	Nej*	God
	*final t silent; final j pronounced y							

	EXCUSE ME	PLEASE	THANKS	WHERE IS...?	HOW MUCH IS...?	YES	NO	GOOD
DANISH	Undskyld	Var venlig*	Takk	Hvor...?	Hvor meget...?	Ja	Nej*	God
NORWE-GIAN	Unnskyld	Vennlist	Takk	Hvor...?	Hvor meget...?	Ja	Nei	God
DUTCH	Pardon	Alstublieft	Dank U wel	Waar...?*	Hoo veel...?*	Ja*	Neen	Goed
GREEK	Sígnome	Parakaló	Efharistó	Poo iné...?	Póso...?	Neh	Ohi	Kalá
HEBREW	Slihah	Bevakashah	Todah rabah	Efoh...?	Kamah...?	Ken	Lo	Tov
TURKISH	Muaf tutmak	Lütfen	Tesekkür	Nereye...?	Kač...?	Evet	Yok	Iyi
SERBO-CROAT	Oprostite	Molim	Hvala	Gdye...?	Koliko...?	Da	Ne	Dobro
SWAHILI	Niwfe radhi	Tafadhali	Asanti	Wapi...?	Kadiri gani...?	N dio	La	Nzuri
RUSSIAN	Izvanít'yeh	Pazhál'sta	Spasíba	Gd'yeh...?	Skólka...?	Da	N'yet	Harashó

*a pronounced ai as in "air"; j as i; final t silent

*j pronounced y; v pronounced f; w pronounced v

	EXCUSE ME	PLEASE	THANKS	WHERE IS...?	HOW MUCH IS...?	YES	NO	GOOD
POLISH	Przepraszam	Proszę* *ę is pronounced nasal en	Dziękuję	Gdzie...?	Ile...?	Tak	Nie	Dobrze
HUNGARIAN	Tessek	Herém	Köszönöm	Hol...?	Mennyi...?	Igen	Nem	Jól
RUMANIAN	Scuzaţi-mi* *ţ pronounced ts	vă rog	Mulţumesc	Unde...?	Cît...?	Da	Nu	Bine
ARABIC	muta asif	Min faadlak (masc.) Min faadlik (fem.)	Shukran	Wen...?	Adeysh...?	Naam	La	Mlih
KOREAN	Silye hammida	...jusipsyo	Komapsúmnida	Oti...?	Kapsi olma...?	Né	Aniyo	Tadanghi chosúmnida
THAI	Khoh thot (mas.) khrat kha (fem.)	Proht	Khop khun	Treh nai...?	Rahk khaa...? tao rai...?	Dja	Plaau	Sabai dii

	EXCUSE ME	PLEASE	THANKS	WHERE IS...?	HOW MUCH IS...?	YES	NO	GOOD
INDONE-SIAN & MALAY	Maaf	Silakan	Terima kasih	Dimana...?	Berapa...?	Ja*	Tidak	Bagus
		*j pronounced y						
HINDI/URDU	Muaf karna	Merher-bani seh	Danyavad Shukria	Kahan...?*	Kitneh paiseh...?	Han*	Nahin?*	Bahut
		*Final n pronounced nasally						
JAPANESE	Moshi moshi	Dozo	Arigato	...doko desu-ka?	Ikura?	Hai	Iyé	Yoi
CHINESE	Shieh^4 kuang^1	Ching^3	Doh^1 shieh^4	...ts'ai^4 na^2 li^3?	Doh^1 shao^3?	Shih^4	Boo^2 shih^4	Hao^3
	TONES: 1 is short, flat; 2 like a question; 3 like drawn-out question; 4 like a command							
VIETNAM-ESE	Xin loi ong	Xin ong	Cam on ong	O dau?	Bao nhieu?	Vang	Khong	Tot lam
	Note: The version below is how Vietnamese is written in the Latin alphabet with tone and pronunciation marks.							
	Xin lỗi ồng	Xin ồng	Cảm ởn ồng	Ở đâu?	Bao nhiêu?	Vâng	Không	Tốt lắm

Numbers, although of the greatest importance, have been left out of this basic phrasebook, inasmuch as written numbers figure on the currency of almost all countries and, if written clearly on any piece of paper at hand, will be understood in any bargaining you are doing.

A tourist can be more polite than these eight words allow by using the local words for "Sir," "Madam," or "Miss." Many speakers of English have already learned these words through foreign travel, but anyone who does not know them can acquire them locally. It is an interesting comment on American customs that "Miss" is often used to address a woman in the North, but "Ma'am," short for "Madam," is favored in the South. In French-speaking countries, a woman is generally addressed as *Madame*, whether the speaker presumes she is married or unmarried. The implication is that it is more flattering to a Frenchwoman to suggest that she is married, while more flattering to an American woman to suggest a single state—and youth.

A number of non-English informal colloquial greetings can be used in the United States, Canada, and the United Kingdom, where foreign-language groups abound. These non-English words are not a basic necessity, but are friendly gestures that give the impression that you have cared enough to learn something about the language of the person you are speaking to. Key words tend to open the door to an immediately friendly atmosphere, even if the conversation is continued in English. The French *ça va bien?* ("Does it go well?") can be answered affirmatively by repeating the same words, or by saying *pas mal* ("not bad"), or even by saying *comme ci comme ça* ("like this, like that"—so-so). The Spanish *¿Cómo le va?* ("How is it going for you?") is often answered with *Así así* ("So-so"). The Italian *Come sta?* ("How are you?") can elicit *Bene, grazie* ("Well, thank you") or the noncommittal *Così così* ("so-so"). The Portuguese say *Come vai?* ("How are you going?"); the answer is *Bem, obrigado* ("Well, thanks"), or *Bem, obrigada* if a woman is speaking.

When someone inquires about your health, be sure to use the words for "good" and "thank you" in the word list above.

Russian is laconic—*Kak Vih?* ("How you?")—and the reply is *Harashó, spasíba* ("Good, thanks").

In German the phrase is *Wie gehts?* ("How goes it?"). A good answer is *Es geht gut* ("It goes well"). In Dutch, *Hoe gaat it?* is an exact equivalent of "How goes it?" One answer is *zo zo* ("so-so"), which is pronounced practically the same as in English. The single Dutch word *Dag* ("day") can mean "hello" and "goodbye."

Chinese offers several colloquial greetings. One is *Hao boo hao?* ("Good, not good?"); one answer is *Hao, ni hao?* ("Good, you good?"). Another is eminently practical—*Ni chih le ma?* ("Have you already eaten?").

A short greeting in Japanese inquiring about health is *Genki desu-ne?* ("Health exists, not so?")

The modern Hebrew speaker asks "What's new?"—*Ma hadash?*—to which a useful answer is *En shum hadash* ("Nothing special").

In Greek, *Ti kánete* means "what are you doing?" which can be answered *Endáxi* ("O.K.") or *Étsi kétsi* ("Not bad"). The informal *Yásoo* can mean "hello" or "goodbye."

When you ask an Arab how he is—*Kif halak?* (to a woman: *Kif halik?*)—he will mention Allah in his reply: *Mabsut, ilhamdulillah* ("Fine, thanks be to Allah"). The word *salaam* ("peace") can be used for "hello" and "goodbye," just as the similar word *shalom* is used in Hebrew.

A point to remember: Unlike Europeans, who constantly shake hands, Moslems do not generally engage in that custom.

The general greeting in Swahili is *Hujambo*; the informal "How goes it?" is *Vi pi?*

For a greeting in Malay, use *Apa kabar?* ("What news?"). An optimistic answer is *Kabar baik* ("News good").

In Hindi, "What's new?" is *Kya khabar hai?* Hindus also greet each other by repeating the name of the god Rama twice.

Among the many different concepts buried in greetings in various languages, perhaps one of the most unusual is expressed in the Mohawk greeting *Skennen kōwa ken?*— "Does the great peace exist?" (a question still without an affirmative answer).

In different sections of the world certain formulas follow compliments or words of admiration. In Spanish-speaking countries a host will often say to a guest *Está en su casa* ("You are in your house"); the formula for reply is *Ud. es muy amable* ("You are very kind"). If you admire his car, he will say *Es suyo* ("It is yours"), and you should respond again *Ud. es muy amable*. But avoid expressing too much admiration for any small or portable article; the host will almost always reply *Es suyo* and may try to force it on you.

In Arabic-speaking countries and among Moslems, it is well to remember to say *Ma sha'Allah* ("May Allah protect") when admiring a child, a picture of someone in the family, a good friend, a new house, a car, a horse, or anything loved or valuable. A compliment without that phrase is believed to bring disaster or the "evil eye" on the esteemed object.

The polite insistence that an acquaintance go first through a
door, expressed in the English "After you" or the French
Après vous, can also be expressed in the form for the word
"Please" given in the eight-word list. If you lose the contest
and are forced to go first, then you can use the equivalent
for "Thank you" in an appropriate language.

A word sure to please while having a convivial drink with a
person is to be able to say "To your health" or "Here's
how" in his or her native language. The following choice of
toast words will prove useful at home and abroad.

German: *Prosit!* .... (from the Latin for
"May it be
advantageous!")

Dutch: *Proost!* .... (from the same Latin
phrase)

Russian: *Za vasheh!* ...... (To yours)

French: *A votre santé!* ... (To your health!)

Italian: *Salute!* .... (Health!)

Portuguese: *Saúde!* .... (Health!)

Gaelic: *Slainte!* .... (Cheers!) (pronounced
slawn-cheh)

Greek: *Is ihien!* .... (To health!)

Hebrew: *Leh hayim!* ...... (To life!)

Indonesian: *Selamat
minum!* .... (Peace while drinking!)

Hindi: *Aapki sehat!* .... (To your health!)

Spanish: *¡Salud!* .... (Health!) *Pesetas*
(Spanish currency) is
often added to *salud*,
and *amor* (love)
frequently follows that.
A good reply to this
toast is "And many
years to enjoy them!"—
*¡Y muchos años para
disfrutarlos!*

Chinese, Japanese, and   ("Dry cup") (the phrase

Korean: *Kan pei!* .... is similar in all three languages; after drinking, people sometimes place the inverted glass over the head to demonstrate that it is really dry.

Arabic: *Fi sahad tak!* ..... (To your health!) However, it is well to remember that the use of alcohol is forbidden by Moslem religious law and also by civil law in some Moslem countries.

Norwegian, Swedish, Danish: *Skål!* .... This Scandinavian drinking toast (pronounced "*skoal*") has a rather macabre background; it originally meant "skull." The word has come down from a custom practiced by the warlike Vikings who used the dried-out skulls of their enemies as drinking mugs, with the evident advantage that the mug held a large quantity of mead and could be easily replaced.

31. *Odd Origins and Changing Meanings*

To be a "cynic" originally meant, in ancient Greek, to be dog-like (*kunikos*) in the sense of being suspicious and critical of people. Members of the Athenian sect of Cynics were believers in stern and virtuous self-control.

"Sardonic" (mocking, scornful) derives from the island of Sardinia. In ancient times an herb peculiar to this island was reputed to cause death by laughing, hence the hollow "sardonic" laughter and the twisted "sardonic" smile.

"Candidate" is derived from the white color (*candidus*— "white," "pure") that Roman candidates for election (*candidati*) wore when running for public office. Another political term, "alderman," comes from the Anglo-Saxon *elderman*, an ancient high priest.

"Botulism" comes from the Latin word for "sausage" (*botulus*). Some of the earliest cases of poisoning through imperfectly canned food were thought to have been caused by sausages.

"Perfume" originally referred to the smoke from fragrant wood burned in temples in ancient times to cover up the smell of blood and burned flesh from sacrifices (Latin: *per fumun*).

"Pornography" is a combination of the Greek words *pórnos* ("prostitute") and *gráphein* ("to write," "writing")— therefore, "writing for or by prostitutes."

The English word "muscle" is descended from *musculus*, the Latin word for "little mouse," a rather apt description of the moving and changing form under the skin, especially of the arms and legs.

"Agony" is from the Greek word *agonía*, referring to the pain incurred in an athletic contest (*agon*).

"Calculus," "to calculate," "calculation" all come from the "pebble" or "counter" (*calculus*) used for counting in the Roman abacus.

"Salary" is based on the word for "salt," *sal*, and stems from the word *salarium*, the salt ration of the Roman legionnaire.

"Money" gets its name from the goddess Moneta, the deity of the Roman temple which also served as the imperial mint.

"Echo" was the name of a legendary nymph who fell in love with Narcissus who, for his part, became enamored with his own reflection which he saw in the waters of a forest pool. When he attempted to make contact with the handsome youth he saw, he fell into the pool and drowned. Echo then pined away until only her voice was left.

The word "dollar" comes from the large silver coins minted in Joachimsthal, a part of the former Austrian Empire. These coins were referred to as *Joachimsthaler*, a name eventually simplified in English to "dollars." The town now belongs to Czechoslovakia and has changed its name to Jachymov. It no longer produces silver dollars—but uranium!

The word "mob" comes from the Latin word *mobile*, referring not to a crowd, which is *vulgus* in Latin, but to its mobile and changeable nature, as in the Latin expression *mobile vulgus*—"the changing crowd."

Vulgus also gives us the word "vulgar," originally descriptive of those not belonging to the nobility. Those of the nobility were generally described by the related words "gentleman," "gentlewoman," "gentility," "gentle," and others, from the French *gentil* for "well-born" or "noble."

The following common words of Norman or Anglo-Saxon origin have changed their meanings since the Middle Ages.

CURRENT WORD	EARLIER MEANING
naughty	poor—of no value
dip	to baptize (dippan)
bid	to pray (biddan)
knave	young fellow, servant
dainty	doughty
lewd	uncultured
crafty	wise, knowledgeable
nice	foolish, silly, wanton
silly	blessed, innocent
crude	bloody
hunch	push, shove
hussy	housewife
harlot	drifter, worthless young fellow
farce	a stuffing for roast poultry; later, an insertion between acts in a play
rascal	member of the rabble; also a rash on the face caused by smallpox or syphilis

———————

Boudoir derives from the French *bouder* ("to pout") indicating, with French *délicatesse,* a special private room in which a woman can be alone when she feels like sulking or pouting.

———————

"Tawdry" (showy, gaudy) is a survival of the seventh century from the name of St. Audrey, once queen of Northumbria and later abbess and patron saint of the Isle of Ely. She was inordinately fond of necklaces and, before repentance, was afflicted with a throat tumor as punishment for her pride and excessive use of elaborate collars and necklaces. Lace neckpieces called "St. Audrey's chains" were later sold at fairs, and the name for the neckpieces was eventually encapsulated to "tawdry."

———————

Other word relics of the Middle Ages are of more indirect origin. The British word "loo" for "bathroom" comes from the French word for water, *l'eau*, used in the warning "Watch out for the water!" (*Garde à l'eau!* or *Gardez l'eau!*) which was used when waste water was tipped into the narrow medieval streets from the high overhead, and often overhanging, windows.

Canter, the slow gallop of a horse, derives from the town of Canterbury, where it was applied to the rather sedate gallop affected by pilgrims en route to the cathedral at Canterbury.

Cinderella's famous glass slipper was really made of fur, as was customary in medieval times for the ladies of the châteaux. This confusion occurred because *vair* ("fur") has the same sound as *verre* ("glass"). The peasants who told and retold the Cinderella story, not having fur slippers themselves, formed the quaint notion that Cinderella's slippers were made of twinkling glass.

Some terms have come down through the centuries from the customs of ancient warfare. "Berserk," meaning "violently crazy," comes from the term applied to the furious warriors among the Norsemen—the *Berserkers*, who kept slaying until their enemies were literally cut apart. But the word really means *behr sekr* ("bear skin"), in other words, a rough fur coat which the warriors habitually wore.

Greek has been the source of many words of war and memorials to former battles. The English word "polemic" comes from *pólemos* ("war"), and "strategy" comes from *strategós*, the Greek word for "general."

A marathon race commemorates the exact distance—26 miles 385 yards—which was run by a Greek messenger from Marathon back to Athens to announce the Greek victory over the Persians. The runner died at the moment he announced the victory, an understandable result of his having fought all day during the battle—after running, over the preceding two days, from Athens to Sparta, and then to Marathon.

The defense of the Pass of Thermopylae is a worldwide example of Greek heroism, but the name of the villain of the battle, he who showed the Persians how to outflank the Greek defenders of the pass, has become a common noun in the Greek language. His name, Ephiáltis, is the regular Greek word for "nightmare."

The Napoleonic invasion of Russia in 1812 left a French expression which changed into a Russian word meaning "useless fellow," "lout," "nogoodnik." The expression arose from occasions when, after the French invaders had captured a village, they would urge villagers to sing and dance for their entertainment. Any recalcitrant Russian who would not participate in these amuse-the-troops events was pushed aside by the French, who would observe that he was useless and lazy and explain: Il ne chantera pas ("He won't sing"), a French observation that entered the Russian language as chanterapá, an insult.

The English word "nitwit" comes from a scornful English imitation of a frequent Dutch answer to a question asked in English—Ik niet wiet ("I don't know").

When Russia began to develop its own railroad system in the nineteenth century, Russian railroad engineers were especially impressed by the railway depot at Vauxhall in London. The place name was so frequently repeated by the Russians that it joined the Russian language as the word for "railway station"—voksal.

The glass transom above a door is called a vassistas in French through a linguistic misunderstanding. Nineteenth-century German invaders and tourists often pointed to the new contraption and asked Was ist das? ("What is that?").

Many French persons thought that was what the Germans called a transom, and the expression caught on as a regular French word.

"Cravat," a somewhat elegant word for "necktie," is derived from pieces of cloth which Croatian cavalrymen habitually tied around their necks. In the Serbo-Croatian language the word for Croat is *Hrvatski*—which, as the custom of tying pieces of cloth around the neck spread, entered most European languages as a word similar to *cravat*.

The familiar French word for a small bar-restaurant— *bistro*—comes from the Russian invasion of Paris after the fall of Napoleon I. As the Cossacks trotted their horses along the boulevards, they were frequently approached by enterprising shills for Parisian restaurants who enticed the Russians into small restaurants where they could eat quickly, leaving their horses outside. The French promoters, in order to convince their Russian clients, had learned the Russian word for "quick"—*beestra*—and used it, accompanied by a pantomime of eating. The Cossacks thought the French were using the name for a small fast-service restaurant, which the word eventually became.

The color "magenta" is named for a battle. A new shade of reddish-purple dye, developed from coal tar in 1859, was named after the Battle of Magenta, fought in that same year and won by French-Italian forces against the Austrians. The battle was especially noted for the quantity of blood spilled on the field.

The word "testimony" comes from ancient Rome and is connected with the age-old custom of swearing to the truth or falsity of events or promises. Although people have sworn by their beards, hearts, lives, fortunes, or family, the real meaning of "testimony" refers to an oath sworn on the testes (testicles)—obviously a serious oath.

Chess, played since remote antiquity, originated in Iran and spread throughout the world. The Russian word for chess—*shakmati*—is closest to its original name. The Iranian term is *shah mat* (meaning, appropriately, "the Shah is dead"); The Anglicized version of this term is "checkmate."

The expression *hocus-pocus* for magical incantations is thought to have been copied in the Middle Ages from the announcement *Hoc est corpus* ("This is the Body") during the Mass.

Mumbo jumbo derives from the Mandingo language of West Africa, in which it means a magician who could make evil spirits, as well as the spirits of one's ancestors, depart.

Malaria was long thought to be associated with the "bad air" (Italian *mala aria*) coming from marshy areas instead of from the mosquitoes who bred in the marshes.

"May Day" has become the international aircraft distress signal. It most probably comes from the French *Venez m'aider!* ("Come help me!") shortened and Anglicized for speedier use.

"High muck-a-muck" does not mean "big chief" but is a more or less phonetic rendition of the Chinook Indian expression for "plenty of food." Apparently the first white visitors mistook the name of the feast for the title of the host.

"Potluck," meaning that one is invited without ceremony to eat whatever is at hand, has just the opposite meaning among Indians on the extreme northwest coast of the United States and Canada, among whom *potlach* means not only a feast but a succession of valuable gifts to the guests by the Indian host—who trusts the guests will reciprocate at some future time.

There is a linguistic relationship between the Italian city of Taranto, the poisonous tarantula spider, and the lively Italian dance, the tarantella. In the Middle Ages a mysterious disease struck the city of Taranto; one of the effects caused the sufferers to jump and gyrate as if dancing. The source of the disease was reputed to be the bite of a local spider, thereafter named, after the town, the tarantula. The tarantella dance is also named for the town, as the steps were inspired by the gyrations of the original frenzied dancers.

"Ghetto" was originally spelled without an *h* and pronounced *jetto*. It comes from *il nuovo getto* ("the new foundry"), the name of the Jewish quarter of Venice and center of trading. The *h* was added to "ghetto" as the name spread to Jewish sections in the towns of northern Europe.

"Royalties," or rights paid to authors of books, plays, movies, and so on, comes from an action of the fun-loving Charles II of England. King Charles settled a perpetual royal grant of income on his illegitimate son, the Duke of Richmond—who, although not an author, was the first recipient of a "royalty."

The three sons of Noah—Shem, Japhet, and Ham—have given their names to language families of the Middle East, Africa, and Europe. Until well into the last two centuries, scholars tended to classify all main languages as either Semitic, Japhetic, or Hamitic. That classification began to change when it became evident that a number of important languages did not fit within the pattern suggested by the Bible. What used to be called the Japhetic languages are now called the Indo-European family. The terms Semitic and Hamitic are still in use, often combined as one family. This family includes the "dead" languages Akkadian, Aramaic, Phoenician, Carthaginian, Libyan, and Ancient Egyptian and some important living languages—Arabic, Hebrew, Berber, Amharic, and Somali.

The term Japhetic has been downgraded from a term covering numerous European and Asian languages to that of a small number of mysterious tongues: Ancient Sumerian, Georgian, Circassian, and Basque, a dialect of which has been found in the Caucasus Mountains. The connection between Japhet, the son of Noah, and these languages remains—the languages come from a very distant past, and originated in the general area where the biblical Ark is said to have come to rest.

Chinese laborers were called *ku-li* (coolie) in the former days of Western domination. The word *ku-li*, Chinese for "bitter effort," is an apt description of the coolie's view of life.

"Croissant"—this tasty pastry owes its name to the battle that saved Vienna from Turkish invaders. At the time the Viennese repulsed the invaders and occupied the Turkish camp, a Viennese baker invented and popularized the croissant (crescent) in imitation of the half-moons, the emblem of Islam that topped the standards and tentpoles of the Turks.

"Pagan" and "peasant" are descended from the same Latin word, *paganus*—"a dweller in the country." Another word for "country-dweller" which has become pejorative is the word "villain," a derivative of *villa*, "country house," in Latin. "Villain" originally referred to the peasants or servants in the area.

"Varlet" and "valet" are both derived from the French chivalric term used to designate a young man-at-arms not yet tried in knightly combat, who meantime served an established knight as an aide and a sort of understudy.

32. Palindromes, Nonstop Words, Tongue Twisters, and Historic Language Puns

A "palindrome," from the Greek words meaning "to run again," is a word or sentence that reads the same backward and forward, as in:
A MAN, A PLAN, A CANAL—PANAMA!
Except for the punctuation, this palindrome reads exactly the same from right to left as from left to right.

A historical palindrome from the nineteenth century is the regretful lament which the British of the period thought applicable to Napoleon:

ABLE WAS I ERE I SAW ELBA.

A humorist has selected as an entry for a very-short-palindrome contest the possible first words spoken by Adam to Eve in the Garden of Eden:

MADAM, I'M ADAM.

An unusual palindrome in German fulfills the rule of the palindrome, even though its meaning is somewhat arcane. It goes:

EIN NEGER MIT GAZELLE ZAGT IM REGEN NIE.
("A Negro with a gazelle never despairs in the rain.")

Ancient Rome enjoyed a romantic palindrome:

ROMA TIBI SUBITO MOTIBUS IBIT AMOR.
("In Rome love will come to you suddenly.")

What is generally regarded as the longest word in English (some compounded chemical and medical words are longer) is "antidisestablishmentarianism," referring to the position of being against the separation of the Church of England from the Church of Ireland.

In German, the tendency is to join a series of qualifying components together, thereby constructing words of often surprising length. But even a rather long word like *Einkommensteurveranlagungskommission* is not really more difficult to understand than would be the same combination in English if it were written together as one word: income-tax-assessment-commission.

But some words seem rather complicated to say in one breath, even to the Germans, for example, the title of a captain of the Danube Steamship Trip Company: *Donaudampfschiffsfahrtsgesellschaftskapitän.*

一 = one   人 = man   中 = China   麗鳥 = oriole

Although Chinese does not have overlong words, some of the written character-syllables, which also combine with other characters to make different words, are made up of an inordinate number of separate lines or strokes, all of which must be executed in a prescribed fashion. Some are easy. The word for "one" is written with one line, and the word for "man" with two, and the word for "China" with four lines. Many syllables, however, are made up of a dozen or more separate strokes. The single syllable needed to write the character for *li* ("oriole," the bird) takes 30 strokes, a feat of writing which would certainly pose a time problem for note-taking bird watchers.

There is a town in Wales, a stop on the railway, whose name on the station sign runs approximately the length of the railway station. The name is Llanfairpwllgwyngyllgoge-rychwyrndrobwyllllandysiliogogogoch. It means "The Church-of-St. Mary-in-the Hollow-of-the-White-Hazel-Tree-near-the-Rapid-Whirlpool-by-the-Church-of-St. Dysilio-by-the-Red-Cave."

Tongue twisters in various languages tend to emphasize letter combinations peculiar to the language which are difficult even for native speakers to say quickly—as in the English tongue twister: "She sells seashells by the seashore."

A French tongue twister featuring the *s* sound focuses on food: *Combien de sous sont ces saucissons-ci? Ces saucissons-ci sont six sous.* ("How much are these sausages here? These sausages here are six cents.")

A Spanish tongue twister emphasizes the importance of rolling the r (pronounced ehr-reh) and appropriately has to do with rolling stock on the railway:

> R con r—cigarro
> r con r—carril
> que rápido corren los carros,
> cargados de azúcar, del ferrocaril.

The verse translates:
> R with r—cigar
> r with r—railroad car
> how rapidly the cars run
> loaded with sugar, of the railroad.

A German tongue twister that offers a lot of practice in the pronunciation of sch portrays a rather dangerous situation: *Zwei schwartze schleimige Schlangen sitzen zwischen zwei spitzigen Steinen und zischen.* ("Two black slimy snakes sit between two pointed stones and hiss.")

The word "quiz" was invented in Dublin in 1791 for the express purpose of winning a bet. A theater manager named Daly, over a series of friendly cups with acquaintances, made a wager that he could add a new, invented word to the language in one night. The next morning a mysterious graffito was seen on streets, sidewalks, walls, and buildings. It was the simple word quiz, which nobody had seen before or knew. Daly won his bet and "quiz," meaning a questioning procedure, eventually joined the language.

Sir Charles Napier, a British officer in India, was given command of an expedition to annex the kingdom of Sind in the middle of the nineteenth century during the British conquest of India bit by bit. Although he strongly questioned the morality of the acquisition, he proceeded to invade and conquer the territory with his customary efficiency. To announce the success of his mission, he dispatched to the headquarters of the British East India Company a one-word message, the Latin word *peccavi*, which means "I have *sinned*." This was only part of the pun: the word *peccavi*, in the Latin version of the Bible, was the key word said by King David as he acknowledged his sins to the prophet Nathan—a biblical reference underlining Lord Napier's ethical opposition to the conquest of Sind.

Frederick the Great of Prussia was an appreciative admirer of French culture and an ardent admirer of attractive women. As a tribute to French culture, he erected a charming palace near Berlin called Sans Souci ("without care"). On one occasion he invited a pretty and lively noblewoman to a royal tête-à-tête by sending her the following cryptic missive written in his own hand:

$$\frac{p}{venez} \quad à \quad \frac{si}{100}$$

The lady correctly interpreted this unusual note as reading *Venez souper à Sans Souci* ("Come to supper at Sans Souci") by reading the combinations from the bottom up and the intervening lines as *sous* ("under"). (The letter *p* in French is pronounced *pay*, and the number 100 is pronounced *sahn*.) The lady replied with two letters only:

$$G \qquad a$$

which the king correctly interpreted as "G grand: a petit," which, when voiced, sounds exactly like *J'ai grand appétit* ("I have a big appetite"), a riposte certainly worthy of royal favor.

After a long and arduous campaign ending in 1926, French colonial troops finally defeated the Moroccan Riff leader, Abd-el-Krim, who had been attempting, with initial success, to free Morocco from French and Spanish domination. For security reasons his place of exile was Reunion Island, an isolated spot in the southern Indian Ocean. Abd-el-Krim's reaction, upon learning of his place of exile, was simply: *Réunion? Mais avec qui?* ("Reunion? But with whom?")

During the persecution of Christians under the Roman Empire, secret Christians developed the sign of a fish, at first recognizable only to other members of the sect, which

could be drawn quickly in sand or earth and then be
stamped out or could even be rapidly sketched in the air.
The choice of the fish comes from a religious pun—the first
letters of each of the Greek words in the formula "Jesus,
Son of God, Savior" make the Greek word for "fish," ἰχθύς
(ikhthus). Another possible reason for choosing a fish as the
sign is that St. Peter's original occupation was fisherman.

A Latin pun applied to some members of the Germanic
Angle tribe (as in "Anglo-Saxon") has survived for 1300
years. St. Gregory the Great, who was pope 590–604, asked
the tribal identity of some newly captured slaves from the
north, including children with blue eyes and blond hair
who were on exhibit in the Roman slave market. When told
they were Angles, he is traditionally quoted as observing:
Non Angli sed angeli ("Not Angles but angels"),a tribute
often repeated in medieval paintings, where angels are
usually portrayed with blond hair.

The aristocrats who fled the French revolution and the
guillotine (1789–1792) generally found asylum in the
countries surrounding France. From these places of refuge
they planned their return with plots for military assistance
from other powers and a stream of propaganda which
nowadays would be termed political or psychological
warfare. One of the most complicated of the pieces of their
counterrevolutionary propaganda concerned the state of
France under the revolutionary regime as indicated below:

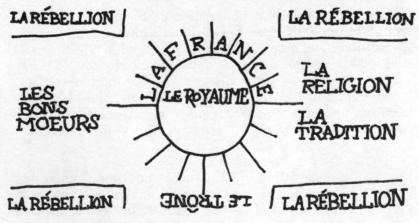

The central circle signifies the sun. Reading from top to bottom, the top indicates: *la France divisée* ("France divided"); *la religion, les traditions, les bons moeurs—à coté* ("religion, traditions, and good customs shoved aside"); *le trône renversé* ("the throne upside down," overthrown); *la rébellion dans tous les coins* ("rebellion in every corner"); *et le royaume dans le plus grand des astres* ("and the kingdom in the greatest of the stars"). This last bit is the final pun, because *les plus grand des astres* sounds exactly like *le plus grand désastre* ("the greatest disaster")—which, according to the royalists, was the state of France without the king. Although cleverly done, this broadside and others like it were largely ignored by the French—the monarchy did not return until the united forces of other European countries made it possible for the émigrés to return to France after the fall of Napoleon.

----

33. The Language of Revolution

An early result of social revolution is the abolition or changing of titles, those of the nobility and sometimes the various polite forms for "Mr.," "Mrs.," and "Miss" customarily employed by the bourgeoisie and throughout society. In the French revolution of 1789, all titles of nobility were abolished and the honorifics Monsieur, Madame, and Mademoiselle were changed to "citizen"—*citoyen* for a man, *citoyenne* for a woman. But this innovation did not long outlast the original revolution. By Napoleon's time, titles of politeness had come back into use and new titles of nobility were distributed to those that Napoleon considered deserving. Then, when Napoleon was defeated, the holders of the old titles of nobility returned. Subsequently, under more kings and one additional emperor, there were more titled persons in France than ever before.

The word "bourgeois," originally meaning simply a person who lived and worked in a town, has gradually acquired a pejorative meaning even among the bourgeoisie themselves. To the social critic, "bourgeois" now implies smugness, lack of taste or imagination, and preoccupation with money. The revolutionary Russians adapted "bourgeois" as *burjúy* and used it as a synonym for capitalist.

The word "capitalist" was popularized in Russia via Karl Marx's *Das Kapital*, written in German in 1847 while Marx was in England. The Russian revolutionaries considered the bourgeoisie a segment of society to be liquidated. In the years of civil war following the Bolshevik takeover of power in November 1917, any individual bourgeois still surviving was often referred to as a *n'yedoryezánniy burjúy* ("a bourgeois whose throat has not *yet* been cut").

Lenin has been credited with a number of observations about capitalists and their relation to the communist world revolution. One trenchant observation was, "The capitalist is eager to sell a rope for himself to be hanged with" (*Kapitalíst gotóv prodát' verióvku na kotóriy yevó poviésiat'*), a proverbial saying frequently alternatively expressed as "When we are about to hang the last capitalist another will suddenly appear offering to sell us a rope."

Another short saying attributed to Lenin is the expressive question *kto-kovó?* ("who to whom?")—which group will vanquish, bury, or supplant its opposing economic system—implying, in short, the improbability of coexistence.

There was even a catchy song, popular through the revolutionary years, indicative of plans for the bourgeoisie, with a chorus that goes:

> Eat pineapples and chew on quails,
> For your last day has arrived, *burjúy!*

It is notable that both pineapples, quails and other gourmet food disappeared from Russia almost as quickly as the *burjúy*.

Red was not originally chosen to be a communist color but was simply a favorite Russian color, probably because of the lack of color in the land and sky of Russia during the long winters. Moscow's Red Square (*Krásnaya Plósh'chad*), named long before communism, means in Russian "beautiful square"; "red" doubles for "beautiful" in Russian. In czarist times, most homes had a special corner of the house where an honored guest was invited to sit, the "red corner" (*krásniy úgol*), with the most comfortable chair or sofa, an icon on the wall, and a hanging lamp in front of the icon. A "red girl" (*krásnaya d'yévochka*) means a very pretty girl, not necessarily a political one. In emphasizing red as the color of the revolution the original revolutionaries chose a color dear to the Russian heart.

The evocative red color for communism is also a good choice in China, where red (*hung*) has proverbially been the color of joy, celebration, and marriage. The color white, which became an epithet for anti-reds in Russia, in China is associated with death and mourning.

Russian censorship and control of civilians by the secret police is traditional in Russia and was as prevalent in czarist times as it is in the U.S.S.R. Deviation from imperial norms of loyal conduct in former times usually found the perpetrators ending up in the "north land," which is the approximate translation of "Siberia."

An unsuspected pun occasioned by the publication of a book bearing the name of an ancient Babylonian king incurred the wrath of the Russian imperial government and the secret police in the troubled years prior to World War I, when the dynasty was struggling to suppress all revolutionary activity and propaganda. It was soon noticed that if you pronounced the innocent title of the book—*Nebuchadnezzar*—you were also saying in Russian "No God and no Czar!" (*N'ye Bog a n'ye Tsar!*). The book was banned, and even requesting by name an oversize magnum of champagne (internationally called a Nebuchadnezzar) came to be tactfully avoided.

After the revolution the dreaded czarist secret police, the *Okhrana*, was succeeded by the equally dreaded NKVD, which subsequently went by a variety of other names. With typically wry Russian humor concerning the fate of persons who disappeared after the NKVD summoned or came to call on them, it soon came to be said that the initials NKVD really stood for *N'ye znáiu kagdá vernúsya domói* ("I don't know when I'll return home").

In the imperial Russian army, enlisted men were obliged to address officers up to the rank of captain as *Váshe Blagaród'ye* ("Your Nobility") and subsequent ranks up to general as *Váshe Visóko Blagaród'ye* ("Your High Nobility"). General officers were addressed as *Prevoshodít'yeltsvo* ("Supreme Excellency"). After the revolution, military officers were simply addressed as *továrish'ch* ("comrade"), followed by their rank, as they are today.

Civilian titles were completely changed, although the former polite terms for "Mr." and "Mrs."—*Gospodín* and *Gospozhá*, which really mean "lord" and "lady"—are still used for foreigners from nonsocialist countries. *Továrish'ch* is used among party members, officials, administrative officers, and in the military; other Russians are officially addressed as *Grazhdanín* ("citizen") or *Grazhdánka* ("citizeness").

Certain "communist" words existed long before communism. *Soviet* is the word for "advice" or "counsel." *Továrish'ch* derives from an old word for "business" (*tovar*), with the connotation of "associate," "partner," "colleague," or "comrade." *Bolshevik* comes from the comparative of *bolshoi* ("big")— bolshevik refers to persons belonging to the "bigger" division of the revolutionary groups that took over power in the October Revolution of 1917 (which really happened in November, according to the present calendar).

Many of the political words of communism have been
adopted directly from German and French; the words
"communist" and "communism" are from Karl Marx's
Communist Manifesto. The Russian word for "revolution"
as a class revolution—*revolútsia*—attained popularity in the
French Revolution of 1792 and subsequent periodic
revolutions, especially the Commune of 1871, an event
much admired by the Russians who, in their own
revolutions against Czarism and capitalism, have always
enthusiastically sung the "Marseillaise." The "Marseillaise,"
translated into a variety of languages, has to this day
maintained a prime position as a revolutionary song
throughout the world.

A few years after the Bolsheviks came to power in Russia,
one of the measures discussed for the program of breaking
with the imperial past and the influence of the Orthodox
church was that Russian be written not in the Cyrillic but in
the Roman alphabet. Although this conversion eventually
proved too difficult to accomplish with the Russian
language, it was attempted for the numerous minor language
groups (well over 100) in Siberia, central Asia, and the
Caucasus. Then, in the early thirties, the policy was
reversed and all the grammars and dictionaries reverted to
the Cyrillic alphabet, with three notable exceptions, Latvian,
Estonian, and Lithuanian, which are permitted to use the
Roman alphabet.

A breach of diplomatic etiquette, tossed off purposely by
Trotsky as a private joke, took place during the confused
period of the Bolshevik takeover of power at Petrograd (now
Leningrad) during and after the renowned "ten days that
shook the world." The new Bolshevik government, in its
sweeping changes of offices and personnel, issued a series
of names for the different bureaus, mostly cut down to
initials for easier reference. In the course of these changes
Trotsky was constantly besieged by foreign reporters trying
to find out the names and initials of the new departments,
especially the ministry of foreign affairs. To repeated
questions about the designation of this important ministry,
Trotsky finally replied that it was called KMIT, without
specifying what the initials stood for. The name of this

ministry and its pronouncements were soberly quoted in the world press. Only gradually, when no further explanation of its name was given, did reporters' suspicions arise that something was amiss. It later was leaked that Trotsky had simply given the first letters of a four-word Yiddish expression, evidently not only as a joke but to express his feelings and those of the regime toward capitalist nations and their capitalist newspapers. For the complete expression was *küss mir im tuchis*, the English equivalent being "kiss my ass."

The most important newspapers in Russia and other parts of the U.S.S.R. are *Pravda* (the name means "truth") and *Izvestia* ("news"). The regular Russian word for "that's true" is *éto právda!* Some critics of these newspapers, either opponents of the current regime or perhaps newspaper readers who would prefer a more realistic and less propagandistic outlook on world news, have kept alive a long-standing quip: "There's no news in the *Truth* and no truth in the *News*"—*V'Právde n'yet izvéstiy a v'Izvestiákh n'yet právdi.*

Although the verb "to have" is an important concept in Western languages, there is no exact colloquial equivalent in Russian. The concept of "having" something in Russian is expressed by "to me," "to you," etc. The sentence "I have an automobile" is, in Russian, "To me is an automobile."

Russian has no specific term for "business" in the commercial sense; the word "affair" (*d'yelo*) is used. The Russian equivalent of the English word "business" is restricted to black-market operations (*bíznes*).

The word *mir* means "peace," "village," "the world" or "universe" according to how it is used in context. An interesting theory suggests itself: does the lack of a verb for permanent possession or an exact word for "business" contribute psychologically to the Russian acceptance of communism, with its prejudice against private property? Does the lack of differentiation between the words for "village," "world," and "peace" foster an innate propensity for worldwide expansion until the Russian version of world peace is attained?

In many world languages the word "communist" is an adaptation of the original German word *Kommunist*. Russian keeps the original spelling; a number of other languages show only minor variations:

Polish	*Komunista*
Czech	*Komunista*
Hungarian	*Komunista*
Greek	*Kommunistis*
Swedish	*Kommunist*
Swahili	*Komunisti*
Hebrew	*Komunist*
Malay	*Kominis*
Italian	*Comunista*
Spanish	*Comunista*
Portuguese	*Comunista*
French	*Communiste*
Turkish	*Komünizt*
Zulu	*Ikhomanist*

In some of the oriental languages, care has been taken to avoid the Russian or perhaps European aura of the word "communist" and to substitute native words in a short descriptive phrase, such as the Japanese *kyo-san-shu-gi-sha* ("common-property-ideology person") and the Urdu *ishtrak* ("sharer among the people"). The Arabic word for communist means "supporter of the common use" but, sex being especially important in Arabic, it must be made clear whether the supporter is male (*shuyuaei*) or female (*shuyuaeiet*).

The most populous communist country, China, carefully avoids any approximation of the European name for "communism" and uses a Chinese one which emphasizes an idea attractive to the majority of the population every time they see it written: *kung ch'an chu i*, meaning simply "share property ideology." The Communist Party is the

kung ch'an tang—"share property association"—a name that
people without property would find not objectionable. The
"capitalist class" is called tze pen chia—"money-origin
house." The term "bourgeoisie," unlike the Russian
adaptation of the same term, has been translated into
Chinese as shao tse pen chia—"small-money-origin house."

The Chinese word for "revolution," ko-ming, meaning "cut
off life," presents a more direct description of a revolution
than the English word and reminds one of Mao Tse-tung's
observation that "a revolution is not like inviting people to
a dinner party." Mao has left a wealth of revolutionary
advice and suggestions. One is especially illustrative of the
Communist technique of alternately attacking and parleying,
the process being repeated until the objective is achieved.
He says it in four words: Ta! Ta! T'an! T'an! ("Fight! Fight!
Talk! Talk!").

Although the Communist revolution in China was to a large
extent directed against the age-old customs and culture of
traditional China, its military success was largely based on
the advice of a Chinese military strategist who lived more
than 500 years before Christ, General Sun Wu, who
condensed a formula for successful guerrilla warfare against
more numerous forces into 16 words. He called these
concepts the "Eight Strategies," and they have been taken as
a model by Chinese, Cuban, and Vietnamese guerrilla forces
in their strategy of wearing down initially larger pacification
forces directed against them. Here are the "Eight Strategies"
in the original words of General Sun Wu:

Di jin: wu tiu	("Enemy advance; I retreat")
Di jirh: wu shün	("Enemy stop; I probe")
Di chuan: wu gung	("Enemy tired; I attack")
Di yin: wu sui	("Enemy retreat; I follow")

The proverbial Russian version of the process of attack and
parley, attributed to Lenin himself, is equally expressive:
"One step backward, two steps forward" (*Shag nazád, dva
shagá v'peryód*).

For almost two hundred years the sounds of Chinese have
been written in letters of the Occidental languages according
to how missionaries (among the first Westerners to learn
Chinese) and other linguists heard them and wrote them
down in Roman letters. The systems that were adopted
scarcely mattered to the Chinese, who went on speaking and
writing their language as they had for so many centuries,
unperturbed by any scheme the "ocean ghosts" might
devise for spelling Chinese words.

The most widely used system of transliterating Chinese into
English, used in almost all English books and newspapers
for over a century, has been the Wade-Giles system. This
system, which helps to keep Chinese mysterious, uses an
apostrophe after certain letters (*p'*, *t'*, *k'*, *ch'*, *d'*, and *tz'*) to
show that they should be pronounced as in English; but no
apostrophe signifies that the letter should be pronounced
differently, that is, as *b*, *d*, *g*, zh, *t*, and *dz*. A number of
other constructions in the Wade-Giles system require prior
instruction: *hs* is pronounced *sh*; *j* is an attempt at a
Chinese *r*.

Since the establishment of the People's Republic of China a
new system of writing Chinese in the Roman alphabet,
pinyin ("transcription"), has come into use. Its official
adoption in 1978 for press reports to foreign countries has
caused flurries of activity in private and governmental
Chinese studies, necessitating a change of spelling on maps
and in books and newspaper reports on China, and cross-
referencing or double filing in records and catalogs. Visitors
to China and readers of newspapers are now becoming
accustomed to the new spelling of names of historical
figures and places: Beijing for Peking, Nanjing for Nanking,
Chongqing for Chunking, Guangzhou for Canton. The name
of Teng Hsiao-ping is now spelled Deng Xiaoping; former

generalissimo Chiang has become Xiang; and the name of
the famous female leader of the Gang of Four, Chiang
Ch'ing, was changed in the Western press to Jiang Qing
during her incarceration.

The English spelling of familiar words in basic Chinese has
changed considerably. "Thank you," formerly *hsieh, hsieh*,
is now *xie, xie*. "Please," once *ch'ing*, has changed to *qing*.
This revolutionary spelling reform is generally more logical
than previous systems and, from a linguistic point of view,
has the advantage that the Chinese invented it themselves.

In schools specializing in Communist propaganda and
psychological and guerrilla tactics, in socialist and Third
World countries, a variety of languages are taught as
important for political and tactical operations against the
democratic bloc of nations of the First World. The number
one language in the curriculum of these schools is not the
language of any large socialist country, such as Russia or
China, or even that of a small one such as Cuba. On the
contrary, the main language taught to revolutionists
throughout the world is English. The reasons are obvious:
English can be used to reach the great majority of all the
world's peoples, in Asia and Africa as well as Europe,
including the British Isles and the Americas. It can also be
employed for worldwide communication and cooperation
between operatives, cadres, groups, and political parties of
different nationalities. So finally, after the historic
revolutionary importance of French, German, Russian, and
Chinese, English has now come to be considered the
language of international revolution.

---

34. Military Codes and Linguistic Deceptions

In the increasingly important science of military cryptology (the establishment and translation of codes), the language in which the code is set is especially important, because combinations of letters vary in different languages. In Japan up to and during World War II, the letters—or numbers referring to them—in the changing ciphers did not stand for letters at all, but for kana syllables. These syllables are quite difficult to understand even after the code is broken because the meaning of each syllable depends on how it is put together with other syllables to form different words.

Prior to World War II, American cryptoanalysts broke the supersecret Japanese "purple" code by constructing their own version of the Japanese encoding machine after a series of experiments based on years-long listening to radio code broadcasts. This U.S. machine could read the radio code emitted by the "purple" encoder. Because of this American breakthrough, prior to Pearl Harbor the cryptographic section of the War Department was able to decode messages to and from Japanese diplomats—enough to judge that negotiations were at breaking point, although the actual attack on Pearl Harbor was launched in complete secrecy and prior radio blackout.

The "purple" code was a supposedly unbreakable Japanese code based on the original German Enigma machine, approximately the size of two typewriters and containing a large number of electronic circuits.

As the war progressed American codebreakers, with practice and improvements in the U.S. copy of the Japanese machine, were finally able to read the secret signals faster than the Japanese for whom they were intended. It is possible that Japanese headquarters was convinced that its complicated purple code was unbreakable by foreigners—not only because of the difficulty of the Japanese language but also because the code used indirect references and a code within a code. The fact that U.S. cryptologists could read these code messages, however, contributed largely to later U.S. successes in the Pacific, particularly in the Battle of Midway. Admiral Nimitz knew as much about Japanese fleet disposition, plans, and strength as did the Japanese themselves, and was able to marshall his forces and strike hard at the proper time, which he did—sinking the four largest carriers of the Imperial Fleet at Midway, an event which marked the beginning of the end of Japanese sea power.

An unusual opportunity was presented to the U.S. Fleet HQ in the Pacific when a Japanese message was intercepted detailing plans for an inspection of the Solomon Islands installations by the fleet commander-in-chief, Admiral

Yamamoto. The message gave the exact date, time, and flight plan. But the Americans had a problem: if the Admiral were attacked and shot down, the Japanese might suspect that the Americans had broken the "purple" code, and change it. However, since Admiral Yamamoto was such a key figure and so important to Japanese morale, a command decision was taken to attack the admiral's flight in force and shoot down the admiral and his escort planes. The operation was successful, but no publicity whatever was given to the exploit. For a while, the Japanese were not sure of exactly what had happened to Admiral Yamamoto. The "purple" code was not changed.

Something of the same sort of agonizing command decision occurred in the air blitz of 1940. The German code, based on the Enigma machine, which was in use in various units and headquarters, had been broken by the British in 1940 by cryptoanalysts—greatly aided by the fact that the British had obtained control of several of these machines, one in North Africa, one from a German submarine, one on the Lofoten Islands off Norway (which had been captured from Germany), and one from a German defector who was really Polish. As a result, the British had established a special isolated facility called Ultra, from which they could easily monitor German code signals, a lucky development that greatly contributed to the salvation of Great Britain. However, when Ultra learned that the Luftwaffe was about to bomb Coventry, the British had to decide whether to supply massive air protection for Coventry, letting the Germans know that their secret plans were being intercepted, or not to supply the protection and continue to be able to read important battle plans. Coventry was heavily bombed but the Ultra secret was preserved.

United States forces in Guam used Navaho Indians to relay field commands in Navaho over the radio communications system to confuse Japanese listeners into thinking the language was a new code and to tie up their cryptographic sections in an effort to crack it.

Before its use in Guam, Navaho had been used occasionally in frontline command post communication in World War I, until ensuing events suggested that someone in the German lines, possibly a university professor called back to active duty, could understand the language. During the invasion of Europe in World War II, Indian radio "talkers" were used once again, this time from the Mohawk tribe, in a unit of General Patton's Third Army. But this time, apparently, there were no Germans around who could speak Mohawk.

Sometimes a cipher can be correctly translated but misread at the same time. When arrangements were being made for Churchill and Roosevelt to meet at Casablanca in 1943, a Spanish source tipped off the Germans by sending them a code message that the meeting would take place in Casablanca. But the German code clerk who deciphered the message decided that the word should be read *Casa Blanca*—the "White House"—the normal place for such a meeting to be held.

Napoleon, for all his military genius, may have lost his last two battles—Leipzig and Waterloo—through difficulty with military ciphers—but the trouble was not that the enemy had captured them. He had evidently ordered them changed after the retreat from Moscow when it was thought that the codes and code clerks had been captured by the pursuing Russians. The new codes he established and used at Leipzig and Waterloo were so obscure that his own generals could not fully understand them, with catastrophic results for the French.

After World War I a number of German war orphans were sent to Norway to avoid starvation in postwar Germany. These same orphans, who grew up as Norwegian citizens and spoke perfect Norwegian, proved to be of considerable help in the German Fifth Column and the German invasion of Norway in World War II.

In 1941 an Italian command opposing the Greeks found itself in immediate danger of being annihilated by two Yugoslavian divisions advancing southward toward the Italian rear. The resourceful Italians composed two messages in Serbo-Croatian, encoded them into the Yugoslavian cipher, and radioed them under a Yugoslavian general's signature to the two divisions closing in on them. The messages ordered each division to retire to the north and prepare new defenses at separately designated points, which they did—unintentionally saving the Italian forces from disaster.

Contradictory orders were beamed to U.S. troops during the Battle of the Bulge by Germans, and even a series of bogus military policemen, Germans in U.S. uniforms, were infiltrated among U.S. forces to direct and confuse traffic. All of the infiltrating Germans spoke American English; some had lived in the United States and others had attended staging areas to perfect their American English and solidify their mastery of typical American behavior. When the Americans became aware of the infiltration, quick tests were made to find out if the MPs were really Americans. Soldiers took to seizing suspects and testing them about facts that all authentic Americans should know. Sometimes this "required" information was the batting averages of well-known baseball players; sometimes it was the identity of comic-strip characters—the name of Little Orphan Annie's dog, of Popeye's girlfriend, or of Blondie's husband. Correct answers were often the passport to survival.

A different rule of thumb, or rather, rule of toe, was often applied to captured Japanese on Pacific Islands who claimed to be Chinese, Japanese Americans, or harmless natives. Suspects had to remove their shoes so that their first two toes could be examined. In the 1940's, Japanese who had grown up in Japan had worn wooden *geta*—sandals with a thong between the first two toes—from childhood, producing a pronounced space between the toes. Another quick test, a linguistic one, was to get the suspect to say "lalapaloosa." Japanese to whom English is not native tend to sound the *l* like an *r* (the Chinese reverse the process, pronouncing an *r* like an *l*).

The maneuver of discovering the enemy through his pronunciation goes back to ancient times, and is found in the Bible (Judges 12:4–7). The Gileadites, in combat against the Ephraimites, "took the passages of Jordan before the Ephraimites: and it was so, that when those Ephraimites which were escaped said, Let me go over; that the men of Gilead said unto him, Art thou an Ephraimite? If he said, Nay; Then they said unto him, say now Shibboleth: and he said Sibboleth: for he could not frame to pronounce it right. Then they took him and slew him at the passage of Jordan: and there fell at that time of the Ephraimites forty and two thousand."

The destruction of great Russian armies by the Germans in the Battle of Tannenberg in 1915 during World War I weakened Czarist Russia and ultimately caused the Russian collapse and the resultant revolution. The Russian defeat at Tannenberg was primarily due to German knowledge of Russian plans, from imperial headquarters down to the lowest troop level. In the élan accompanying the initial Russian invasion of Germany, the Russians planned to trap German forces in East Prussia between two enormous Russian armies. However, the Russians lacked telephone equipment and were indolent in using military codes; insufficiently trained Russian units took to sending radio messages to each other "in the clear" (uncoded), possibly supposing that the opposing German units did not understand Russian. But the Germans did, and were able to concentrate on knocking out the Russian armies one at a time, at such an enormous cost in Russian lives that the initial Russian enthusiasm for the war and confidence that it could be won began to evaporate.

An eminently successful linguistic deception was accomplished by the U.S. army prior to the Allied invasion of "Fortress Europe" (Ger.: *Festung Europa*). Under conditions of great secrecy, troops were trained in the

Boston area in winter warfare and survival and also took intensive courses in basic Norwegian, emphasizing the military vocabulary. All military personnel connected with the training were constantly reminded of the penalty for breach of the TOP SECRET security classification. All civilian specialists, such as ski instructors and Norwegian language teachers recruited from all over the United States, were carefully cleared by security checks. When the project was completed the troops were given winter equipment, including skis, and shuttled aboard a convoy of transports. After several days at sea the winter equipment was collected again and exchanged for summer field dress and equipment—more suitable for the invasion of Tunisia. For it was to Tunisia that the troops had been destined from the beginning—while German reinforcements waited for them in Norway. The planners of this operation would certainly give their assent to an aphorism coined by Mao Tse-Tung: "You want something made known? Tell people it is secret."

A British Indian army unit was captured during Rommel's advance in North Africa and guarded by a small contingent of German Afrika Korps troops. The British commanding officer, a major, before being separated for internment in officer POW camp, asked permission to say goodbye to his troops, mentioning that he had served with them for years in India. Granted permission, he said what seemed to be some words of farewell: *Jub main ishara kara asi khamla karna!*—"When I give the signal, attack!" He then quickly gave the signal, knowing that his troops no longer had their rifles but did have—by Sikh religious custom—their knives, hidden on their persons. After some rapid infighting with knives, the unit and its commander escaped to fight again.

The United States, because of its multinational and multiracial population, possesses more than any other nation the potential for training operators and infiltrators for what is often referred to as "unconventional warfare." Members of foreign groups from all parts of the world have maintained their linguistic and national ethnicity for generations, especially in large cities. Extreme care, however, should be taken in training second and third generation Americans to be familiar with present conditions in any area where they might operate. They must be prepared to speak the current version of the language they already know and to be aware of *current* local habits and customs. In World War II, American operatives of Italian or French background were betrayed not only by a failure to react correctly to some current comments familiar to all local residents, but even by their way of holding a knife and fork or smoking a cigarette. Some Arab-Americans, infiltrated into North Africa and the Middle East, blended perfectly with the local population, being familiar with Arab customs, but did not know the simple commands given to camels which were still an important part of daily life at the village level.

35. *Secret Languages, Crime, and Slang*

Slang, jargon, and argot are all variations of the same linguistic phenomenon: a specialized language or vocabulary used by members of a particular group for ease of expression, usually devised with the intent of restricting understanding to members of the group.

"Jargon" comes from the old French word *jargoun*, "twittering," the sound made by birds, incomprehensible to others. *Argot*, the French word for "slang," can be traced to an old French word meaning "to tear," from the torn clothes of beggars and thieves who first developed *argot* during the Middle Ages.

Much of the secrecy of criminal slang developed and kept constantly changing so that it would not be understood in snatches of conversation overheard by the guardians of the law or possible victims. Numerous words of American slang came from prison or from the criminal "industries," such as smuggling, bootlegging, prostitution, and, most recently, dealing in drugs. The greater part of this vocabulary is composed of substitute words for police, money, firearms, sex, types of crimes, victims, and punishments. After a word becomes generally understood by the public it is usually changed.

Occasionally the translated form of a slang word appears in another language. The American "bread" for money is also used in French (*pain*) with the same meaning. "To pinch" in the sense of "arrest" also exists in French (*pincer*) with the same basic and subsidiary meanings.

Slang terms related to crime often join the popular language because of their humorous, sometimes grimly humorous, suggestion. "To go west," although usually considered to refer to the happy hunting grounds where Indians go at death, appears to come more directly from prisoners' slang at Newgate Prison in London. The West Gate led to the scaffold, so the expression "to go west" came to mean a journey from which there was no return.

An example of criminal slang applicable to the 1980's is the expression "square grouper" (groupers are large warm-water fish), referring to bales of marijuana smuggled into the U.S. by what are ostensibly fishing boats.

An involved example of rhyming slang was developed in London among convicts and spread by them as they were shipped out to penal colonies. In this system a pair of associated words uses the last one to rhyme with the word the speaker wishes to disguise. Thus "gin" is expressed by "needle and pin"; "crook" by "babbling brook"; "wife" is "storm and strife"; and "bees and honey" stands for "money." The original duo for "girl" was "twist and twirl" and by a further encoding the nonrhyming "twist" came to mean "girl." In the case of "bacon and eggs" for "legs," the "bacon" has come to stand for "legs" in an effort to complicate the code.

A somewhat taxing method of using a quick, spoken code language temporarily incomprehensible to the police and others is used in the southeastern cities in South America. It involves saying some or all of the words backwards. Because Spanish uses so many vowels, reversing the words and saying them quickly makes them sound like normal words. *Mujer* ("woman") would be *rejum; carcel* ("jail") would be *lecrac; matar* ("to kill") would be *ratam;* and *escapar* ("escape") would be *rapacse.* A popular tango in Buenos Aires had a mysterious name, *Samsemoton,* until listeners realized it was simply ¡*No tomes más!*—"Don't drink any more!"—in reverse.

In most languages there are language tricks, perhaps first developed as conversational scramblers in prisons to confuse guards. Most are easy to understand, as is pig Latin in English: the initial letter is changed to a position at the end of the word and followed by *ay.* ("Let's go!" becomes *Etslay ogay!*). A French code language puts an *av* before vowels (Paris becomes *Pavaravis*). German has a code which repeats every syllable a second time but changes the first letter of the repeated syllable to *b* (*Kindergarten* would be *Kinbinderbergarbartenben*). Any of these codes can be used effectively only if the speed at which they are spoken is fast enough to confuse the listeners.

Underworld code languages exist in metropolitan areas throughout the world. There are even special thieves' languages in India, and the ubiquitous Gypsies may still be using the vocabulary of one of these. The word "Gypsy" is an adaptation of "Egypt," which the Gypsies were alleged to have crossed during their migration from India to Europe. "Pal" is a Gypsy word that has been adopted into idiomatic English. A Gypsy word for "prison"—*staripen*—has become the English slang term for "prison"—"stir."

Although police have generally adapted to underworld slang by learning it themselves, a complete police language, used only by police, has been developed by the native constabulary in Papua New Guinea. This language even has a regular name on the language list: *Polis-motu* ("police talk"). It has not been reported, however, whether local criminal elements have attempted to learn it.

A number of slang terms having to do with crime have been accepted into idiomatic English. Some of them have interesting linguistic backgrounds, often historic.

kidnap: .... a combination of "kid" (small goat) and "napper" (thief).

Mafia: .... in Sicilian dialect; probably from the Arabic *mah'yah* ("boastful").

big shot: .... the projectile of a 90-millimeter cannon used by Garibaldi against the Austrians, translated into English by Italian immigrant admirers of Garibaldi.

hijack: .... from the highwayman's informal but potentially deadly invitation to the driver of a stagecoach to raise his hands: "Hands up high, Jack!"

derrick: .... Derrick was a famous English hangman who practiced his trade at Tyburn about 1600. His name had such notoriety among criminals and others that in

	thieves' slang his name applied to anything that hoisted or lifted.
yen:	from the Chinese word "to smoke" (opium); has come to mean an insatiable craving.
cop:	initials of "constable on patrol"—not from copper buttons or a copper badge.
gat:	from Gatling gun, predecessor of the machine gun.
thug:	from Hindi, to describe a religious sect whose members made friends with and then killed, robbed, and buried unsuspecting travelers.
goon:	Hindi for "hired killer," *goonda* (not specifically for religious purposes).
hoodlum:	originally members of Irish vigilante strongarm squads in San Francisco directed against Chinese laborers. "Hoodlum" is reputedly Muldoon spelled backward (and misspelled).
vandal:	from the Vandals, a German tribe with a special penchant for destruction, who put the finishing touches on the declining Roman Empire in the West.
hash:	short for hashish. Hashish has contributed an important term to the language of today, the term "assassin," which comes from *hashishin* ("the hashish ones"), applied in the Middle Ages to a selected group of potential killers fostered by the so-called Old Man of the Mountain, the religious and political leader of a Moslem Shia sect in northern Persia. Secure in his mountain fortress, he kept his young

executioners happy with hashish,
luxury, and women, and also
convinced that they had died and
gone to Paradise. These killers
were, from time to time, sent
back to "earth" with instructions
to murder whoever was on the
assassination list of the Old Man
of the Mountain. If successful,
and not killed themselves during
the assassination attempt, they
were readmitted to "paradise"—
from which, the Old Man assured
them, they had been only
temporarily absent.

Crime-related slang from the United States has achieved
wide recognition in other languages as, for example, in the
French words *le gangster, le hold-up, le racket,* and *le
kidnap.*

Military slang has had a two-way influence on languages,
infiltrating the local language and bringing words from the
local language into the home language. Examples of military
slang entering local languages persist in the Latin languages,
which retain forms of slang terms used by Roman
legionaries, notably in the following three words:

ENGLISH	head	leg	horse
LATIN	caput	crus	equus
LEGIONARY SLANG	testa ("pot")	gamba ("hoof")	caballus ("nag")
FRENCH	tête	jambe	cheval
ITALIAN	testa	gamba	cavallo

Of these three, Portuguese and Spanish have kept only the
word for horse (*cavalo, caballo*). The Italian *gamba,*
pluralized to "gams," has become a slang term in American
English for legs, especially female ones.

Military occupation influences the local language in proportion to the duration of the occupation. This is one reason why there are many more English terms in Japanese and German than vice versa. In former times, however, the language of the occupiers became the dominant language of the country—English in India, French in Indo-China, and French or English in various parts of Africa.

Occupation troops usually pick up certain key expressions which become part of slang and, if persistent enough, eventually join the language. Arabic words used by French soldiers that have passed into colloquial French include: *toubib* ("doctor"), *baroud* ("fight"), *kif-kif* ("it does not matter"), *maboul* ("crazy"), *bled* ("arid wasteland"), and *blédard* (a soldier who spends most of his time in the *bled*)—all indicative of harsh military life.

Hindustani words brought back from India by British troops include: "veranda," "punch" (the drink), "tiffin," "bungalow," "curry," "bearer" (servant), "pajamas," and "jodhpurs," all descriptive of a not unpleasant life style.

An effective force in the growth of a new crop of American English slang has been the worldwide expansion of jazz and rock music with an elaborate slang of musicians' terms. The names applied to this music—jazz, rock, rock and roll, boogie—and the words "swing" and "jive" were originally all associated with the act of sex, coincidental but certainly not detrimental to the general acceptance of the music. Titles of songs circulate in most countries without translation, spreading slang and English idiom at the same time (French: *le jazz hot* and *un slow* for a blues song).

There are over a million words in English, and 100,000 of them are considered slang. The special "in" language connected with an activity and used by the members of a group but not understood by outsiders is jargon or slang— until it becomes so generally used that it enters the language as accepted idiomatic speech. New words and expressions are constantly being formed as new activities develop, whether in the professions, industry, the arts, or the media. Some of the new jargon now being developed in rocketry, robot development, transistors, or computers will soon gain general acceptance in English, while older slang or jargon words will be swept into the dustbin.

Some slang words and expressions have lasted for hundreds of years without attaining true linguistic respectability. Shakespeare used a number of popular expressions that are still in use but seem only a little old-fashioned in our day: "Tell it to the marines!" "Beat it!" "Oh boy!" "not so hot" "it's Greek to me" and the expression from flapper days "flaming youth," now almost as outdated as the era of Elizabeth I.

If slang does not enter the idiomatic language it dies, preserved only as a quaint relic of a certain point in language time. The expression "twenty-three skiddoo" popular in America in the early '20s is one of these. At Twenty-third Street in New York City, facing a park, stands the Flatiron Building, an early skyscraper shaped roughly like a flatiron or a slice of cake. Because of its situation the corner is a windy one and the wind was apt to lift women's skirts—to the appreciation of a habitual audience of loungers who, being periodically scattered by the police, gave rise to the evocative warning.

Slang disappears when a situation changes. A very old French term for a sentence to forced labor as a rower in the galleys was "to scythe down the big prairie" (faucher la grande prairie), the scythe being the great rowing oar and the "big prairie" standing for the sea.

In several Spanish-American countries there exist a number of supposedly slang terms which are not really slang at all, but somewhat modified relics of the Indian languages spoken before the Spanish conquest. These slang survivals are used in Mexico, Central America (from Aztec and

Maya), the former Incaic lands of South America, along the
west coast and central plateau (from Quechua and Aymará),
and in Paraguay (from Guaraní, which is still spoken
extensively). In Mexico today a profiteer is called a *coyote*,
and the Aztec rather than the Spanish names for certain
animals are still used: *zopilote* ("vulture"), tecolote ("owl"),
among many. The final *te* in these words stands for the
Aztec *tl* ending, similarly modified in other words familiar
to Americans, such as *chocolatl* ("chocolate") and *jitomatl*
("tomato"). Another interesting example of current Mexican
slang is the word *escuincle* ("kid," "young child"), from the
Aztec *xolo-escuintle*, a kind of dog—a fat chihuahua—often
used for food. The dogs did not survive the Spanish
conquest. Another example in Mexican Spanish is *cuate*,
meaning "friend" or "pal," from the Aztec *cuatl*, "twin."

"Posh" meaning "elegant" or "luxurious" is said to come
from the first letters of the phrase "port out—starboard
home" referring to the preferred cabins (those on the north,
away from the sun) on the ships which transported British
personnel back and forth between Great Britain and India
during the halcyon days of the British Raj.

Another slang word, perhaps hundreds of years old, is not
only still with us but may well be one of the most
frequently uttered words on the planet—"OK." Almost
everyone, English-speaking or not, knows what it implies,
although there is considerable doubt about its origin. It has
been traced to an Algonkian word of assent or greeting,
okeh. Another theory explains it as a misspelling of the
initial letters of "all correct," purportedly used by President
Andrew Jackson to show he approved documents submitted
to him. It was used in the presidential campaign of Martin
Van Buren. Van Buren was born in Kinderhook, New York,
and was often referred to as the "Kinderhook Fox." During
the campaign he was supported by the Democratic OK Club,
the "OK" standing for "Old Kinderhook," which would give
the word a Democratic origin. A more pleasant explanation
(at least to rum drinkers) would seem to be traceable to the

approximate French pronunciation (Oh Kay) of an excellent colonial rum called *Aux Cayes* ("at the Cays"). This rum, made in Haiti, was so good that its satisfied imbibers used its name to apply to anything they considered good or perfect.

---

36. *Languages in Space*

If we make contacts with beings from other
worlds, what language will we use to
communicate with them? The principal
languages that have been used up to now
by explorers from earth have been English
and Russian, the languages astronauts
speak when talking to mission control
centers.

Satellite messages are usually given in digital codes destined to be decoded when received on earth. An eminent exception was the first Chinese satellite, which continually broadcast the message *Tung fang hung—Mao Tse-tung*, meaning "The east is red—Mao Tse-tung."

The American-launched space probes Pioneer 10 and 11 and Explorer 1 and 2, now approaching the outer limits of our solar system, will take English and other languages past the solar system to the far corners of our galaxy and eventually beyond. Explorer 2 emits recordings of earth's languages, messages from earth's leaders, mathematical formulas, and earth sounds and an assurance of earth's peaceful intentions toward extraterrestrial populations taped by President Carter. Pioneer 10 contains images of the dominant species of earth (a man and a woman, nude), a diagram of conception, and identifying information about the hydrogen atom, in the supposition that any intelligent life capable of getting the message will understand it and try to communicate with the sender.

Names for the planets and many of the stars and star constellations come from Greek and Roman mythology and have been adopted by most countries in the world. The words "astrology" and "astronomy" both come from Greek, "astronomy" meaning "arrangement of the stars," and "astrology" meaning "speaking of the stars."

The zones between the earth and the cosmos are named "spheres" (from the Greek *sphaira*):

"atmosphere"	"steam sphere"
"troposphere"	"revolving sphere"
"stratosphere"	"spreading sphere"
"ionosphere"	"violet sphere"

"Galaxy" comes from the Greek *galaxia*, "circle of milk," referring to the Milky Way, and "cosmos" is derived from the Greek word for "order."

Modern astrology deals largely with the zodiacal band of constellations usually referred to by their Latin names, Pisces, Scorpio, Taurus, Capricorn, etc. The word "zodiac" comes from Greek, meaning "circle of animals."

The planets are named for the Roman and Greek gods and goddesses, the Roman versions of the names being the ones now in use. The Greeks identified the earth with a Greek goddess, Gaia, whom they also considered to be the earth itself.

In ancient popular tradition the planets were the abodes of the gods they were named for or represented the gods themselves, although advanced thinkers such as Plato suggested that the stars were given the names of the gods, animals, and legendary monsters to make it easier to remember them.

In the Far East the main planets, with one exception, have different associations:

WESTERN	EAST ASIAN
Mercury	water star
Mars	fire star
Venus	gold star
Saturn	earth star
Jupiter	wood star
Neptune	star of the sea king

Arab astronomers, who kept the science of astronomy alive during the European Dark Ages, gave names to many of the first-magnitude (brightest) stars, such as:

Altair	("flyer")
Aldebaran	("follower")
Deneb	("tail")
Betelgeuse	("giant's shoulder")
Rigel	("foot")

As modern telescopes have expanded their range, so many thousands of new stars, constellations, and even new galaxies have come into view that names from classical tradition have become scarce, and discoverers have assigned names made up of letters and numbers to new stars and novas. Names of newly discovered celestial objects are listed in the International Astronomical Registry. But in a variant of the sale of "pet rocks," a name-a-star company has been established in Toronto, Canada, which offers to assign a person's name to a star for $30 and list the name, together with the star's location, in a new book of star names.

The original Russian satellite had a neutral name: Sputnik, a combination of put' ("travel"), s ("with") and nik (a diminutive suffix designating a person)—in other words "a traveler that accompanies" or "a fellow traveler."

Of the several thousand space satellites that have been successfully launched in the past fifteen years, well over a thousand are still in orbit. Although launched by a variety of nations, including America, the U.S.S.R., the United Kingdom, Australia, Canada, France, Germany, Japan, China, the Netherlands, Spain, Italy and India, consortiums of countries and industries, and even individual companies, the names of the satellites have not been politicized, generally having names pertaining to space, exploration, weather, or even a combination of letters and numbers. A like procedure has been followed for naming new heavenly bodies or recognizable features on the planets.

Recently, however, the Soviets have been naming asteroids that they have discovered after heroes of the Russian revolution. As a countermove, U.S. and European astronomers have named a new one after Andrei Sakharov, a Soviet dissenter.

One might hope that future propaganda contests in space will be avoided and that if any particular people are immortalized, they will be chosen not for their political overtones but for other reasons—perhaps because they express the positive side of human aspirations. On the seventh anniversary of Kenya's independence in 1970, a satellite was launched by the Center for Aerospace Research from Kenya. It was called Uhuru—Swahili for "freedom."

In postulating what the future holds for languages in space, we must also accept the possibility that there may already be a number of languages in space among the myriad of planets which may be circling the millions of suns in our own galaxy. (No one has yet seen planets circling a star other than our own sun, but considering the number of planets circling all the sun stars of our galaxy, there is a good possibility that hundreds of millions of these planets support life, and that many millions have developed a civilization as advanced or more advanced than ours.) Whatever languages or means of communication inhabitants of such planets may be using, it has occurred to a number of reputable earth scientists that we have long been hearing, on earth, extraterrestrial communication signals without recognizing them. Light flashes or radio signals noted since the present age of science began may have included intergalactic communications, not just radio waves generated by turning planets or circling stars.

Guglielmo Marconi, inventor and developer of radio communication, in 1920 expressed the opinion that unidentified radio signals over the Atlantic which were picked up in America and Europe and on the ocean might be signals from another planet.

A suggestion made by Karl Friedrich Gauss, a renowned mathematician and astronomer in the first half of the 1800's, was typical of the early scientific desire to communicate with other planets in our solar system. At a time when a number of astronomers including Percival Lowell thought the planets, especially Mars, were inhabited, Gauss suggested that geometric messages be drawn on earth in the hope that they would be seen in space and interpreted as the work of intelligent beings. He proposed that the outline of a huge right-angle triangle be cut in a wooded area of Siberia and planted with wheat in order to make it more visible, and that the process be repeated with great squares and other geometrical figures, and that other planets be observed to see if a like message appeared on their surfaces—which would signify a return of our signals and a willingness to communicate.

Nikola Tesla, a Croatian-born scientist who discovered the rotary magnetic field and pioneered many modern technological developments in electricity, prophesied that the first recognizable cosmic message that earth would someday receive from space would be the simple arithmetical progression 1, 2, 3 spelled out through radio signals or some other means. Having noticed a series of unidentified periodic impulses himself, he reflected, "The feeling is constantly growing on me that I had been the first to hear the greeting of one planet to another."

As more and more radio signals are being received from space, some of which may prove to be other than those generated by rotation, there have been a number of announcements that messages from space were being detected. In what was called Project Ozma, undertaken at Greenbank, Tennessee, in 1969, an astronomer named Frank Drake aimed the Greenbank radio telescope at the star Tau Ceti, which is fairly near as stars go, in the constellation of the Whale. He detected regular signals —eight in each second—which continued for two weeks. But when he moved the telescope away from Tau Ceti he got the same signal, indicating that it probably was coming from somewhere on earth.

In 1965 Russian astronomers created a sensation when they reported receiving messages from the quasar CTA 102 in a regular 100-day cycle, although this report was later downgraded. Despite these temporary disappointments the

Greenbank Observatory in Tennessee, the enormous telescopic installation at Arecibo in Puerto Rico, the National Radio Astronomy Observatory Very Large Array installation in New Mexico, and other units throughout the world continue to function as "listening posts on the universe."

If extraterrestrials have, as millions of the earth's population and some astronomers believe, penetrated earth's space, the most likely communication they could make with us or we with them would be through mathematics and geometry and certain universal constants, such as the speed of light or the wavelength of the hydrogen atom. Several European space scientists have suggested that reported UFO landing sites in France, Italy, and Spain contain messages in imprints that have allegedly been burned into the earth by landing UFOs. Measurements of these imprints have been reported in the French press to give equivalent measures for pi (3.14159 . . .), "the golden section" (1.618 . . .) and the square root of each, as if alien intelligence were testing technological recognition signals on the population of a possibly civilized planet. Until more conclusive proof is obtained, it is interesting to speculate that a mathematical dialogue may already have been initiated.

---

37. *English vs. American*

Some time has elapsed since George
Bernard Shaw referred to Great Britain and
the United States as "nations separated by
a common language." And despite a certain
rapprochement between the two main
varieties of English, certain differences still
plague the foreign student of English and
even native English speakers themselves.

American books published in Great Britain are usually reset in type before publication, not because of American slang, which the British usually find quaint and even expressive, but because of certain differences in spelling common words. These include the British use of "u" in words like "colour," "honour," "labour," "neighbour"; c instead of the American s in words like "defence" and "offence"; the verb ending ise as in the British "practise" instead of ice as in the American "practice." The British use re instead of er ("theatre," "centre"); spell "check" as "cheque," "tire" as "tyre"; and use certain conjunctions ("whilst" instead of "while") which most Americans find old-fashioned.

A further divergence in the language is in the accent, a regional difference that no longer affects the common language. Most differences in accent are not marked enough to create inability to understand or be understood. The exceptions are the speech of the Scottish highlands and offshore islands in Great Britain, the American Gullah dialect of Blacks on the Sea Islands off the coast of Georgia, South Carolina, and Florida (which contributed "juke" as in "jukebox" and "voodoo" to English), and the English dialects of the Caribbean. There are no true dialects in the United States but rather language pockets where other languages have mixed with English: Spanish in the southwest United States, German (creating "Pennsylvania Dutch") in central Pennsylvania, and Cajun (a form of old French) in the up-river parishes of Louisiana. Big cities also have language areas created by ethnic majorities, but these are simply language pockets. General American English is becoming constantly more standardized through radio, television, and movies.

Up to the end of the 1800's Great Britain was still divided into a number of true dialect areas, and some of these dialects were almost incomprehensible to a speaker of standard English. Standard British English is now comprehensible almost everywhere in the British Isles through the same forces that have standardized English in America. If this standardization did not exist, English dialects—such as those of Somerset, Sussex, Lancashire,

Devonshire, Dorset, Sheffield, Westmoreland, Yorkshire, Wiltshire, Norfolk, Northumberland, and Cornwall—would still be on their way to developing as separate languages.

Louis-Lucien Bonaparte, who was more peaceable and studious than his famous uncle, made a study of these English dialects, which he considered potential languages, for the purpose of making translations of the Bible.

The nearest approaches to a separate dialect in the United States are dialectical pockets on the Sea Islands, where Gullah is spoken, and in the Ozarks, where a form of Elizabethan English survives. The reason for its survival has been the isolation of its speakers, who have held onto the form of English their ancestors brought to America hundreds of years ago, just as the French population of Canada has preserved its European language heritage. As isolation breaks down, dialects tend to disappear, although regional accents are considerably more persistent.

The British accent generally sounds better to Americans than the American accent sounds to the British. This may be an American linguistic tribute to the country that formed the language and originally colonized the land. (But the linguistic tribute is tempered from time to time by resentment of the mother country—as when "Big Bill" Thompson, running for his third term as mayor of Chicago in 1927, threatened to punch King George V on the nose should the opportunity arise.)

Differences of vocabulary in British and American English are noticeable principally in the words used in the ordinary run of daily life. These words are in themselves familiar to Americans; what is unfamiliar is the way in which the words are used in the United Kingdom. Americans frequently find English usage of a familiar expression somewhat startling; for example, if someone there tells you he is "really fagged out," he means simply that he is very tired.

Translation services on the continent of Europe differentiate as much as possible (often erroneously) between British English and American English. A customer is generally asked which of these "languages" he wishes to be used in translating his material. While such distinction is valid for industrial terminology and especially for machine parts, the two languages are nevertheless constantly moving closer together. The English and the Americans have always shared a common literature, formerly principally the literature of Great Britain, although at present there is a more equalized exchange of literature across the Atlantic.

A number of British terms for cars and roads take some time for an American to get used to. A divided highway is called a "dual carriageway" in England and an overpass is, rather imaginatively, called a "flyover." A traffic circle is a "roundabout," except in some of the larger cities, where it is a "circus." The hood of a car is a "bonnet"; the trunk is the "boot" and a muffler is a "silencer."

Considerable differences in vocabulary occur in other categories:

OCCUPATIONS

AMERICAN	BRITISH
ticket agent	booking clerk (pronounced *clark*)
traveling salesman	commercial traveller (or) rep.
trial lawyer	barrister
lawyer	solicitor
elevator	lift
elevator operator	liftman
garbage collector	dustman
hardware dealer	ironmonger
cleaning lady	charwoman
druggist	chemist
realtor	estate agent
visiting nurse	district nurse

HOUSEHOLD ITEMS, CLOTHES, AMUSEMENTS

installment plan	hire purchase (or) never-never
baby carriage	pram (perambulator)
diaper	nappy
check stub	cheque counterfoil
water heater	geyser
faucet	tap
apartment	flat
garbage can	dustbin
transom	fanlight
wrench	spanner
broiler	grill
TV	telly (or) the box
run for election	stand for election
nothing	nil
soccer	football
long-distance call	trunk call
spool of thread	reel of cotton
run (in stocking)	ladder
suspenders	braces
garter belt	suspender belt
rubber boots	gumboots
vest	waistcoat
undershirt	vest

FOOD

tenderloin	undercut
roast	joint
string bean	French bean
candy store	sweet shop
biscuit	scone
cookie	biscuit
dessert	sweet
hot cereal	porridge

English is the most widely studied language in the world today. As the predominant language of business and travel, it offers many professional and business advantages as a second language. Increasingly students of English on the continent of Europe, in South America, and in Asia study with American teachers in order to understand American speech (reportedly more difficult for a foreign student than British speech) and to acquire an American accent. It is interesting to note that while foreign students attempt to acquire an American accent, the British accent is still much admired by most Americans.

38. *The Export of English Words*

Since the 1940's, not only has English spread to all parts of the world but separate English words have also infiltrated the vocabulary of most important languages. Many of the adopting languages already have a vocabulary that can express the concept of the English word completely, but English words are adopted because they are shorter and because they are increasingly familiar through use by tourists, business travelers, advertising, films, and television.

Since World War II French has suffered such an invasion of English words (1,500 in general use, and a total of 2,600, according to a recent French dictionary survey) that French language authorities are constantly engaged in attempts to keep French French. It is historically interesting that French has contributed—through the Norman conquest of England—40 to 45 percent of all English words, yet the French reaction to the invasion of English words is determined resistance.

———————

British imports in French include *le week-end, le shake-hand, le five o'clock tea, le building, le sandwich, le smoking* (for "tuxedo"), *le fair play, le dancing* ("dance hall"), *le camping, le football* ("soccer").

———————

American words in French include more recent imports such as: *le businessman, le drugstore, le snack-bar, le gangster, le racket, le parking, le gag* ("joke"), *le gadget, le bluff, le star* ("actor"), *le boy-friend* and *le mobile-home*, all masculine gender. The feminine words are *la girl, la script-girl, la cover-girl*, and *la starlette*.

———————

Exceptions could be made, according to linguists, only for such difficult-to-translate terms as *le gang, le job, le cowboy, le far-west, le jazz, le derrick, le bulldozer, le hot-dog, le hold-up, le cash, le self-service*, and *la baby-sitter*.

———————

An attempt to find a French word for "striptease" brought forth a tongue twister: *déshabillage agacerie*—"undressing-teasing." For "striptease artist" the word *effileuse* (a female person who unravels tissue piece by piece) was suggested. Both words were dropped and the term is still *le strip-tease*.

———————

Special consideration was given by French language experts to "cocktail." They decided the word should be kept, as it was possibly a French invention anyway. But it was recommended that it should be spelled *coqueteyle*, a decision successfully resisted by the cocktail set.

———————

Germans adopt English words with facility and without any special prejudice against them since German linguists consider English an offshoot of German in any case.

Among the thousand-plus English words in modern German, each with its masculine, feminine, or neuter definite article (*der, die, das*) or its plural article (*die*), are *der Bestseller, der Manager, der Hobby, das Apartment, die Cocktail-Party, der Bartender, der Drink, der Cocktail, der Boss, der Job, der Gangster, der Computer, der Clown, der Teenager, das Baby, der Babysitter, die Kleenex, das Makeup, die Chips* ("French fries"), *der Toaster, der Swimmingpool, Start!, Stop!,* and *TV* (pronounced *tay-fow*), *Rollerskating* and *Jogging.* The last two are not considered as nouns but simply as part of the verbal construction.

Some new coinages in German combine German and English: *Buttondownhemd* ("button-down shirt").

On rare occasions an English word has been shortened (an unlikely feat in German), as in the case of a word for a young post-teenager—*der Twen* ("a person in his or her twenties").

Many words recording the passions of *die Teenager* are also in common use—*die Jeans, die Boots, das Sweatshirt, das Teeshirt, die Shorts, die Taperecorder, der Tapedeck, das Rock and Roll, der Stereo,* and *die Party.*

The long-standing German word for "grapefruit," *die Pampelmuse,* has, under the influence of American short forms, been supplanted by *der Grape.*

English adjectives—*single* ("unattached"), *happy, simple,* and *super!*—are all used in German without case forms.

American slang terms, some originating in a spreading drug culture, have also attained popularity in colloquial German: *in* ("with it"), *cool, down* ("depressed"), *high* ("elated"), *die Mafia,* and *der Trip* (a drug one).

Baseball is a popular game in several Spanish-speaking countries, and American terms for the game have been adopted with spelling modifications: *béisbol, jonrón* ("home run"), *aut!* ("out!"), *batero* ("batter"), *al bate* ("at bat"), and *estraik* ("strike").

Other Spanish colloquial terms taken from English include *yanqui* (not always a compliment), *suéter* ("sweater"), *boxeo* ("boxing"), *nócaut* ("knockout"), *pancakes* (among other American edibles), and the ubiquitous *jeans,* often spelled *yiens.*

A number of English words have been incorporated into Italian. They are principally concerned with films, television, and shopping, and each has one of the Italian words for "the" (this list includes *il*, masculine; *la*, feminine; *lo*, masculine before a double consonant).

il supermarket
il luncheonette
il marketing
lo shopping
il poster
lo spray (for hair)
lo slip (male swim trunks or undershorts)
la pop art
il popcorn
il play
lo script

lo speaker ("announcer")
lo show (TV)
la TV (pronounced *tay-voo*)
il cameraman
il drink
il weekend
il party
la boxe (boxing)
il match (sports)
jeans

Swahili, one of the widely spoken languages of Africa, has adopted a number of Arabic words through the centuries. As the Swahili-speaking countries have become more developed, a number of technical words from English have joined the language, including:

post office	*posta*
police	*polisi*
operator	*opereta*
bank	*banki*
blanket	*blanketi*
movies	*sinema*
brakes	*brek*
petrol (gas)	*petroli*
machine gun	*mashingun*
wire	*waya*
picture, photograph	*picha*
bar	*baa*
car	*kaa*

Swahili names for the months of the year have also been taken from English: *Januari, Februari, Machi, Aprili, Mei, Juni, Julai, Agosti, Septemba, Octoba, Novemba, Disemba.*

There are about 10,000 foreign words in Japanese, mostly adopted from English—assuredly a record for English words in a foreign language, especially since Japanese has no common language roots with English. The katakana syllabic alphabet allows the Japanese speaker to adopt foreign words into Japanese with ease, requiring only modification of pronunciation for Japanese speech patterns (u, for instance, is pronounced lightly or not at all, especially at the end of a word). Many of the English adoptions come from contacts through business and business products. There are hundreds of words in this category alone, such as:

meka	maker, manufacturer
surogen	slogan
moderu	model
ado	ad
depato	department store
erebeta	elevator
serubisu	service
taipuraita	typewriter
birudingu	building
rajio	radio
teipu rekoda	tape recorder

sutereo	stereo
kaa	car
mota	motor
motosaiku	motorcycle
gasorin	gasoline
toranjisuta	transistor
kamera	camera
saresmanu	salesman

Many American words have been shortened in Japanese—
maskomu for "mass communication," *komu* for
"computer," *terebi* for "television."

The Japanese enthusiasm for baseball (*beisuboru*) is equal to
that of the United States. Their versions of the American
baseball terms include:

boru	ball
sutoriku	strike
batto	bat
pitchingu	pitching
ranna	runner
kyatcha	catcher
auto!	out!
seifu!	safe!
hoomurun	home run

Japanese includes hundreds of English words for non-
Japanese foods, among them *supu* ("soup"), *hotto dogu*
("hot dog"), *sandoichi* ("sandwich"), *suteiki* ("steak"),
hambagu ("hamburger"), *biru* ("beer"), *uisuki* ("whisky"),
desato ("dessert"), *pai* ("pie"), *aisukurimu* ("ice cream")
and the inevitable *koka-cora*, which needs no translation.

As industrial prosperity has increased in Japan, English
words for elements of the good life (*manshon raifu*,
"mansion life") have been adopted: *aparto* for apartment,

manshon for "mansion" or "country house," *yotto* for "yacht," *daiyamondo* for "diamond," private *puru* ("pool"), *teresu* ("terrace"), *gorufu* ("golf"), *tenisu* ("tennis"), and *sanpen* ("champagne").

There is even a modern tendency in Japanese to use two or more foreign words together. A Japanese may refer to *mai kaa* ("my car"), *mai taoun* ("my town"), or *mai homu* ("my home") instead of using equivalent Japanese words. Ken Ishii, a Japanese writer, has recently suggested a temporary slowdown in the importation of English for Japanese words, pointing out in an article that a popular television program for teenagers (*chiieneija*) is called *rettsu go yangu!* ("Let's go young!") without translation.

The wholesale Japanese adoption of English words (but not English as a language) may be an example of how the spread of English worldwide may be facilitated by the previous adoption of and familiarization with English words.

From time to time the invasion of English into other languages is counterpoised by strong local resistance—as, for example, in the French-speaking community Quebec. Canadian French speakers tend to disapprove all English imports, even those accepted in France, and avoid using English words as much as possible.

In the vocabulary of clothing, one of the most prevalent words in the entire world is the word "jeans," for the uniform of the world's youth. This apparently American word, however, is really a French name for an Italian city, Genoa. A certain resistant material imported by the French was referred to as coming from Genoa—*Gênes*—in French—a name Americanized to "jeans" and reimported to France and the world as an American word.

Within the United States itself there exists a linguistic pocket, the Navaho-speaking lands, which steadfastly refuse to adopt any English-language imports, even mechanical terms. A car is called a *chidí*, for the noise it makes; its parts are named as if the car were an animal.

The other parts of the *chidí* have the following meanings in Navaho:

headlights	the eyes of the *chidí*
brakes	you pull a cord against the *chidí*
carburetor	the heart of the *chidí*
wheels	the legs of the *chidí*
tires	the moccasins of the *chidí*
gasoline	the juice for the *chidí*
radiator fan	in the front of the *chidí* it whirls around

In Navaho a caterpillar tractor is called "the *chidí* that crawls around," and an airplane is "a *chidí* that flies here and there."

The Navaho word for "train" means "many wagons, no horse."

The Navahos do not recognize in their language the names of the states whose boundaries pass through their reservation, but consider only their own boundaries, an enormous reservation called by them simply "the land of the people," a connected enclave covering large areas of Utah, Arizona, Colorado, and New Mexico.

In their own language the Navahos do not use the English names of nearby cities (Gallup, Denver, Phoenix), but names that describe events important to the Navaho tribe or nation that occurred at the place.

Even nationalities are described according to how they looked to the Navahos. Germans (*Béésh bich ahii*), for example, are identified as "the ones their hats are iron," a reference that comes from the First World War when American Navaho soldiers came into contact with the Imperial German army.

Even in the U.S.S.R. there are increasing indications of English words being adopted by younger Russians. Recently a Soviet philologist, N. Gorbanevsky, specifically complained about such trendy imports as *fahzer* ("father"), *bahton* ("button"), and *votch* ("watch"), among others popular with younger Soviet citizens.

---

39. *Someday—a World Language?*

Legends of an ancestral common language
that broke into a variety of tongues occur
all over the world. The "confusion of
tongues" described in the biblical legend of
the Tower of Babel in Genesis and other
ancient records was recognized by the
Spanish conquerors of Yucatan when they
found the legend among the Maya referring
to a land to the east where all men once
spoke a common language, since lost.

Chinese legends tell of a common language for all men which, when it split up into various languages, caused the universe to "deviate from its right way."

In Persian mythology Ahriman, the Spirit of Evil, caused man's original language to be divided into thirty tongues, from which the others descended.

According to Greco-Roman legend, men lived under the rule of Jupiter, the Father of the Gods in the Golden Age, speaking a common tongue until Mercury changed the tongue into a variety of dialects that became languages.

Herodotus, Greek historian of the fifth century BC, records a linguistic experiment carried out by one of the later rulers of Egypt, Pharaoh Psamtik. The pharaoh was convinced that if babies were not taught a language they would eventually begin to speak the original language of mankind. He therefore ordered that twin infants be taken from their mother and raised by a shepherd. The shepherd was enjoined, under pain of death, never to speak a word to them in any language. At the age of two the children's food supply was cut off, in the belief that they would eventually speak under the pressure of hunger. The report to the pharaoh was that one of the hungry children had finally said "bread" in Scythian. By this somewhat overcontrolled experiment Pharaoh Psamtik established, to his own satisfaction at least, that Scythian (formerly a tongue of what is now the southern Ukraine) was the original language of mankind. (This experiment was repeated by the German emperor Frederick II in the thirteenth century—but these twins died.)

From time to time, one or another country's seemingly successful struggle for empire and world supremacy has appeared to be establishing a unified political world and with it a world language that would be learned and spoken by all people. The first Western example of the possibility of "one world" was Alexander the Great—but in his meteoric career of world conquest, he was more interested in empire than in a world language. The dominance of one language, Latin, was later established by Roman conquest and long control of the Mediterranean world and points north and east. Even after the fall of the Roman Empire, Latin continued its sway in modified forms, the popular "native" languages of Rome's former provinces. It continued to be the language of the Catholic Church and of study, research, the professions, and official communication during the Middle Ages and still exercises its influence today in medicine, law, and science. In fact a simplified modern form of Latin, Interlingua, has been developed for international scientific communication.

With the spread of Islam, Arabic also spread throughout the world (not, however, to the New World), and is still spoken wherever Islam exists. Its claim to being a world language is reinforced by the fact that it is the national language of over twenty nations in Africa and Asia. If the spread of Islam had not been arrested in several crucial European battles, Arabic might have been not only one of the world's important languages, but the single most important language in the world.

The Mongol and Turkic invasions of the West almost conquered the known world, but their incursions qualify as temporary conquests that did not involve the creation of a world language. The survivors that the conquerers had not destroyed were usually permitted to retain their own language and culture as long as they remained submissive and paid their taxes.

In the fifteenth and sixteenth centuries it seemed possible for a while that Spanish would become the world language, or at least the most important one, a possibility terminated by the fate of the Spanish armada (in Spanish, *la gran armada*) in 1588 and further Spanish defeats by the French, who in the 1650's became the new leading power in Europe.

Waterloo put an end to French political dominance of
Europe and perhaps the world but did not interfere with the
diplomatic and cultural importance of the French language.
French continued to be the diplomatic language of Europe,
which dominated the world throughout the nineteenth and
early twentieth century—and French is still the national
language of many countries. French is also one of the two
working languages of the United Nations (the other is
English).

During World War I in Germany, a professorial group was
assigned the task of simplifying German for prospective
subject populations of the extensive territories to be
conquered in Europe and throughout the world. (One is
reminded of the German slogan: *Heute gehört uns
Deutschland—morgen die ganze Welt.* "Today Germany
belongs to us—tomorrow the whole world.")

Russian, which is spoken throughout the world's largest
contiguous land area, is another possible candidate for a
common future world (and space) language. (A joke recently
current in Europe recounts that European optimists are
having their children taught Russian while European
pessimists are having them taught Chinese.)

Chinese is spoken by the largest segment of the world's
population, even considering that certain local Chinese
dialects or languages, which are not mutually
comprehensible, are spoken by many millions of people.
The national language, Kuo-yü, formerly called Mandarin,
is spoken by approximately 800 million people, more than
twice the number that speak any other language. When
Kuo-yü becomes the spoken language of all China, as the
government intends, one out of every four people in the
world will speak the same language, Chinese.

The world's second language, by number of native speakers, is English. Its spread is no longer based on conquest but on political weight, commerce, travel, and long-distance communication—certainly a more commendable way of spreading a language than the destructive military conquests of the past.

In the last two hundred years a number of attempts have been made to invent an international language which would be easy to learn and equitable to many national language groups. The languages invented toward the end of the nineteenth century were all seen by their creators and supporters as a contribution to world peace. The two world wars of the twentieth century, while certainly confirming the need for peace, have helped to spread English rather than fostering any one of the new inventions. There are more than a dozen of these invented languages, including such intriguing names as Kosmos, Monoglottica, Universalsprache, Neo-Latine, Veltparl, Idio Neutral, Mundolingue, Dil, and Volapük, all dedicated to the idea of establishing (or reestablishing, if the ancient legends are to be believed) one international language for the entire planet.

The most persistent of these invented languages is Esperanto. According to its supporters' count, it has more than a million speakers, many in Brazil and Japan. Esperanto has taken on the characteristics of a movement; adherents recognize each other by wearing buttons bearing a green star—an invitation to be addressed in Esperanto.

Esperanto offers the advantage of an extremely simplified grammar and a vocabulary based on the Romance languages, Latin, German, and a smattering of Russian and Greek. There is no masculine or feminine article; "the" or "a" is *la*; all nouns end in *o* ("the father" is *la patro*, "the mother" is *la patrino*). The plural is indicated by *j* (pronounced *i*) ("man" is *viro*, "men" is *viroj*). Verbs end in *s*, and a noun which is the object of a phrase ends in *n*. "The boy kisses the girl" is *La knabo kisi la knabinon*. A more intense kiss is called a *shmaco*.

Esperanto was invented by Dr. L. L. Zamenoff in 1887. Dr. Zamenoff, a native of Poland, did not include Polish words in his international language, with one notable exception. When it came to choosing a word for "sausage" he was apparently unable to resist the memory of the delicious Polish *kielbasa*, so the words for "a sausage" became *la kolbaso*.

Esperanto has the advantage of a very simplified grammar, attractive to speakers of European languages with their often involved grammatical structures. The disadvantage of Esperanto as an international world language is that its vocabulary, being based on the Romance and Germanic languages, leaves out the languages of Asia and Africa spoken by the majority of the world's peoples. In addition Esperanto, having no national base, has a tendency to subdivide into national "dialects" or offshoots, such as Esperantido, Nov-Esperanto, and Ido.

After World War I Charles Ogden, an English psychologist, invented a system which he called Basic English. Designed as a means of worldwide communication, this system uses 850 preselected English words—600 nouns, 150 adjectives, and 100 words classified as "other." A number of articles, short stories, and books have been "translated" into this system, whose principal difficulty is not for the foreign student but for a native speaker of English trying to understand what the foreign student is saying as he uses, with often considerable circumlocution, the limited number of words available in Basic English. This difficulty stems from the attempt to freeze the vocabulary of a language— which, like any other living organism, is constantly changing.

Among all the possible candidates, standard English would seem to be, under present conditions, a good choice for a common world language. It is spoken as a national language by a greater number of nations than any other and over more of the world's surface than any other.

English has a vocabulary more than twice the size of any other language (German is the closest competitor). English has over one million words, and new words are constantly being added, not only from foreign languages, but from current scientific and industrial developments as well.

There has never been a language so influenced by a combination of so many other languages; English is not only a world language but an assimilated mixture of most of the world's languages.

To the original crucible of Anglo-Saxon, Celtic, and Norman French have been added thousands of other words from Dutch, the Scandinavian languages, Spanish, Italian, German, Portuguese, modern French, Arabic, Russian, Hebrew, Yiddish, Malay, Hindi, Chinese, Japanese, and the Amerindian tongues.

Some of the new words from languages formerly considered exotic from an English point of view are now common English words. Their basic translations have interesting meanings.

Japanese	*judo*	"passive way"
	geisha	"art person"
	harakiri	"stomach cutting"
	kamikaze	"spirit wind"
	kimono	"wearing thing"
	tycoon	"great prince"
Chinese	*chow*	"fried"
	gung-ho	"work harmoniously"
	typhoon	"great wind" (*taifung*)
	kowtow	"bump head"

Hindi	punch (drink) ...	"five ingredients"
	pariah	"drum" (parai, a shunned caste of drummers)
	shampoo	"massage" (champna)
	bangle	"bracelet of glass" (bangri)
	chit	"letter" (citta)
Sanskrit	sugar	"gravel" (sakara)
Amerindian	squaw	Natick, "female creature"
	papoose	Narraganset, "very small"
	wigwam	Massachuset, "their dwelling"
	possum	Algonkian, "white beast"
	tepee	Dakotah, "tent"
Russian	samovar	"self-heating"
	vodka	"little water"
Gaelic	whisky	"water of life" (uisge beatha)
	slogan	"war cry" (sluagh gairm)
Hebrew	shibboleth	"ears of corn"
	kosher	"according to law" (kasher)
	amen	"certainly"
	sabbath	shabbath; from shabhath, "to rest"

Arabic	*sofa*	"carpet" (*suffah*)
	magazine	"storehouses" (*makhazin*)
	alcohol	"eye shadow" (*alkohl*)
	mattress	"place to throw something" (*matrah*)
Persian	*julep*	"rose water" (*gulab*)
	paradise	"hunting park" (*pari daeza*)
Turkish	*tulip*	"turban" (*tulibend*)

Expressive words in any language can easily be incorporated into English, facilitated by the fact that English nouns are not divided into genders, adjectives do not form plurals or have cases, and verb tenses are simple and easy to understand.

During the last sixty years a liberal approach to grammar and construction has developed in English. Radio, television, advertising, and the press customarily change nouns to verbs at will and create adjectives and adverbs from nouns and verbs—hallowed practice in English. Words are coined and used for illustrative or explosive effect.

English and Chinese are, grammatically at least, among the world's simplest languages, as languages tend to simplify with time and extensive use. In other words, the more people that speak a language the simpler it becomes.

Old rules change, gradually or suddenly. The once scrupulously observed rule on the correctness of saying "It is I" (not "me") was delivered a telling blow during World War II by no less a master of the language than Sir Winston Churchill. As the British army in France was reeling in defeat and a Nazi invasion of Great Britain loomed on the horizon, Churchill made a special broadcast in an attempt to restore morale. His voice, broadcast to every corner of the empire and the world, began with the words "This is me, Churchill, speaking." (One wonders what effect his speech would have had, had he begun "This is I . . .")

Churchill also struck a blow against the stylistic prohibition of ending a sentence with a preposition. When he was shown an edited version of a speech he had written, he noted that the editor had changed what was an effective sentence solely because it ended with a preposition. He restored the original, writing in the margin, "This is the sort of thing up with which I will not put."

English has at least one great disadvantage as a potential world language—its nonphonetic spelling. One splendid example is the phrase "though a rough cough and hiccough plough me through"—in which -ough is pronounced six different ways.

Many reformers, including Theodore Roosevelt and George Bernard Shaw, have tried to simplify English spelling. (Shaw even left a legacy in his will for this purpose.) If spelling modification is eventually successful, it will alter the greater part of English and American literature, perhaps an excessive price to pay to avoid memorizing word spellings.

English in its present form is used more in print than any other language. Of all the books published in the world, 50 percent are printed in English; 70 percent of the world's mail is written in English; and 75 percent of the world's cables are sent in English.

English is by far the most frequently used language in all international conferences, scientific, political, or industrial. More than half of all chemical abstracts and scientific treatises are written in English.

Despite the high literacy rate of many foreign nations (including Japan, the most literate of all), more literate people speak English than any other language.

About 300 million people speak English as a native language and perhaps 300 million more speak it as an acquired language. These non-native speakers bring English close to the total number of speakers of Chinese, because comparatively few foreigners speak Chinese as an acquired language and many Chinese inside and outside China do not yet speak Kuo-yü (Mandarin).

Although Chinese has considerably more native speakers than English, English-language areas exist throughout the world. In many non-English-speaking countries—Denmark, Norway, Sweden, the Netherlands, Switzerland, India, Pakistan, Malaya, and other countries in Asia and Africa, more than 10 percent of the population speaks English. In Germany and some parts of the Spanish-speaking world, the percentage of English-speaking persons is approaching 10 percent of the population. In Japan the study of English is widespread, and even in the U.S.S.R., English is the principal foreign language taught in the educational system.

It might be appropriate, in the space age, to suggest that English became the principal world language through the air. All international flights communicate with the passengers and with the ground in English as well as in the national language of the particular airline. (An attempt to suppress English in airport communication in Quebec was, understandably, of short duration.)

In telephone conversations the ascendancy of English is especially striking. In 1980 there were about 472 million telephones (not counting the People's Republic of China) in the entire world. About 238 million of these were in English-speaking countries or English-speaking enclaves.

The United States has over 175 million telephones, and Japan, with 55 million, is the closest runner-up. Adding up all the "English-speaking" phones, more than half of all the telephones in the world turn out to be in English-speaking countries. In addition, the majority of all international telephone calls are made in English, even business calls between Asian and African or European countries which do not share a common language.

The present use of English as an auxiliary world language for long-distance communication, in travel, and in business is still no proof that it will be the one world language of the future. What will probably happen is that certain words will become understood everywhere on the globe. Three of these words—"hello," "OK," and "stop"—may already be the unrecognized precursors of a future world language.

Additional words that are internationally recognized (some originally from English, French, or other languages), are already in almost universal use, and may eventually form part of a future world language. They include:

> automobile
> bus
> taxi
> plane
> motorcycle
> bicycle
> airport
> hotel
> cinema
> football
> polo
> bank
> post (office)

theater
concert
opera
ballet
dance
music
sport
tennis
golf
camera
passport
telephone
television
radio
program
menu
steak
salad
coffee
whisky
soda
cigarette
dollar

A number of common words pertaining to clothes and household items will eventually be added as they attain worldwide usage, joining "jeans," "Coca-Cola," "aspirin," "spray."

These possible beginnings of a common world language are recognized virtually everywhere, partially because they have been used by so many travelers and English-speaking residents, and partially because they are the same or very similar to words in the native languages. These basic words have not been chosen by linguistic committees but have been created by necessity and linguistic similarity; the list will eventually grow to several hundred, then to a thousand, and at that point, barring unforeseen events, may in the next century serve as the foundation of a worldwide tongue based on English. That tongue will include words and phrases from the world's major (and minor) languages that express particularly useful and general concepts.

Whether or not a word standing for "mother" is the natural first word uttered by babies everywhere, words for "mother" tend to begin with or emphasize the m sound in most of the world's languages:

mère (French)
madre (Spanish and
    Italian)
Mutter (German)
mãe (Portuguese)
mama (Swahili)
umame (Zulu)
umm (Arabic)
imeh (Hebrew)
moeder (Dutch)
moder (Swedish and
    Danish)
man (Hindi and Urdu)
mitir (Greek)
mam (Welsh)
mor (Norwegian)
mat' (Russian)
me (Vietnamese)
mu (Chinese)

Two notable exceptions to this "m-for-mother" tendency are the Japanese ha-ha and the African west coast word, which is Ewe da-da.

———————

Whether or not a common world language does develop in the future, a number of major and minor languages will undoubtedly continue to flourish, kept alive by the pull of a common memory based on tradition, history, literature, national pride, and love of country.

———————

A national language is more than a means of communication; it is the total memory of a tribe's or a nation's existence. It represents the character and individuality of the group, tribe, or nation to which a person belongs. In Cymric (Welsh), an ancient language struggling for existence in Great Britain, there is a proverb about language peculiarly applicable to the persistence of language: *Cenedl heb raith; cenedl heb galon*—"A nation without a language (is) a nation without a heart."

Acknowledgments

The author wishes to express his appreciation for the assistance in the preparation of this work to Valerie Seary-Berlitz, author, linguist, and artist, for her aid in its written preparation and in the research, selection, and placement of the illustrations.

Further grateful acknowledgment is made to the following persons, living or deceased, who have been a help or an inspiration in my own study of languages or in the preparation of this book: Professor Mark Baldwin, Latinist; Ehud Beneliezar Benyehuda, lexicographer, specialist in modern Hebrew; Lin Berlitz, linguist, researcher; Dr. George Frangos, historian, author, linguist, specialist in Balkan languages; Dr. Alexei Gierowski, historian, linguist, author, specialist in East European languages; David C. Frost, editor, linguist; Charles Hughes, linguist, philologist, ethnologist, specialist in American Indian languages; Dr. Constantine Mertvago, multilinguist; Roger Montfort, historian, educator; William Morris, lexicographer, author, lecturer, columnist, specialist in word origins; Professor W. Max Müller, Egyptologist, linguist, historian, translator of the *Mahabharata*; Antonio Pascual F, historian, classicist; Dr. Mario Pei, linguist, philologist, author, specialist in Romance languages; Maxime Berlitz Vollmer, author, lecturer, linguist, philologist; King Wang, specialist in classical Chinese; and King-Mau Wu, linguist, specialist in Chinese dialects.

Index

A

J

R

S

T

W

Y

Z